"To live or to exist in less than aliveness or deadness. Such is the profound question at the heart of contemporary psychoanalytic theory and treatment and this expertly curated volume brings together the leading writers on the vitalizing possibilities that inhere in contemporary psychoanalytic theory and practice. We encounter patients dominated by states of non-aliveness, absence, dysregulation, trauma and neglect; and clinicians who utilize elements of their own presence, reverie, countertransference and sheer courage to facilitate, kindle and ignite life, libido and vitality. Reading this book is an exercise in parallel process: each unique chapter will itself inspire, enliven and vitalize the reader; and will help all clinicians as we struggle with our most difficult and challenging patients."

—**Robert Grossmark**, Ph.D., teaches and supervises at NYU Postdoctoral Program, The National Institute for the Psychotherapies, The Eastern Group Psychotherapy Society

"Since the Winnicottian and Bionian ontological revolution in psychoanalysis, analysts have been more focused on helping our patients 'to be' than 'to know.' As Winnicott outlined what allows a person to develop a capacity to be, we began to understand more about ways that we are also not allowed to be. A focus on deficits in symbolization, parental absence and deadness have now led to an increasing interest in experiences and metaphors of vitalization. This volume is a gift in helping us to understand how profoundly stark life can 'be' without a sense of aliveness. A talented collection of analysts from the Independent, Kleinian, and Relational traditions contribute to our understanding of this crucial concept in contemporary psychoanalytic theory. These essays probe intersubjective processes of how vitalizing processes emerge, are enacted, and integrated. There is also a keen interest in the kind of object the analyst is becoming in the analytic process, one who can find new parts of the patient's inner life and play. Schwartz Cooney and Sopher's volume embodies how analytic concepts such as deadness continue to evolve as key analytic writers bring to the matter their own struggles with finding vitality inside their patients and aliveness within the analytic process."

—**Steven Cooper**, Training and Supervising Analyst at the Boston Psychoanalytic Society and Institute; Associate Professor of Psychology at Harvard Medical School and Chief Editor Emeritus at *Psychoanalytic Dialogues*

"This is a rich and absorbing book, full of original descriptions of the void and its place in psychopathology. There seem to be myriad ways of arriving at empty states, but even more interestingly, a variety of routes out of them. The clinical accounts are very moving, and read like chapters out of a terrific novel: there is endless patience, endurance, stamina, terrible boredom, suspense and real excitement for patients and analysts alike. Read and enjoy."

—**Anne Alvarez**, Ph.D., M.A.C.P, Consultant Child and Adolescent Psychotherapist and teacher and retired Co-Convener of the Autism Service, Child and Family Dep't. Tavistock Clinic, London

"This important volume highlights some of the most essential aspects of human existence: enlivenment, desire, generativity and hope. In highly creative and sophisticated ways, it brings to life critical ideas on therapeutic action, transformation, the capacity for a full existence and the role of psychoanalysis in reviving vitalization."

—**Dr. Galit Atlas**, faculty member in the postdoctoral program in psychotherapy and psychoanalysis at New York University and author of *The Enigma of Desire*

Vitalization in Psychoanalysis

In *Vitalization in Psychoanalysis*, Schwartz Cooney and Sopher develop and explore the concept of vitalization, generating new ways of approaching and conceptualizing the psychoanalytic project.

Vitalization refers to the process between two people that ignites new experiences and brings withdrawn aspects of the self to life. This book focuses on how psychoanalysis can be a uniquely creative encounter that can aid this enlivening internal process, offering a vibrant new take on the psychotherapeutic project. There is a long tradition in psychoanalysis that addresses the ways that the unique subjectivities of each member of the therapeutic dyad contribute to the repetition of entrenched patterns of relating, and how the processing of enactments can be reparative. But this overlap in subjectivities can also bring to life undeveloped experiences. This focus on generativity and progressive action represents a significant, cutting-edge turn in psychoanalysis. *Vitalization in Psychoanalysis* represents a deep meditation on this transformational moment in the history of psychoanalytic thought.

Pulling together work from major writers on vitalization from all the main psychoanalytic schools of thought, and covering development, theory and clinical practice, this book will be an invaluable guide for clinicians of all backgrounds, as well as students of psychotherapy and psychoanalysis.

Amy Schwartz Cooney, Ph.D., is on faculty at the New York University (NYU) Post-Doctoral Program in Psychoanalysis and Psychotherapy. She is on the Board of Directors and is faculty/supervisor at the National Institute for the Psychotherapies (NIP) and at the Stephen Mitchell Center for Relational Studies. She is Joint Editor in Chief of Psychoanalytic Dialogues and is in private practice in New York City.

Rachel Sopher is Board Director, Faculty and Supervisor, National Institute for the Psychotherapies (NIP) Training Institute; Faculty and Supervisor, National Training Program for NIP; and Faculty, Stephen Mitchell Center for Relational Studies. She is Editor-in-Chief of *Psychoanalytic Perspectives* and maintains a private practice in New York City.

RELATIONAL PERSPECTIVES BOOK SERIES

The Relational Perspectives Book Series (RPBS) publishes books that grow out of or contribute to the relational tradition in contemporary psychoanalysis. The term *relational psychoanalysis* was first used by Greenberg and Mitchell[1] to bridge the traditions of interpersonal relations, as developed within interpersonal psychoanalysis and object relations, as developed within contemporary British theory. But, under the seminal work of the late Stephen A. Mitchell, the term *relational psychoanalysis* grew and began to accrue to itself many other influences and developments. Various tributaries—interpersonal psychoanalysis, object relations theory, self psychology, empirical infancy research, feminism, queer theory, sociocultural studies and elements of contemporary Freudian and Kleinian thought—flow into this tradition, which understands relational configurations between self and others, both real and fantasied, as the primary subject of psychoanalytic investigation.

We refer to the relational tradition, rather than to a relational school, to highlight that we are identifying a trend, a tendency within contemporary psychoanalysis, not a more formally organized or coherent school or system of beliefs. Our use of the term *relational* signifies a dimension of theory and practice that has become salient across the wide spectrum of contemporary psychoanalysis. Now under the editorial supervision of Adrienne Harris, Steven Kuchuck and Eyal Rozmarin, the Relational Perspectives Book Series originated in 1990 under the editorial eye of the late Stephen A. Mitchell. Mitchell was the most prolific and influential of the originators of the relational tradition. Committed to dialogue among psychoanalysts, he abhorred the authoritarianism that dictated adherence to a rigid set of beliefs or technical restrictions. He championed open discussion, comparative and integrative approaches, and promoted new voices across the generations. Mitchell was later joined by the late Lewis Aron, also a visionary and influential writer, teacher and leading thinker in relational psychoanalysis.

Included in the Relational Perspectives Book Series are authors and works that come from within the relational tradition, those that extend and develop that tradition, and works that critique relational approaches or compare and contrast them with alternative points of view. The series includes our most distinguished senior psychoanalysts, along with younger contributors who bring fresh vision. Our aim is to enable a deepening of relational thinking while reaching across disciplinary and social boundaries in order to foster an inclusive and international literature.

A full list of titles in this series is available at www.routledge.com/Relational-Perspectives-Book-Series/book-series/LEARPBS.

Note

1 Greenberg, J. & Mitchell, S. (1983). *Object relations in psychoanalytic theory.* Cambridge, MA: Harvard University Press.

Vitalization in Psychoanalysis

Perspectives on Being and Becoming

Edited by Amy Schwartz Cooney
and Rachel Sopher

Routledge
Taylor & Francis Group
LONDON AND NEW YORK

First published 2021
by Routledge
2 Park Square, Milton Park, Abingdon, Oxon OX14 4RN

and by Routledge
52 Vanderbilt Avenue, New York, NY 10017

Routledge is an imprint of the Taylor & Francis Group, an informa business

British Library Cataloguing-in-Publication Data
A catalogue record for this book is available from the British Library

Library of Congress Cataloging-in-Publication Data
Names: Schwartz Cooney, Amy, 1961– editor. | Sopher, Rachel, 1974– editor.
Title: Vitalization in psychoanalysis: perspectives on being and becoming / edited by Amy Schwartz Cooney and Rachel Sopher.
Description: Milton Park, Abingdon, Oxon; New York, NY: Routledge, 2021. | Includes bibliographical references and index.
Identifiers: LCCN 2020044235 (print) | LCCN 2020044236 (ebook) | ISBN 9780367687892 (paperback) | ISBN 9780367687885 (hardback) | ISBN 9781003139065 (ebook)
Subjects: LCSH: Self psychology. | Psychoanalysis.
Classification: LCC BF175.5.S44 V58 2021 (print) | LCC BF175.5.S44 (ebook) | DDC 150.19/5–dc23
LC record available at https://lccn.loc.gov/2020044235
LC ebook record available at https://lccn.loc.gov/2020044236

ISBN: 978-0-367-68788-5 (hbk)
ISBN: 978-0-367-68789-2 (pbk)
ISBN: 978-1-003-13906-5 (ebk)

Typeset in Times New Roman
by Newgen Publishing UK

Contents

Contributors

Christopher Bonovitz, Psy.D., is Training and Supervising Analyst, William Alanson White Institute; Adjunct Professor and Clinical Consultant, NYU Postdoctoral Program in Psychotherapy and Psychoanalysis; and Associate Editor, Psychoanalytic Dialogues & Contemporary Psychoanalysis. He is coauthor with Andrew Harlem of the book, Developmental Perspectives in Child Psychoanalysis & Psychotherapy, published in 2018 as part of the Relational Book Series.

Jody Messler Davies, Ph.D., was Co-Editor-in-Chief of Psychoanalytic Dialogues from 1998 to 2008. She is a supervisor, faculty member and former co-chair of the Relational Track at New York University (NYU) postdoctoral program, founding vice-president of the International Association for Relational Psychoanalysis and Psychotherapy (IARPP), and a founding board member of the Stephen Mitchell Center for Relational Studies.

She is co-author (with Mary-Gail Frawley-O'Dea) of *Treating the Adult Survivor of Childhood Sexual Abuse: A Psychoanalytic Perspective*; and of over 50 published papers on the topics of trauma, dissociation, multiple self-states, erotic transference and countertransference, termination, and analytic love.

Lisa Director, Ph.D., is Adjunct Clinical Associate Professor of Psychology and Clinical Consultant at the New York University Postdoctoral Program in Psychotherapy and Psychoanalysis. She is a faculty member and supervisor at the Stephen Mitchell Relational Study Center and at the Psychoanalytic Psychotherapy Study Center. She is an associate editor of *Psychoanalytic Dialogue*s and is in private practice in New York.

Dianne Elise, Ph.D., is a personal and supervising analyst and Faculty member of the Psychoanalytic Institute of Northern California, a training analyst member of the International Psychoanalytic Association, and has served on the editorial boards of the *Journal of the American Psychoanalytic Association* and *Studies in Gender and Sexuality*. Her over 30 publications include wide-ranging papers on the subjects of gender, sexuality, and erotic transference, appearing in the *Psychoanalytic Study of the Child, The Psychoanalytic Quarterly, Journal of the American Psychoanalytic Association, Psychoanalytic Dialogues, Studies in Gender & Sexuality,* and *Psychoanalytic Inquiry,* as well as several book chapters. Elise's book, *Creativity and the Erotic Dimensions of the Analytic Field* (Routledge, 2019), expands her work in innovative ways and presents her contemporary thinking on erotic life in psychoanalysis. She is in private practice in Oakland, California.

Daniel Hill, Ph.D., is a psychoanalyst, educator and a leading proponent of the affect regulation model. He is the author of *Affect Regulation Theory: A Clinical Model* (2015). His publications and presentations include topics ranging from the clinical use of multiple models to religious fundamentalism. He was the founder/director of PsyBC and CSAR (1996–2017). For the past 15 years Dr. Hill has conducted on-going study groups focused on an in-depth understanding of the regulation of affect. He is in private practice in NYC where he is on the faculties of the National Institute of the Psychotherapies and the New York University Postdoctoral Program in Psychoanalysis and Psychotherapy. Dr. Hill can be contacted at danhill@psybc.com

Margaret Black Mitchell, LCSW, is a psychoanalyst in New York City. She is a founding Board Member and Vice-President of the International Association of Relational Psychoanalysis and Psychotherapy (IARPP), a Founding Board Member and faculty, The Stephen Mitchell Relational Study Center and Board Director at NIP. She is the co-author, with Stephen Mitchell, of Freud and Beyond, a History of Modern Psychoanalytic Thought and Associate Editor of Psychoanalytic Dialogues.

Joseph Newirth is a Professor at the Derner School of Psychology at Adelphi University. He is a supervisor at the NYU Postdoctoral Program in Psychotherapy and Psychoanalysis New York University, and is on the faculty and a supervisor at the National Training Program at the National Institute of the Psychotherapies, New York, NY. He received his BA from the City College of New York, his Ph.D. from the University of Massachusetts and his psychoanalytic training at the William Alanson White Institute. He encourages dialogue, critical thinking, and opportunities for students and supervises to deepen their understanding of how psychoanalytic theories relate to the practice of psychoanalysis and psychotherapy. He has published numerous articles in professional journals and frequently presented papers at national and international conferences. His first book, *Between Emotion and Cognition: The Generative Unconscious* (2003), received the Gradiva prize for critical analysis and interpretation in 2004. His second book, *From Sign to Symbol: Transformational Process in Psychoanalysis, Psychotherapy and Psychology* (2018), was published by Lexington Books and received the American Board and Academy of Psychoanalysis annual book award in clinical psychoanalysis.

Rachael Peltz, Ph.D., is a personal and supervising analyst, Faculty member and Co-director of the Community Psychoanalysis Track at the Psychoanalytic Institute of Northern California. She is an associate editor of *Psychoanalytic Dialogues*. She has a private practice in Berkeley, California, and works with adults, adolescents, couples, and families.

Amy Schwartz Cooney, Ph.D., is on faculty at the NYU Post-Doctoral Program in Psychoanalysis and Psychotherapy. She is on the Board of Directors and is faculty/supervisor at the National Institute for the Psychotherapies (NIP) and at the Stephen Mitchell Center for Relational Studies. She is Joint Editor in Chief of Psychoanalytic Dialogues and is in private practice in New York City.

Boaz Shalgi, Ph.D., is a clinical psychologist; a senior lecturer at the Department of Psychology, Bar-Ilan University, Israel; Head of the Doctoral Unit: "Psychoanalysis and its interfaces", The

Psychotherapy Program, Sackler Faculty of Medicine, Tel Aviv University, Israel; Editor in chief, "Sihot" – Israel Journal of Psychotherapy.

Rachel Sopher is Board Director, Faculty and Supervisor, National Institute for the Psychotherapies (NIP) Training Institute; Faculty and Supervisor, National Training Program for NIP; and Faculty, Stephen Mitchell Center for Relational Studies. She is Editor-in-Chief of *Psychoanalytic Perspectives* and maintains a private practice in New York City.

Steven Stern is a faculty member of the Massachusetts Institute for Psychoanalysis and the Institute for the Psychoanalytic Study of Subjectivity, and is Clinical Associate Professor of Psychiatry at Maine Medical Center and Tufts University School of Medicine. He is a member emeritus of the International Council of the International Association of Psychoanalytic Self Psychology and serves on the Editorial Board of Psychoanalysis, Self, and Context. He has been a frequent contributor to the contemporary psychoanalytic literature, with a particular interest in theoretical integration. His book, Needed Relationships and Psychoanalytic Healing: A Holistic Relational Perspective on the Therapeutic Process, was published by Routledge in 2017 in the Psychoanalysis in a New Key Book Series. Dr. Stern practices in Portland, ME, with specializations in psychoanalysis, psychodynamic psychotherapy, couples therapy, and clinical supervision.

Acknowledgments

We would like to thank the teachers, supervisors, colleagues and analysts who have touched and inspired our professional and personal growth. We are indebted to our patients, students and supervisees who have moved us, challenged us and deepened our passion for this work. We would also like to thank Steven Kuchuck for his guidance, support and friendship throughout this process. Above all we would like to thank our families for their love and support. Amy thanks her husband for his belief and encouragement in this project and her children who are her pride and joy. Rachel would like to thank her family for being her heart and her rock, and for constantly amazing her. Lastly, we are so grateful for the opportunity we have had to enter into this creative partnership, which has been not only generative but joyful and vitalizing, too.

Chapter 1

Schwartz Cooney, A. "Vitalizing Enactment: A Relational Exploration," *Psychoanalytic Dialogues* 2018, reprinted by permission of the publisher (Taylor & Francis, www.tandfonline.com).

Chapter 2

Sopher, R. "An Allegiance to Absence: Fidelity to the Internal Void," *The Psychoanalytic Quarterly* 2018, reprinted by permission of the publisher (Taylor & Francis, www.tandfonline.com).

Chapter 3

Peltz, R. "Activating Lifeness in the Analytic Encounter: The Ground of Being in Psychoanalysis," *Psychoanalytic Dialogues* 2020, reprinted by permission of the publisher (Taylor & Francis, www.tandfonline.com).

Chapter 8

Elise, D. "Moving from Within the Material," *Journal of the American Psychoanalytic Association* 65:1, copyright © 2017, reprinted by permission of SAGE Publications.

Chapter 11

This chapter is derived from an article originally published in Psychoanalytic Dialogues (2016), 26: 685–697, copyright Taylor & Francis.

Introduction

We write this introduction in March of 2020 just as COVID-19 has begun to spread throughout the world. Never in our lifetimes has the fragility of human life come so clearly into our awareness. Never has time compressed so acutely, bringing existential themes of vitality and death, chaos and order, isolation and connection into sharp focus. The crunch of the pandemic has brought about much anxiety and pain, putting us in contact with the precariousness of life. But this unprecedented crisis also carries the potential to place us in contact with the fundamental being-ness of human experience – the very essence from which all generativity emerges. It is spring here in New York, and in the midst of the dread of quarantine and grief of disease, the beauty of nature has resurfaced in our parks; intensified forms of aliveness and deadness cyclically advance and recede. This is the historical moment we are living through as we contemplate our topic, the context in which we engage vitalization in psychoanalysis.

The idea for this book began in another time, seemingly long ago, when we found ourselves again and again returning to certain questions and themes in our talks together as analysts and friends. We found that we had both been thinking about the conditions and qualities that spark novel experience and can generate contact and movement in the psychoanalytic encounter. Since then, we have been occupied with the questions of how the old relates to the new, how loss relates to discovery and how the analyst can meet the patient in ways that both recognize the injuries of the past and instill hope for the future. What is needed to bring life to deadened states? What do we do with the experience of deadness in itself? And what might we do that transforms it, or makes the creation of new life possible? In short, we have become increasingly engaged with the theme of *vitalization in psychoanalysis*. This collection represents both a culmination and an expansion of our conversation on this topic which we regard to be at the forefront of psychoanalytic thought today.

There are multiple roots and many contributors to the construct of vitalization, but we have both been singularly inspired by the work of Anne Alvarez. Alvarez (1997) speaks specifically of patients who need the analyst to rouse them to life, so they may be "called into awareness of the human world outside themselves, [and thus be] called into awareness that they themselves exist" (Alvarez 1992, p. 73). Her concept of reclamation refers to the need to reach out to patients who are in withdrawn or "undrawn" states. She theorizes that reclamation is a response to states of lifelessness, in which an action is necessary to promote connection and reclaim vital aspects of the self. An analyst may respond to experiences of deadness in the therapeutic relationship by actively reaching out to a patient, spurred by countertransferential urgency that emerges in the analytic relationship; the therapist's movement in these moments creates something new, instills life, curiosity and interest in the mutual exchange. Alvarez' thinking is infused with a sense of hope and possibility, a willingness to look beyond deficit to consider capacities that may be underdeveloped and that may, through the analytic relationship, come to life and newly thrive. Her articulation of vitalization has animated our thinking as relational analysts and enlivened our work with a range of patients at diverse clinical moments. These ideas have since germinated, evolving over time into the collection which engages a range of thinkers on this very meaningful topic.

Vitalization in psychoanalysis

This book aims to explore the phenomenon of vitalization in psychoanalysis from a variety of vantage points. With the field's move away from the archaeological metaphor of unearthing repressed mental contents towards a focus on the emergent properties of the analytic relationship, contemporary psychoanalytic theory has become engaged in questioning what can be uniquely generated through human connections. There is a long tradition that addresses the ways that the unique subjectivities of each member of the analytic dyad contribute to the repetition of old and entrenched patterns of relating and how the living through and processing of these enactments can be reparative (e.g. Bass, 2003; Benjamin, 1990; Black, 2003; Bromberg, 1998, 2006; Davies, 1996, 1998; Mitchell, 1993, 2000; Stern, 2010). But the overlap in subjectivities inherent to the psychoanalytic encounter can also be generative of the new, and thus bring to life embryonic affects and undeveloped experiences, in a propulsive movement towards authenticity, connection and transformation.

The term vitalization signifies the engendering of novel experience, the ignition of an enlivening internal process that can come about through deep engagement with the other. We have arrived at an important moment in the history of psychoanalytic thought, in which a confluence of ideas centering on vitalization has gathered concerning the creation of new experience, progressive action, generativity and emergence in psychoanalysis. This book will bring together these and other ideas about enlivenment and vitalization from diverse vantage points. For example, within relational thought there has been recent exploration of the ways in which the analyst can be a catalyst for change (Director, 2016) and how enactment itself can be generative and vitalizing (Aron and Atlas, 2015; Schwartz Cooney, 2018). Within contemporary object relational perspectives, a dialogue is underway considering how new objects and internal structures can be created throughout the lifetime beginning with transformation in the analytic encounter (for example, Levine, 2012). Neo-Kleinians are considering how the analyst can reach the patient in areas of non-symbolized autistic experience and in so doing potentiate unlived aspects of self (for example, Alvarez, 2012; Newirth, 2003). Theories that have grown out of attachment research explore the ways that non-symbolized, implicit interactions can create "now moments" and "moments of meeting," providing unique opportunities for change at procedural levels (Boston Change Process Study Group, 2010). Contemporary self-psychological approaches emphasize the expansion of the self through encounters with the analyst as a vitalizing self-object (Kohut, 1971, 1984). By highlighting differing theories of vitalization, this book provides a unique integrative platform, allowing for a deeper and more focused study of this significant turn from a predominant emphasis on uncovering and mourning the old, towards the study of creating and generating the new.

Part I

The book is organized into two sections that interrogate the themes of therapeutic action and the analyst's use of self. This delineation is in many ways artificial: the ideas explored in this collection resonate and share striking similarities, though the theoretical perspectives and languages or idioms of individual authors are often distinct and vary widely. We were surprised to find that many of the chapters in this collection seemed to engage one another to create a meaningful dialogue and in so doing extend our thinking in exciting new directions. In the first part, titled "Vitalization as unconscious action: enactment, dreaming and emergence," the various chapters contemplate ways in which vitalizing processes emerge unconsciously in the analytic encounter, generating vibrant, spontaneous, visceral and novel experiences for both partners in the dyad. In this section, the authors often draw on and integrate object relational and relational perspectives, creating a rich interweave of ideas that uniquely contribute to our understanding of what is most enlivening in the psychoanalytic process. Therapeutic action here often has its genesis in entwining fields of unconscious experience. Many of our theorists in this section explore the place of representation and symbolization in vitalizing action.

The section begins with two chapters by the co-editors that address different ways of using unconscious process and intersubjective contact to generate new experience in the analytic dyad. The first chapter, "Vitalizing enactment: a relational reconsideration," by Amy Schwartz Cooney introduces a concept she developed that expands on and relationalizes aspects of Alvarez' formulations. Here she describes vitalizing enactments as uniquely generative, spontaneous interactions that can draw the analytic dyad from deadened impasse into enlivened exchange. Such enactments, which are initiated by the analyst's unconscious sense of countertransference urgency, rapidly engage the patient in untapped areas of psychic experience, creativity and play. Vitalizing enactments are unique because they are progressive and they are understood to be transformative as lived experiences rather than in the retrospective processing of pathological, repetitive patterns or dissociations.

Rachel Sopher describes a phenomenon she terms allegiance to absence, an early experience of loss or neglect that comes about at a time when the difference between self and non-self is still developing. This overwhelming experience of absence creates a sense of deadness that cannot be accessed through verbal or other symbolic forms of communication. Treating an allegiance to absence requires that the primary attachment, or absence thereof, becomes actualized in treatment in the analytic encounter – in the here and now where it can be experienced and transformed, first on a non-verbal, enactive level, then on different levels of development and of reality through shared experienced and reclamation of lost and undeveloped parts of self, these deadened places become potentiated with life and meaning.

In her essay, "Activating lifeness in the analytic encounter: the ground of being in psychoanalysis," Rachael Peltz focuses on vitalizing presence, a ground-level contact that is made in the field, creating what she terms "transformation in action." Through such unique and often unrepresentable meetings, vitality may be kick-started and development rebooted. Peltz draws on a myriad of contemporary theoreticians in her own unique integration, illustrating her ideas through a rich and moving clinical presentation. Closely related to Peltz's theoretical formulations is Joe Newirth's innovative chapter, "The generative unconscious and the capacity to be fully alive." In this piece, he extends his work on the generative unconscious (Newirth, 2003), which views the mind as a developmental structure that has the capacity to create novel subjective meaning through the analytic encounter. He suggests that, when working with patients who live in fragmented concrete worlds, as "orphans of the real," the analyst must tolerate experiences of deadness and overcome dissociations in order to access reverie and vitalizing imaginative processes through the generative unconscious.

Drawing on and integrating various object relational theories, Boaz Shalgi takes up the notion of vitality through psychic transformation. He delineates alternative theories of change through either rational understanding or through non-linear, emergent and spontaneous processes. Here, he locates the capacity for growth in the infusion of impersonal reality with personal meaning, lending vitality to the magic of one's life. In this rich formulation, therapeutic action lies in the creative use of the psychoanalytic encounter as a powerful vehicle for imparting life with expanded personal meanings. Margaret Black expands this section with a historical overview of the unique contributions of relational project and its contemporary iterations. She theorizes the analyst's unique clinical sensibilities and the way the analyst draws on and interweaves distinct theories in each clinical encounter to meet the patient in an enlivening way. Black beautifully illustrates her ideas through two moving clinical vignettes, showing how vitalization was achieved through very different kinds of clinical processes, one informed by ideas originating with the Boston Change Process Study Group and one drawing from Ogden's thought. She utilizes these examples to show how unconscious and conscious processes can enter into and vitalize the therapeutic relationship.

Part II

In the second grouping of chapters, titled "The analyst's vitalizing use of self: love, play and provision," the authors explore and theorize different ways that analysts can participate in enlivening interchange with patients. These articles lean towards a consideration of developmental deficits in comprehending states of internal deadness and lack. Similarly, they share a focus on the way the analyst's presence can provide a new and ameliorative experience that is uniquely generative. The authors in this section speak from various contemporary perspectives, drawing on affect regulation theory, self psychology and relational and object relational thought. Together these chapters provide a creative consideration of the various ways we can conceptualize the analyst's vitalizing role in the psychoanalytic project.

In her novel formulation, illustrated by an extended clinical vignette, Jody Messler Davies offers an innovative reconceptualization of shame and links vitalization with the reawakening of desire. In this original piece, Davies proposes that shame results from cumulatively refused desire in the early parent–child relationship. She suggests that, as the analytic dyad engages in a deep, mutual process of shared imagination, analytic love can facilitate the rekindling of desire. The patient then becomes able to reclaim feelings of aliveness that had been foreclosed developmentally and sealed over in shame. Dianne Elise explores another important manifestation of analytic love in her chapter titled "Moving from within the maternal." In this provocative formulation, she likens the therapeutic encounter to the erotically charged interplay and choreography of dance. She theorizes that the analytic role plays an important structuring function in the treatment couple, and emphasizes the vitalizing potential contained in the erotic and creative aspects of embodied experience. For Elise, the analyst acts as a libidinal energizer, stimulating new life in the patient and in the analytic couple.

In his theoretically sophisticated chapter, titled "Vitalization as a case-specific emergent process," Steven Stern extends his self-psychologically informed notion of the "needed relationship" to suggest that, within each treatment, a unique form of therapeutic action is co-constructed to vitalize the patient and the therapy. Working through repeated enactments leads to a progressive increase in the analyst's understanding of the patient and the kind of provision that is needed in the relationship. This in turn results in a uniquely vitalizing engagement of increased fittedness in the intersubjective realm, which he illustrates through a generous clinical vignette. Daniel Hill draws on regulation theory in his rich elaboration, defining vitality as a state in which one is open to and capable of utilizing both positive and negative affect adaptively. He cogently highlights how, for individuals who have experienced neglect in early childhood, growth through mutual attunement may not be possible. In such cases, Hill deftly demonstrates how therapeutic action occurs through the provision of an attuned relationship that addresses affect on a cognitive level, and then through shared implicit understanding within a mutually regulating analytic process.

Drawing on the work of Anne Alvarez and integrating relational conceptualization, Lisa Director explores the role of the analyst as an "enlivening object" – a catalyst who can kindle life within deprived and neglected patients who suffer in prolonged deadened states due to developmental injury. Through a beautifully rendered vignette she demonstrates the vitalizing potential of the therapeutic relationship in cases in which psychic structure is missing or underdeveloped. She shows how therapeutic action can originate in the countertransference response of the analyst who then summons the patient to life by introducing new capacities to relate and make meaning in the dyad. In his original article, "What makes time fly? Loewald's concept of time and the resuscitation of vitality," Christopher Bonovitz suggests that building the capacity for vitality entails "playing" in the transference in ways that can enliven a deadened or dissociated past. Therapeutic action occurs in and through transference engagement that re-establishes links that have been severed due to trauma and loss. Bonovitz beautifully illustrates his novel integrations with vignettes from a treatment with a widowed man and a bereft child, each entrenched in states of timeless foreclosure.

The process of creating this edition has been an enlivening one for us – enabling us to mine old ideas, mull over differences and areas of common sensibilities, while also creating new ideas out of our exchanges with each other and with the authors who have contributed to this project. We hope that this book will similarly touch and inspire the reader and the analyst to approach each new encounter with a sense of hope, aliveness and possibility.

References

Alvarez, A. (1992). *Live Company: Psychotherapy with Autistic, Borderline, Deprived and Abused Children* . London: Routledge.

Alvarez, A. (1997). Projective identification as a communication: Its grammar in borderline psychotic children. *Psychoanalytic Dialogues*, 7:753–768.

Alvarez, A. (2012). *The Thinking Heart. Three Levels of Psychoanalytic Therapy with Disturbed Children*. London: Routledge.

Aron, L. and Atlas, G. (2015). Generative enactment: Memories from the future. *Psychoanalytic Dialogues*, 25(3):309–324.

Bass, A. (2003). Enactments in psychoanalysis: Another medium, another message. *Psychoanalytic Dialogues,* 13:657–676.

Benjamin, J. (1990). An outline of intersubjectivity: The development of recognition. *Psychoanalytic Psychology*, 7(Suppl.):33–46.

Black, M. (2003). Enactment: Analytic musings on energy, language, and personal growth. *Psychoanalytic Dialogues*, 13:633–656.

Boston Change Process Study Group (2010). *Change in Psychotherapy: A Unifying Paradigm.* New York: Norton.

Bromberg, P. (1998). *Standing in the Spaces: Essays on Clinical Process, Trauma, and Dissociation.* Hillsdale, NJ: The Analytic Press.

Bromberg, P. (2006). *Awakening the Dreamer: Clinical Journeys*. Hillsdale, NJ: The Analytic Press.

Davies, J.M. (1996). Linking the "pre-analytic" with the postclassical: Integration, dissociation, and the multiplicity of unconscious process. *Contemporary Psychoanalysis*, 32:553–576.

Davies, J.M. (1998). Multiple perspectives on multiplicity. *Psychoanalytic Dialogues*, 8(2):195–206.

Director, L. (2016). The analyst as catalyst: Cultivating mind in the shadow of neglect. *Psychoanalytic Dialogues,* 26(6):685–697.

Kohut, H. (1971). *The Analysis of the Self.* New York: International Universities Press.

Kohut, H. (1984). *How Does Analysis Cure?* Chicago: University of Chicago Press.

Levine, H.B. (2012). The colourless canvas: Representation, therapeutic action and the creation of mind. *International Journal of Psycho-Analysis*, 93(3):607–629.

Mitchell, S.A. (1993). *Hope and Dread in Psychoanalysis*. New York: Basic Books.

Mitchell, S.A. (2000). *Relationality: From Attachment to Intersubjectivity*. Hillsdale, NJ: The Analytic Press.

Newirth, J. (2003). *Between Emotion and Cognition: The Generative Unconscious.* New York, NY: Other Press.

Schwartz Cooney, A. (2018). Vitalizing enactment: A relational exploration. *Psychoanalytic Dialogues*, 28(3):340–354.

Stern, D. (2010). *Partners in Thought: Working with Unformulated Experience, Dissociation, and Enactment.* New York, NY: Routledge, Taylor and Francis.

Part I

Vitalization as unconscious action

Enactment, dreaming and emergence

Chapter 1

Vitalizing enactment

A relational exploration

Amy Schwartz Cooney

Introduction

Drawing on her years of experience as a child psychoanalyst, Alvarez (2012) theorized a form of intervention termed "vitalization" in which the analyst reaches out to "reclaim" severely disturbed patients, drawing them from states of near psychic death into live contact. For Alvarez, these active interventions are aimed at the introjection of a new good object and the development of a more enriched sense of self in children whose primary object has been disastrously deficient. I have found Alvarez's ideas compelling and hopeful, offering a vision of the progressive action of psychoanalysis. I have also found her ideas applicable in a broader theoretical context and with a wider population, particularly in therapeutic impasses that feel inert and with adult patients who struggle to feel alive emotionally.

My project in this chapter is twofold. I consider Alvarez's notion of vitalization through the lens of relational thought. From this perspective, I regard vitalizing interventions as enactments that can be enriching and transformative in their lived experience rather than in retrospective processing. I also advance a broadened conception of enactment as not only repetitive of old conflicts or expressive of dissociated affect but also opportunities for potentiating new experiences in the analytic dyad. I begin by briefly reviewing Alvarez's ideas. I then introduce the concept of *vitalizing enactment*, contextualize this idea theoretically, and present a clinical vignette from my work with a withdrawn and despairing patient to illustrate this chapter's themes.

Anne Alvarez: interventions at the level of vitalization and reclamation

In her most recent book, *The Thinking Heart*, Alvarez (2012) articulates three modes of therapeutic intervention that are intended to match her patient's level of development and the severity of their difficulties. In treating children who are able to make causal linkings, Alvarez works at the explanatory level, using "why–because" interpretations that relate emotions to experience, past to present. For patients who are not yet able to make these kinds of connections, she proposes working descriptively. Alvarez focuses on the "whatness" of experience, helping her patients identify their emotions, naming and amplifying what they are feeling. For children who are chronically dissociated, or "undrawn," she suggests that treatment may need to focus on *vitalization and reclamation*, helping the child connect with feeling themselves. Vitalizing interventions involve the analyst using herself actively as an enlivening transferential object: initiating contact, insisting on meaning, reaching out to (re)claim the patient and draw him into the world of objects and feelings.

Alvarez integrates a contemporary Kleinian/Bionian perspective with attachment and regulation theory, proposing that psychopathology results from environmental trauma and failure in the original container. From this standpoint developmental and emotional disturbance is understood in relation to deficits in her patients' senses of self and in their internal objects. Alvarez is particularly concerned with introjective processes and facilitating the internalization of a good object in cases where the child's earliest relationships have been severely lacking.

Alvarez (1997) rethinks symptomatology, questioning when defenses are best understood as efforts to mask underlying conflicts and anxieties and when they may represent efforts to overcome and develop new capacities. For example, she distinguishes between omnipotent defenses and nascent efforts to establish a sense of potency. In a similar vein, Alvarez extends Bion's (1963) concept of the container/contained. Where Bion focused on the analytic function of metabolizing unbearable affects, Alvarez suggests that the container can *also* hold and make meaning of a range of other unsymbolized mental contents, including joy, efficacy, and a sense of future possibility. When working with severely disturbed children, Alvarez uses herself as a uniquely generative container, metabolizing different kinds of unformulated experiences, negative and positive, in an effort to realize her patient's capacities.

A relational interpretation of vitalization as enactment

Alvarez's work resonates with a sense of hope, compassion, and a vision of the progressive action of analysis. She concerns herself both with what has been damaged and lacking and what has not yet taken form. To my reading, Alvarez's unique personal involvement and willingness to work with her subjective responses have the feel of relational psychoanalysis. In this chapter I suggest that the enlivening interactions Alvarez describes in her efforts to connect with acutely "undrawn" children can be creatively reconceptualized and applied to relational work with despairing adults in deadened impasse.

For example, in illustrating vitalization and reclamation, Alvarez (2012) presents her work with an autistic child named Robbie who has become increasingly inaccessible and unreachable in advance of the summer break. "Desperate" to make contact, "to say good-bye and consider the possibility of remembering each other" (p. 22), Alvarez is stirred by what she describes as "countertransference urgency." She writes,

> Nothing reached him. I felt more and more worried that I had lost him for good. I found myself moving my head into his line of vision and calling his name. He suddenly looked at me in surprise, like someone surfacing from the deep and said "Hello–o–o" wonderingly and sweetly, like someone greeting a long lost friend.
>
> (p. 22)

In the clinical process that follows, Alvarez shows how her patient moved from his "undrawn" state into contact with her and the world of feelings. "Here Robbie came verbally, musically and dramatically to life" (p. 22).

In this extraordinary interaction she seemed to breathe life into Robbie, his objects, and the treatment. I imagine this moment was meaningful and vitalizing for Alvarez as well. I understand the analyst's "countertransference urgency" as an expression of *her* subjectivity. Alvarez's response reflected the unique and inchoate ways that this relationship had touched her and created intrapsychic disruption *within her*. This Robbie was *her Robbie*. While doubtless other clinicians would have been moved differently, Alvarez's reactions emanated from *her* psyche and *her* connection to this boy and to some part of herself that was stirred by him. Robbie's responsiveness was also specific to *this relationship* and his dynamics as they emerged with *this* analyst.

Through my own relational lens I am conceptualizing this moment as an enactment in which patient and analyst met in a way that was progressive and alive. This encounter was an enactment in that it was an unconsciously driven, spontaneous, and seismic action. While clearly asymmetrical (Aron, 1996), this was a mutual exchange between two people, two minds meeting, touching, and transforming one another. The interaction between Alvarez and Robbie led to intrapsychic movement, which in turn altered the relational field for patient and analyst alike. While mindful of the unique characteristics and parameters of psychoanalytic work with children, I suggest that the analyst's enlivening use of herself in such moments of therapeutic crises can be usefully generalized to work with adults and considered as enactments.

Vitalizing enactment

I am proposing that *vitalizing enactments* are interactions in which the analyst reaches out to draw the patient from their most necrotic zones, enlivening the treatment and generating new experiences. These enactments are distinct in that they can potentiate underdeveloped affects and capacities for the patient and analyst alike. Vitalizing enactments represent efforts to progress consciously and unconsciously rather than to re-create old pathological patterns or manifest dissociated experience. In working with such enactments the emphasis is on creating novel feelings and ways of being rather than interpreting what Alvarez (2012) describes as the "why–because" or "whatness" of the experience. Narratizing, reflecting on process, or linking old to new may follow as different "grammars" develop (Alvarez, 1997). *In vitalizing enactment the action is in seizing the moment and creating something new.*

The concept of enactment has generally been understood as a repetition of aspects of the past. Jacobs (1986) first identified "enactment" as an unconscious countertransferential action that occurs in response to the patient's psyche and the pulls of the relationship. Since then and across theoretical orientations enactment has widely been regarded as ubiquitous and been seen as more or less problematic (see Aron, 2003, for discussion). It has alternately been conceptualized as an unconscious replaying of past trauma, troubled internal processes, or dissociated experience (Benjamin, 1990; Bromberg, 1998, 2006; Davies & Frawley, 1994). Enactments have come to be understood as high-risk encounters that hold the potential for great rewards if they can be survived and processed (Bass, 2003).

What I am suggesting here is a different take. *Just as Alvarez* (1997) *posited that the container can be a medium for the transformation of a range of feelings, I am suggesting that in enactment a range of unconscious experiences can also emerge.* I am building on the assumption that the unconscious is a repository for negative feelings and fantasies *as well as* positive and embryonic affects and that the analytic couple is in continuous unconscious dialogue (Ferenczi, [1932] 1988) in multiple ways from the start. It follows that patient and analyst can respond to each other from unconscious areas that contain nascent feelings of love, joy, and hope as well as conflict and painful dissociated affect. All of these interactions can be intense, spontaneous, and destabilizing; all of these meetings can be forms of enactment. From this perspective enactments need not inevitably be repetitive and problematic. Enactments can also be progressive and can lead to the creation of novel feelings and capacities in the here and now. Consistent with this view, enactments need not be seen as problems to which the *solution* is enriching. The enactment itself can be transformative for patient and analyst, bringing to life experiences that have been submerged or unborn.

Theoretical convergences and expansions

Aron and Atlas (2015) proposed a conception of enactment as generative: a way of practicing novel possibilities that can subsequently be lived out in the evolving future for both partners in the analytic dyad. Building on Jung's notion of the prospective function, they suggested that through enactment we can anticipate, envision, and construct new possibilities, paving the way for their subsequent realization. My notion of vitalizing enactment shares with Aron and Atlas's work a view of enactment as potentially creative and forward moving. But our conceptualizations differ because in vitalizing enactment the action is in seizing the moment and creating something new rather than in rehearsing future outcomes.

Lisa Director's (2009, 2016) recent work is also relevant. Extending Alvarez's thought, Director has proposed that the relational analyst can function as an enlivening object, catalyzing intrapsychic change within the patient. Director (2009) is centrally concerned with intrapsychic development in patients whose "curtailed object relations confine them to primitive forms of engagement" (p. 120). I am interested in an expanded conceptualization of enactment as carrying the potential for vitalization and in exploring the interplay of intrapsychic and intersubjective processes in the analytic dyad that can potentiate such creative transformations.

Newirth's (2003) work on the "generative unconscious" also relates to the concept of vitalizing enactment. He has theorized that the unconscious can be a source of creativity and energy rather than only a site of pathological conflict. Stern (2003) proposed that, as dissociations are lifted unformulated experiences can emerge that not only are defensive but also can be creative and lead to joint discovery. Echoing both of these theorists, I'm suggesting that vitalizing enactments involve the creation and emergence of novel and enriching experiences through analytic interaction.

Stephen Mitchell has advanced a theoretical shift in psychoanalysis from a model of damage and cure to one of mutual growth and enhancement of subjective experience. His exploration of the creation of new meaning rather than reworking old tapestries is spelled out in his chapter "Penelope's loom" (1988) and in his explication of analytic intention (Mitchell, 2000). He emphasized the mutative potentials in the analytic relationship as a different form of interacting in the here and now. Similarly, in vitalizing enactment the focus is on the creation and enhancement of experiences for both partners in the analytic dyad.

Loewald's (1960) focus on growth, development, and the dimension of the future is germane, as is Cooper's (2000) work on the role of "futurity" in the analytic process. As with vitalizing enactment, these ideas go to the progressive potentials of the therapeutic relationship. Hoffman's (2009) advocacy of "passion in the countertransference" relates to vitalizing enactment in his notion of the analyst's active role as a new good object, particularly against the looming inevitabilities of loss and mortality. Vitalizing enactments, however, involve developing nascent capacities and new object experiences rather than confronting malevolent introjects in the manner Hoffman has advanced.

The idea of living though, rather than interpreting, vitalizing enactment jives with several strands of analytic thought. For example, in recent work Grossmark (2012) explored the value of *being in* rather than directly interpreting the "enactive flow" when working with patients who do not experience themselves as psychically alive. Similarly, Black (2003) has suggested that at certain moments it is the shared experience of the enactment rather than subsequently processing it that is transformative. Fiscalini's (1988) work on the transformational role of "living through" new experiences in the interpersonal matrix of the analytic dyad is also resonant. From an object relational perspective, Rosenfeld (1987) and Williams (2010) have each explored the importance of interpretive restraint, particularly when working with vulnerable patients who may find verbal interventions shaming or invasive. These are some of the formulations that animate my understanding. In the vignette that follows I illustrate and explore these ideas further.

Clinical vignette

Joel was a middle-aged man who came into analysis to treat chronic insomnia, anxiety, and depression, explaining that he was disaffected in every area of his life. Handsome, educated, bright, he had been unable to establish relationships or meaningful work. He felt lifeless and humiliated by his sense of inner lack. He spent his days at a job that was rote and his nights alone or scrolling through Internet dating sites in search of ever-elusive connections.

Joel was the only child of parents who had fled persecution in South America, to escape massive violence and avoid the fate of family and friends who had disappeared. Although he was told that family life had been happy and full, Joel had no memories of these early days.

Joel's family settled in this country when he was 2 years old, living a life of alienation and exile. The shades of their home were always drawn. Joel was a shy and lonely child. He described his father as gruff and authoritarian, largely absent. His mother had "a breakdown" soon after the family immigrated, which resulted in a psychiatric hospitalization. He described her as a quiet and frail presence, unfailingly good and beloved. He valorized her suffering and her endurance. She was irreproachable as a person and unapproachable as a psychic object for our exploration. The only conflict Joel remembered with her was a struggle with language. She would speak to him in Spanish and he, desperately wanting to be "like the other kids," insisted on responding in English. This stubborn bilingual exchange persisted through his youth. As an adult looking back on these battles, he regretted the conflict, had given up the effort to "fit in," and existed in an alienated nether world, deeply entrenched in shame, self-loathing, and contempt.

I empathized with Joel's experience and attempted to explore his current life, considering his difficulties in the context of his past relationships: his mother's fragility, his father's absence. I tried to think with him about the ways he was emotionally replicating his parents' life of exile and holding their unmetabolized trauma (Faimberg, 2005; Gerson, 2009), but he could not consider any way in which his past had shaped or impacted his life today. He was fiercely protective of his parents and rejected any exploration that might remotely "implicate" them in his present struggles. He knew he was self-loathing and loathed himself for it. Most sessions ended with a scowl.

I tried in different ways to reach Joel. I attempted to connect with his little-boy experiences of alienation and exclusion. I attempted to interpret his resistance to exploring his internal world to his childhood conflicts with his mother, suggesting that we were reenacting his early refusal to "speak her language" and their inability to find a common tongue. I endeavored to explore the intersubjective field, focusing on what he felt in the room with me or imagined I experienced with him as we struggled to engage. Each effort was dismissed. A pattern developed between us: he would bring in experiences in which he felt disgusted either with himself or with someone he encountered (a date that failed, an interaction that fizzled), and I would try to delve into what had occurred. I would point to the intensity of his self-criticism and sharp devaluation of others. I'd try to explore these feelings or consider them in relation to his inner world and his formative relationships. He would scoff at such linkings and retreat further, his self-blame and protectiveness toward his objects intensified. There seemed to be no way to open up reflective space or think about his life as other than fated and doomed.

Joel spoke of his difficulty finding anything to say in sessions because there was nothing to talk about, nothing inside him. He came dutifully, paid promptly, but seemed to get nothing out of our work. This was the environment in which we lived, immersed in a kind of dead zone. I fell into a shared "situational illness" (Bollas, 1983) as a sense of hopelessness pervaded our sessions. Whether I attempted to question, clarify, resonate with, or interpret what was going on in Joel's inner or outer world or in the room, Joel shut down. Throughout the treatment I had been holding and containing Joel's loneliness and despair. Under the ongoing weight of his refusal I found myself shutting down too. The "no-thing" within Joel was between us and within me as well.

I conjectured that Joel's mother might have initially been more emotionally alive but that he lost her during her hospitalization. When she returned she was a frail and ephemeral presence, unable to be present for Joel in a vitalizing way. Consistent with Green's (1986) ideas, I understood Joel to be yoked to a damaged object, identified with a sense of inner lifelessness (no-thingness), and fiercely loyal to this depriving connection (Fairbairn, 1952). While I found these ideas useful intellectually and turned to them in an effort to enliven myself in the increasingly stalled climate of our work, I was unable to reach Joel or help him consider, recognize, symbolize, mourn, or even be curious about anything.

I felt useless and helpless in the countertransference. I came to experience myself both as the "dead mother" analyst who could not breathe life into the treatment and the bereft child, locked into psychic deprivation. While I wanted very much to help Joel, I also felt angry with his internal objects and thwarted by their ghostly presence. The treatment felt deadened and stalled.

In one session Joel was telling me of his deepening sense of disconnection. He was floating, barely moored to anyone or anything. He seemed to be sinking deeper and deeper into withdrawal. As he spoke, my mind trolled back to "memories in feelings" (Klein, 1975). Images of the past and present fused. As I looked at Joel, my father, who had struggled with severe depressions during my childhood, took form. I returned to an image of him at night, alone in the quiet of our parlor floor, clutching himself and crying. He was inaccessible and unapproachable. I watched from my hidden perch on the stairway above until I silently turned away and retreated to my room. In this moment of reverie I connected with a longing to have been close to him. I wished there could have been more.

Now here was Joel before me threatening to float away, sitting alone in his darkness. Here was Joel, the child he had been: alienated and bound to a mother who could barely survive. Here was Joel, the adult he had become: encased and rejecting. Here we were now in shifting relational configurations: mother/son; father/daughter; analyst/patient; siblings living with our shadows. To echo Alvarez, I was stirred then by my own "countertransference urgency." I leaned forward, facing him, calling out his name, "Joel, you are not alone, I am here. You matter to me and our relationship matters." He looked at me then, and I said, "I want to be important to you and I don't want you to drift away." There was silence, and I was unsure if I had alienated him further or drawn him near, perhaps neither, perhaps both. The session ended.

This heightened response was a marked departure from my usual style with Joel and certainly a wake-up from the torpor that had set in between and within each of us. I now see this intense moment as the beginning of a vitalizing enactment. In retrospect, I believe my "countertransference urgency" expressed my wish to stir Joel and his deadened internal objects to life and to reach and vitalize my retreating father and the parts of myself that were identified with him. My reverie had connected me in a visceral way to buried wishes and longings and brought me into a different relationship to Joel, as a complementary and concordant figure (Racker, 1957). *Moved by these identifications and Joel's deepening retreat, I reached out to Joel, insisting on meaning and connection.*

In our next meeting, Joel came in hesitantly, sat down. We looked at each other. He began, "Sometimes I think I keep coming in here because you're the only person in the world that knows that I'm alive as I wander around out there. This is—you are—important to me." I was touched by this admission and said, "Thank you for telling me that." There was a long silence. Something was stirring. I sensed that asking how this felt or what it was like to talk this way would be derailing.

He said then, quite unexpectedly, "Are you a sports fan?" In our time together he had rarely asked me anything about myself or expressed curiosity about me. I said in a playful way, "I remember a few years back when I saw newspaper headlines about the 'subway series' and thought it was an exposé on mass transit." He smiled a little and I continued, "So no, not much of a sports fan, how about you?" He replied, "I don't think I ever told you but I love basketball, always have. When I was a kid I always wanted to watch games, go to the Garden. My mother would say, 'I don't understand, it's just a game …' and I couldn't explain."

I felt the presence of the "bad" and beloved object, the dead mother. Part of me wanted to "go after her" and point out her failings. But I held back, sensing that to do so would return us to a deadlock in which I criticize his objects and he defensively withdraws. This was one of the rare occasions in which he considered a lack in his mother. I felt that to amplify it would interfere with his nascent capacity to view her in a more nuanced way and would polarize us.

So instead I said, "Tell me more about the game." He explained to me that it was the NBA Championship and the New York Knicks were playing. Last night had been a major victory for New York—a team that rarely wins, hadn't even been in the finals for years. They had done well in the first game, then fell apart and kind of gave up in the second. But last night they were on fire. There was a player who had never been special, usually just sat it out on the bench, but last night he was amazing. He made one basket after the other and led his team to victory! While the championship was not over, this was an extraordinary win.

I was taken with this story of redemption and hope—succeeding against all odds and coming to life when least expected. Although I had many clever connections to make, I said only, "How amazing, how great!" He was checking in to see if I was really enjoying this, and I was. He was alive. We were alive. We were relating as two people in the room. At the same time he was a little boy sharing his excitement with a mother who meets him there. He was a father enjoying his child. He was a man on a date, and I was with him in each of these pairings.

He continued, "So I was watching at home. I know it's pathetic I can't even go to a sports bar and sit around with other people, but I huddle in my apartment." He looked at me for the challenge of his self-rebuke, but I was not going there.

Instead I said, "Tell me about last night. Was it fun?"

"It was. And you know what else?"

There is such delight in sharing secrets. "No, what?"

"I have some pot that I got when I had that knee operation, so I smoked some and I got this nice buzz, not the nervous kind, but just mellow and I was watching the game, and this guy was winning and I felt …"

The air was ripe with possibility and he continued in hushed tones: "I felt manly, watching the game, watching my team win."

I was so thrilled with him and the memory of this feeling—the image of him stoned, flexing his muscles, cheering his team on to victory.

Then he paused and said, "Can I ask you something?"

The encounter felt packed with possibility. There was a back and forth we simply had never had in a session before. I paused and said, "Yes, what is it?"

He said, "Do you ever smoke pot?"

I thought for a moment about the question and his taking a chance by asking me something intimate and slightly subversive. I thought about the courage this suggested. I wondered what he wanted to know about who I was and what we might do together. There was an erotic charge, a vitality and uncertainty in the air.

Would a personal revelation be seductive? Would a direct response be taken as a promise to maintain this level of intensity and disclosure? Would refraining from a response be felt as a rejection or a refusal to speak this new language? I was concerned with safeguarding the boundaries of our relationship and keeping it analytic and also wanted to stay with and in this expansive moment. I struggled with how to reply and what to explore. Should we think about the meaning or timing of the question? Should we talk about "what's going on here" now and why this is occurring in relation to my strong reaction to him in our last session and our exchange today? Should I answer or reflect or deflect?

I recalled Davies's (1994) work with a withdrawn, despairing man in "Love in the afternoon" in which she disclosed that she had fantasies about him in an enactment that ultimately enabled the patient to claim dissociated aspects of himself and his traumatic past. Balancing concerns about self-disclosure with an appreciation for this novel experience, I plowed ahead and replied, "I smoked once in a while in college, but it made me nervous, then silly, then I got the munchies." We laughed together.

After a few moments Joel's laughter faded and he said, "When I was at school everyone else used to get stoned and silly and I never could." I felt him heading down a rabbit hole into his feelings of disgust for the boy he had been, and I said, "You wanted so much to be hanging out with the group, to be a part of things and feel connected." He said sadly but without self-contempt, "I did, but I never knew how to join in and somehow people always figured that out and lost interest." His words, laced with hurt and regret, were reminiscent of older reflections but also new in that Joel was rueful rather than ashamed. He continued, "I wish I could have been like everyone else. I wish I could be silly." This brought tears to my eyes as I felt the pain of his sense of exclusion and lack. I also felt a stirring of something else: the possibility of having more. I said, "Yes, of course you do. It is wonderful to be silly sometimes." We looked at each other, and we both smiled a little. There was no scowling as the session ended. He walked out and I was left bemused, confused, energized.

Our interaction felt different, uncertain and new. There had been risk taken, questions asked and responded to. We kept the old objects backgrounded while creating novel experience together in the here and now of our relationship. He approached but we did not pursue the feelings of being pathetic, being a loser. We stayed close to what Joel longed for rather than what he criticized in himself for never having. We touched on feelings about the past without foreclosure or contempt. There was a whisper of hope.

I felt myself teetering back and forth: in the moment and involved, and also making choices to go with what felt most alive (Ogden, 1995). I was aware of the pull of the black hole (his and my own) and the tug away from it toward something vibrant, chancy, and even sexy. In this enactment aliveness was not related to the content of the material or the valence of the emotions expressed. Aliveness was in the way Joel and I related to each other and to the experiences we were exploring. Aliveness was in the spontaneity, freedom, and vibrancy of the emotions we discovered and shared.

During this session I felt a strong urge to tell Joel what I knew through and with him: how utterly painful it is to be tethered to and haunted by a desolate object. How confusing it is to want more when the other can barely sustain themselves. I did not say these words to him. But I believe this knowledge informed and altered our work in unspoken ways. My thoughts here are in line with Bass's (2015) elaboration of Ferenczi's "dialogue of unconscious" in which he articulated the ways in which the analyst's capacity to use her own subjectivity and reach blind spots within herself can lead to new openings and mutual growth.

Something had changed in my relationship to my own internal world and to Joel's. I felt more empathy for and recognition of his attachment to his mother. I felt less of a need to wrest him away from her as I drew nearer to my retreating father and the wish to reach him. As my internal relationship to these split-off introjects (his and mine) softened, Joel became freer to respond in different ways (similar to Cooper, 2014; Davies, 2004; also Coltart, 1986; Symington, 1983). Somehow through an uncanny process of wordless transmission (Ferenczi, [1932] 1988) Joel seemed to grasp these shifts and respond in kind. He was able to resist being drawn back into his depressed internal states and allegiances. He began to experiment with new ways of relating to me and to his own experience. Space opened up within him and in our relationship for emotions that were new: for feeling potent and hopeful, for sharing secret longings and sad regrets, for wanting and asking for more. These were the nascent experiences that emerged through this vitalizing enactment that enlivened both of us and the treatment.

Discussion

Vitalizing enactment: formulating the process

I am conceptualizing this interaction as a vitalizing enactment that drew the patient and the treatment out of impasse into dialogue. This enactment involved a shared movement from dissociation to connection to the creation of novel experience. It was spurred by internal shifts that ricocheted between us and resonated intersubjectively. I believe that we had reached a "tipping point" when this enactment began. A number of different forces coalesced in Joel and in me that were specific to our relationship and this moment in time that propelled us forward.

In entering treatment Joel had found a partner with whom he could powerfully re-create the emotional environment of his youth and his inner world. For a very long time we had lived in that eerily familiar place, playing out mirroring internal relational dynamics. My efforts to reach Joel interpretively were experienced as reproaches that led to despair and impasse as the treatment fell into deadlock. I had to fully enter Joel's subjective world and find myself there. Through my reverie I connected with the most deadened parts of myself, my own "bad" objects that had been backgrounded and dissociated through much of our earlier work. In so doing I could better know, accept, and converse with Joel from the inside out.

This knowledge, Joel's increased withdrawal, and my own sense of urgency led me to reach out to him so intensely. In responding to my entreaty Joel was signaling that the shifts within me were reverberating in him as well. We had dwelled together in the still life of the interior past and could begin to inhabit the unpredictable world of the here and now. Feelings of potency, excitement, curiosity, and surprise began to take shape as we interacted in new ways. Longings for contact and closeness emerged, as did embryonic feelings of hope and the possibility of accepting loss without shame. This enactment vitalized both of us and enlivened the treatment. It drew us out of impasse into dialogue that potentiated these new experiences for us as an analytic couple and as individuals.

"Going first," self-disclosure, and vulnerability

In this enactment with Joel, I had to "go first" (Burton, 2012), disclosing my own vulnerability and need by letting him know "I want to be important to you and I don't want you to drift away." Joel replied with a disclosure that expressed his recognition and appreciation of me for holding him in mind and not giving up on him. "Sometimes

I think … you're the only person … that knows that I am alive … out there. [You] are important to me." His words were a gift that I accepted with gratitude.

I am not suggesting that the analyst should always make personal disclosures of this nature when faced with such inertia or that she work so directly from her own vulnerability (see Levine, 2016) in vitalizing enactments. There was a synergy in this moment that is difficult to pinpoint and impossible to prescribe. With another patient or at a different time, this kind of disclosure might have been experienced as intrusive or misattuned. It might have represented a manic flight from depression or a demand for affirmation. These are the risks that the analyst grapples with in using herself in such an active and enlivening way, that warrant ongoing consideration and reflection. Notwithstanding these concerns I believe that what occurred emerged uniquely from our relational matrix and was mutually transformative. As a couple we had reached our limit of containment. I could no longer hold the deadness and Joel, I believe, was ready at last to emerge.

Mutative action: intersubjective and intrapsychic transformations and growth

In terms of my understanding of the mutative action, a confluence of intrapsychic and intersubjective processes within and between us entwined to generate change. My direct plea to Joel to stay with me and the treatment, my assertion of his importance, and my wish to be important too represented different ways of relating in the real world. In this sense the interpersonal experience was transformative. The relationship between us as two adults responding to one another in vibrant new ways was progressive and growth promoting.

I also believe my words articulated buried unconscious wishes and had transference analogues that spoke to Joel's object world (and mirrored unarticulated longings of my own). I voiced what Joel in that quiet house of his youth had never been able to say. He wanted to be important. He wanted his love to be valued and returned. Speaking from the position of his object I was able to offer myself to Joel as "live company" (Alvarez, 1992), providing a kind of connection he had scarcely known. In responding with appreciation and animation

Joel was forging novel experiences. The affective mutuality and internal symmetry contributed to the power of this vitalizing enactment.

In sharing his sports story Joel found a partner who was eager and enthusiastic, who could enjoy and celebrate with him. The story of the basketball game was full of meaning and hope for victorious participation, for winning and coming through. During our interaction Joel repeatedly checked in with me. I believe he was checking to see if I could be a partner who would hold him in mind both as the person he was (Fonagy & Target, 1997) and the person he might become (Cooper, 2000; Loewald, 1960). He needed to know that I could recognize the boy who had spent his life sidelined and ashamed and the man who might someday join the game. These were new ways of being seen and known.

In questioning me about my own secret delinquencies Joel was probing (Ghent, 1990), experimenting with the limits between us. He was feeling out who I was as a new object and a person and what our connection could be. Without inhaling, we were getting high in the giddy back and forth of our generative exchange. All at once we were two college kids in a quad passing a joint; we were the children of our youths retranscribing the past; we were two adults in the here and now enjoying one another. We were patient and analyst in a vitalizing enactment creating, discovering, and progressing together.

Alvarez (2012) has cited Trevarthen's (1993) work on the importance of a child's experience of delighting the other. This occurred as Joel seemed to radiate in the glow of our encounter. It was also a joy for me to delight in him. The room filled with a shared pleasure and sense of mutual recognition (Benjamin, 1990) that was transformative. In voicing his regret for what had not been and the wish "to be silly," there was no defensiveness or self-reproach. There was poignancy and hope. This moment was very alive as we found a new way to relate to the old and intractable. We did not dislodge old objects. We accepted their presence and began to create novel ways of relating to self and other in the present moment.

Enactment as a progressive lived experience

Although I have thought often about those sessions, we have not analyzed what occurred. As the enactment was under way, reflections on the process would have taken us out of the moment. We were traversing unknown territory rather than pausing to map out where we had been or where we might go from there. In vitalizing enactment the action is in the lived experience, rather than the verbal understanding of what has unfolded or the linking of old to new. Attempts to symbolize the interaction might have been clunky or intellectual, pulling us away from the vibrancy of the moment.

I muse that when enactments involve pathological repetitions of dissociated or traumatic experience analytic progress may require surviving, unpacking, and verbally making meaning of what has transpired. But when enactments are vitalizing, the lived process is itself transformative. I do not see vitalizing enactments as techniques but as relational events that can be uniquely generative and can move the analytic dyad through deadened impasses into novel areas of creation.

Ongoing process

My work with Joel continued and is midsentence as I write this. We have never again fallen into such deadened impasse nor been propelled through the kind of vitalizing enactment that I have explored in this chapter. We are closer and our dialogue is more fluent. There have been no dramatic shifts in Joel's representations of his objects. But there is more wiggle room, and we are more adept at sidestepping our old rabbit holes. I believe that through the treatment Joel is taking in good object experiences. He has also begun to try out new ways of relating in and out of the consulting room, contributing to greater relational freedom (Stern, 2015) and intersubjective growth.

I have found that keeping my finger on the pulse of what is generative—the desire to connect, the wish to be silly, the longing for more—tends to be facilitative. Interpreting the pull of the old readily becomes an enactment of the old. I work delicately and with greater compassion around Joel's introjects, remembering how dearly he holds these troubling and beloved figures. I imagine that in the future we might converse with Joel's past and inner world in different ways. For now I stay as near as I can to how things feel and the parts of Joel that are emerging.

In a recent session, Joel came in to tell me about something "interesting" that had happened (his "interest" in himself is a new and exciting phenomenon!). He was on a date with a woman who asked him about his past relationships. This was usually a dreaded question to be avoided at all costs. This time he ventured, "I'm kind of a loner and never really had a long-term relationship. It's been hard for me to get close to people." While he girded himself for the inevitable rejection and humiliation, he was surprised that his date murmured some kind of assent and ordered a drink.

In exploring his feelings Joel said, "I figured as soon as she got a sense of who I am, what a freak I am, she would have just walked away, even been mad at me for wasting her time."

Shaking my head, I said, "But that didn't happen. She didn't think you were as bad as you fear."

"It's always been my story, since I was a kid," he said.

"It's always felt like the only story you could tell. I wonder though about other stories ..."

Joel looked at me—with skepticism, with curiosity?

I continued, "What was it like, to just say something simple and true about yourself?"

Our eyes met. Even before he responded there was a subtle easing in the room, like a sigh. He leaned back. "It was a relief and it felt good. I don't even remember what we talked about after that because it was all such a surprise to me."

We laughed and shared in the wonder of surprise.

Here, very gently, we were considering the way his inner life and past experiences had shaped his perceptions and could compel and constrain him. Without directly implicating his objects or delving deeply into history, we focused on the present and what it feels like to accept oneself and try out different ways of being. We were working intrapsychically and engaged intersubjectively, relating to one another with a deepening sense of freedom and possibility. Potential space opened in a way that felt almost tangible. In this and subsequent sessions we began questioning fate and the malleability of destiny. *Did Joel have to forever be the child of his youth?*

Conclusion

This chapter was inspired by Alvarez's notion of vitalization and reclamation. Alvarez's ideas go to the generative potentials of the analytic relationship. Taking creative license with her formulations, I have reconceptualized a construct that originated in work with children and applied it to adult psychoanalysis, proposing the notion of *vitalizing enactment*. Echoing Alvarez's (1997) expanded interpretation of Bion's container/contained, I have suggested that enactment can represent the potentiation of a range of novel and positive experiences and capacities in the here-and-now moment of the analytic encounter. I have suggested that in deadened impasse the analyst, moved by her own internal exigencies and working from within the relational matrix, may reach out to her patient and initiate a vitalizing enactment that can enliven the pair and bring new experiences to life.

Acknowledgments

Thanks to Noah Glassman for his thoughtful feedback on an early version of this paper. I'm also grateful to Rachel Sopher for our ongoing dialogue on vitalization in psychoanalysis.

References

Alvarez, A. (1992). *Live company: Psychoanalytic psychotherapy with autistic, borderline, deprived and abused children*. London: Tavistock/Routledge.

Alvarez, A. (1997). Projective identification as a communication: Its grammar in borderline psychotic children. *Psychoanalytic Dialogues*, *7*, 753–768. doi:10.1080/10481889709539218

Alvarez, A. (2012). *The thinking heart: Three levels of psychoanalytic therapy with disturbed children*. New York, NY: Routledge.

Aron, L. (1996). *A meeting of minds: Mutuality in psychoanalysis*. Hillsdale, NJ: The Analytic Press.

Aron, L. (2003). The paradoxical place of enactment in psychoanalysis. *Psychoanalytic Dialogues*, *13*, 623–631. doi:10.1080/10481881309348760

Aron, L., & Atlas, G. (2015). Generative enactment: Memories from the future. *Psychoanalytic Dialogues*, *25*, 309–324. doi:10.1080/10481885.2015.1034554

Bass, A. (2003). "E" enactments in psychoanalysis: Another medium, another message. *Psychoanalytic Dialogues*, *13*, 657–675. doi:10.1080/10481881309348762

Bass, A. (2015). The dialogue of unconsciouses, mutual analysis and the uses of the self in contemporary relational psychoanalysis. *Psychoanalytic Dialogues*, *25*, 2–17. doi:10.1080/10481885.2015.991235

Benjamin, J. (1990). Recognition and destruction: An outline of intersubjectivity. *Psychoanalytic Psychology*, *7*, 33–47. doi:10.1037/h0085258

Bion, W.R. (1963). *Elements of psycho-analysis*. London, UK: Heinemann.

Black, M. (2003). Enactment: Analytic musings on energy, language, and personal growth. *Psychoanalytic Dialogues*, *13*, 633–655. doi:10.1080/10481881309348761

Bollas, C. (1983). Expressive uses of the countertransference: Notes to the patient from oneself. *Contemporary Psychoanalysis*, *19*, 1–34. doi:10.1080/00107530.1983.10746587

Bromberg, P. (1998). *Standing in the spaces: Essays on clinical process, trauma, and dissociation*. Hillsdale, NJ: The Analytic Press.

Bromberg, P. (2006). *Awakening the dreamer: Clinical journeys*. Hillsdale, NJ: The Analytic Press.

Burton, N. (2012). Getting personal: Thoughts on therapeutic action through the interplay of intimacy, affect, and consciousness. *Psychoanalytic Dialogues*, *22*, 662–678. doi:10.1080/10481885.2012.735588

Coltart, N. (1986). "Slouching towards Bethlehem" ... or thinking the unthinkable in psychoanalysis. In G. Kohon (Ed.), *The British school of psychoanalysis: The independent tradition* (pp. 185–199). New Haven, CT: Yale University Press.

Cooper, S. (2000). *Objects of hope; Exploring possibility and limit in psychonalysis*. Hillsdale, NJ: The Analytic Press.

Cooper, S. (2014). The things we carry: Finding/creating the object and the analysts' self-reflective participation. *Psychoanalytic Dialogues*, *24*, 621–636. doi:10.1080/10481885.2014.970963

Davies, J.M. (1994). Love in the afternoon: A relational reconsideration of desire and dread in the countertransference. *Psychoanalytic Dialogues*, *4*, 153–170. doi:10.1080/10481889409539011

Davies, J.M. (2004). Whose bad objects are we anyway? Repetition and our elusive love affair with evil. *Psychoanalytic Dialogues*, *14*, 711–732. doi:10.1080/10481881409348802

Davies, J.M., & Frawley, M.G. (1994). *Treating the adult survivor of childhood sexual abuse*. New York, NY: Basic Books.

Director, L. (2009). The enlivening object. *Contemporary Psychoanalysis*, *45*, 120–141. doi:10.1080/00107530.2009.10745990

Director, L. (2016). The analyst as catalyst: Cultivating mind in the shadow of neglect. *Psychoanalytic Dialogues*, *26*, 685–697. doi:10.1080/10481885.2016.1235444

Faimberg, H. (2005). *The telescoping of generations: Listening to the narcissistic links between generations*. London: Routledge.

Fairbairn, W.R.D. (1952). *Psychoanalytic studies of the personalities*. London: Routledge.

Ferenczi, S. ([1932] 1988). *The clinical diary of Sandor Ferenzci* (J. Dupond, M. Balint, & N.Z. Jackson, Eds.). Cambridge, MA: Harvard University Press.

Fiscalini, J. (1988). Curative experience in the psychoanalytic relationship. *Contemporary Psychoanalysis*, *24*, 125–142. doi:10.1080/00107530.1988.10746225

Fonagy, P., & Target, M. (1997). Attachment and reflective function: Their role in self organization. *Development and Psychopathology*, *9*, 679–700. doi:10.1017/S0954579497001399

Gerson, S. (2009). When the third is dead: Memory, mourning, and witnessing in the aftermath of the Holocaust. *The International Journal of Psychoanalysis*, *90*, 1341–1357.

Ghent, E. (1990). Masochism, submission and surrender: Masochism as a perversion of surrender. *Contemporary Psychoanalysis*, *26*, 108–136. doi:10.1080/00107530.1990.10746643

Green, A. (1986). The dead mother. In *On private madness*. London, UK: Hogarth Press.

Grossmark, R. (2012). The flow of enactive engagement. *Contemporary Psychoanalysis*, *48*, 287–300. doi:10.1080/ 00107530.2012.10746505

Hoffman, I. (2009). Therapeutic passion in the countertransference. *Psychoanalytic Dialogues*, *19*, 617–637. doi:10.1080/10481880903340141

Jacobs, T. (1986). On countertransference enactments. *Journal of the American Psychoanalytic Association*, *34*, 289–307. doi:10.1177/000306518603400203

Klein, M. (1975). *Envy and gratitude and other works, 1946–1963*. New York, NY: Delacorte Press.

Levine, L. (2016). A mutual survival of destructiveness and its creative potential for agency and desire. *Psychoanalytic Dialogues*, *26*, 36–49. doi:10.1080/10481885.2016.1123511

Loewald, H. (1960). On the therapeutic action of psychoanalysis. *The International Journal of Psycho-Analysis*, *58*, 563–572.

Mitchell, S.A. (1988). Penelope's loom. In *Relational concepts in psychoanalysis: An integration* (pp. 271–308). Cambridge, MA: Harvard University Press.

Mitchell, S.A. (2000). *Relationality: From attachment to intersubjectivity*. New York, NY: Routledge.

Newirth, J. (2003). *Between emotion and cognition: The generative unconscious*. New York, NY: Other Press.

Ogden, T.H. (1995). Analyzing forms of aliveness and deadness of the transference–countertransference. *The International Journal of Psycho-Analysis*, *76*, 695–709.

Racker, H. (1957). The meaning and uses of countertransference. *The Psychoanalytic Quarterly*, *26*, 303–357.

Rosenfeld, H. (1987). *Impasse and interpretation: Therapeutic and anti-therapeutic factors in the psycho-analytic treatment of psychotic, borderline, and neurotic patients*. London, UK: Tavistock.

Stern, D. (2003). *Unformulated experience: From dissociation to imagination in psychoanalysis*. New York, NY: Routledge.

Stern, D. (2015). *Relational freedom: Emergent properties of the interpersonal field*. London, UK: Routledge.

Symington, N. (1983). The analyst's act of freedom as agent of change. *International Review of Psychoanalysis*, *10*, 263–291.

Trevarthen, C. (1993). Playing into reality: Conversations with the infant communicator. In L. Spurling (Ed.), *Winnicott studies* (Vol. VII). London, UK: Karnac.

Williams, P. (2010). *Invasive objects: Minds under siege*. New York, NY: Routledge.

Chapter 2

An allegiance to absence

Fidelity to the internal void

Rachel Sopher

Jennie

It is the end of a session with my patient Jennie; she rocks back and forth as she speaks, her hands covering her face. We have spent the hour experiencing the depths of her despair, traveling back in time together to a harrowing episode in which her mother drove while under the influence of mind-altering drugs, crashing the car, almost killing them both. Towards the end of our time I ask Jennie how she feels. "I feel like a hole," she tells me in a tiny voice. "Like you're in a hole?" I ask her. "No, like I *am* a hole. Like there is a pit, an indentation, a negative space in the place where I am supposed to be," she answers. I wonder if my question, together with the approach of the end of the hour, have left her feeling emptied out, traumatized by the experience of merger as we relived her trauma together, followed by the abrupt separation, a ripping apart into "a devastating sense of two-ness" at the session's end (Tustin 1981, p. 106). Work with Jennie is characterized by just the type of absence she describes: there is a hole in her, and in me, an emptiness that suffuses the heart of the intersubjective space between us, hollowing out our interactions at their core.

Separation and absence

Many describe encounters with patients suffused with feelings of deadness, emptiness, and lack in what has been referred to as the black hole or void in internal experience (Balint 1963; Eshel 1998; Gerson 2009; Green 1986; Gurevich 2008; Peltz 1998; Tustin 1972). Because this black hole is an often unformulated internal state defined by what is not there rather than what is, both patients and psychoanalysts lack adequate ways of communicating about this experience of early, traumatic absence and its consequences. One intention of this chapter is to continue the discussion about these preverbal states, to elaborate the language for the presence of absence in treatment, both in the internal worlds of patient and analyst, and in the intersubjective overlap created in the relationship between them (Ogden 2004). The internal absence is most often conceptualized as a deficiency in psychic structure, an area of weak or non-representation. Rather than defining the psychic void solely as a lack of internal development leaving a passively experienced impoverished inner world, this chapter highlights the phenomenon of libidinal investment in the original black hole in the early care-taking environment, creating an allegiance to absence, an emotional investment in a state of nothingness that actively impedes experiences of vitality and psychic growth, and shutting down elaboration of the generative unconscious.

The internal void or absence is often formulated in terms of the ongoing structural consequences of a profound lack in early maternal care, a zone of deadness or emptiness that pervades psychic space. Because the infant has not yet developed the ability to symbolize the absence of the object, it is dependent on the concrete presence of the mother to feel safe. According to Winnicott (1971), if the mother is apart from the child, her image remains alive in his mind for x minutes. After x minutes, her image starts to fade; if she stays away $x + y$ minutes the child is in distress but still has not been irreversibly transformed, but:

> in $x + y + z$ minutes the baby has become traumatized. In $x + y + z$ minutes the mother's return does not mend the baby's altered state. Trauma implies that the baby has experienced a break in life's continuity, so that primitive defences now become organized to defend against a repetition of "unthinkable anxiety"
>
> (p. 97)

When a child experiences the loss of the mother that is too sudden, too early, or too long, it brings up the "nameless dread" (Bion 1962) of catastrophic abandonment. Traumatic separation evokes "unthinkable anxiety" that must be defended against at all costs as all ensuing separations bear the threat of this paradigmatic, unendurable separateness: the gap between self and other having become an infinite, timeless void experienced as too painful to bear (Lombardi 2015).

Winnicott (1971) elaborates that, from the child's perspective, there is a time when the mother is dead but can come back to life, and past that, a point when she is felt to be dead forever. As this change takes place, the child experiences a moment of anger, a protest, that is passed over then lost as the new reality of the mother's indelible absence takes hold of his psyche. There are thus dual dangers looming, according to Winnicott: there is the menace of catastrophic aloneness threatening breakdown from without, and the unexperienced violent reaction to the original separation threatening fragmentation from within.

In order to avoid re-experiencing the trauma of early abandonment, the child may attempt to deny his separateness using omnipotent fantasy and autistic defenses, creating an unrelated shell-self built around a fragmented interior that must exert energy to plug up the hole at his vulnerable core, remaining mortally defended, isolated, and related to an enclosed world of internal objects and inanimate things (Tustin 1986). This encapsulation keeps the child safe from experiencing his separateness and from the traumatic knowledge of his need for the other.

In his discussions of internal absence Winnicott's (1971) predominant emphasis is on the structural impact of the neglectful environment of the original parenting relationship on the dependent child victim and the way this manifests internally; that is, he foregrounds the passively experienced consequences of early abandonment and their sequelae later in life. To illustrate, he uses a quote from a patient who had suffered repeated abandonments throughout her childhood; referring to her previous analyst, she told Winnicott that, "The negative of him is more real than the positive of you" (p. 23), which he interpreted to be representative of an internal world in which absence and loss served as the nucleus around which she organized her self-experience. Winnicott highlights the experiential quality of the void in the patient's psyche, the long-ranging impact of early neglect on the patient, which led her to feel that what was unavailable was more real than the immediately available objects around her. Green (1997) similarly explains that, for Winnicott's patient and others like her, "The non-existence will become, at some point, the only thing that is real" (p. 1082). These understandings illustrate one side of a self–other configuration, the position of child victim in relation to an absent parent.

Though these formulations and others like them accurately describe the psychic experience of internal absence as inner reality, they privilege the encapsulated experience of early infancy and the long-ranging consequences of being the passive object of neglect. This construction, though eminently useful, leaves out another side of the story—the child's identification with the absent non-object and subsequent attachment to and investment in the experience of emptiness. The originally traumatic absence becomes introjected as a libidinally invested attachment to lack, the tie to the non-present object bringing about a sense of futility and cynicism about the power of available human bonds in favor of an internal relationship to absence. Winnicott's patient, mentioned above, must hold on to the nothingness, the gap having become the barrier beyond which lies certainty of annihilation. As she continued she told Winnicott, "All I have got is what I have not got" (p. 23). Her expression belies the powerful attachment to the absent object and her fidelity to what she has "not got," hence her loyalty to the absence in intersubjective relationships, including the one with her analyst. The nothingness is her everything; it is her attempt to maintain a connection with her primary objects which were defined by their non-presence through absence and neglect.

In a similar example, a patient once told me that, though she had been in a harrowing situation over the weekend in which she lost control while skiing and injured herself, she had felt "safe because *no one* was watching." In exploring this phrase it became clear that the "no one" that was watching her was her internal absent mother. This patient's mother in her lack was still the main object of attachment, the source of safety even as defined by her non-presence.

At an early stage in development, the child needs the mother's presence in order to symbolize, and digest his experiences, to make them meaningful. When the mother is absent, there is no containing presence available to help the infant to understand the overwhelming affect associated with her absence. In the child's state of omnipotence, he infers that his neglected state is a consequence of the mother's desire in relation to him (Aulagnier 2001). In other words, he surmises that the mother wants him to feel her absence and neglect. The child attaches this meaning to the early experience of abandonment in order to maintain a connection to the absent maternal object—this state of affairs being more preferable than the catastrophe of having no object at all. The child makes a secret pact with the absent mother, promising to cut off his own needs to fulfill her desire for absence; this in exchange for his continued existence. The need to maintain this meaning, that the mother wanted the child to experience abandonment, creates a strong bond with the absent object, and inhibits other experiences with present objects that might threaten this important primary link.

The allegiance to absence is analogous to Fairbairn's (1963) model of the internalization of and the attachment to the bad mother, but in this case the mother is bad because absent or neglecting (rather than angry, critical, or intrusive). In other words, the child cathects to a non-object as representative of the original absent bond with the mother. Later in life, he will continue to unconsciously look for similarly absent objects to enact (and attempt to master) the original traumatic experience of absence. The neglectful parent is not only taken in, becoming the source of the internal absence, but also libidinally invested, such that there is an emotional attachment to what wasn't there. This is a powerful devotion to absence, an allegiance to the lack that exemplified the child's early primary relationships. There is an imperative attached to the link with absence, as the persecuting absent object requires the constant presence of the child so that she may continually fulfill her wish to absent herself from him. Aloneness thus takes on the masochistic morality of allowing oneself to be absented, enacting the central primal relationship.

This allegiance to absence is a bond with nothing, a fidelity to nothingness that fills up all the internal space so that no novel experience may take root and grow. Vitality, spontaneity, and other emanations from the authentic self subsequently must be repressed as they threaten the link with the absent non-object. To break the bond with the absent object would mean suffering the original disorganizing catastrophe of her absence, as well as coping with the affective understanding of what one has given up in the maintenance of this early connection.

Patients with this type of "negative investment" are eternally drawn to what is not there, the absence haunting with a powerful hold that pervades all psychic space. The ensuing disavowal of early need leads to a state of suspended animation, the deadness fencing in the private madness of totalizing desire that might otherwise be unleashed (Emery 2002; Green 1988). As such, instead of experiencing a potentially generative bond suffused with creative possibility between self and other, there is a menacing danger perceived in the intersubjective space, one that threatens to break the bond with absence such that the original breakdown and its resultant overwhelming affect are re-experienced. The original catastrophic abandonment becomes encapsulated, avoided as the affect it encases is indigestible; there is no way to symbolize what was not there, making it impossible to mourn.

An unarticulated non-presence

An allegiance to absence differs from Green's (1986) dead mother in that this type of object relationship is a pre-symbolic connection to an unarticulated non-presence. Where the dead mother was once available to the child as an intelligible live object who then fades away, the allegiance to absence is a relationship to a state of lack, a more diffuse attachment to a process that defies representation. This results in a connection to an object that is defined by a state of non-generativity, a cathexis to the blanking out of the possibility of creative expansion, in order to maintain loyalty to the absent object and protect oneself from the painful knowledge of what has subsequently been lost. Attachment to a bad object that defies representation leads to a freezing of the original traumatic scene in a concrete space without the capacity to elaborate the internal object world. Instead, the opposite occurs: the absent objects must be protected by keeping the natural development of the generative unconscious in a rigid, stagnant state.

Instead of developing new and more complex internal object relationships (Green 1993) there is a necessary withdrawal of investment in others in order to maintain the link with the original absent object. This leads to a reciprocal wish to eliminate the desire for the other in the self with an ensuing attack on internal objects. This process impairs the capacity for symbolization as new objects cannot be stably represented internally (Reed & Baudry 2005), leaving an internal void that cannot be filled. This early habituation to withdrawal of investment leads to difficulty creating and maintaining internal representations later in life, often leaving only affect and impulse as surrogates for meaningful object relations. This illustrates the way the allegiance to absence, rather than a passively experienced lack of internal structure, is an active and ongoing process of divestment from external reality that inhibits the path to mourning deemed too painful to approach, let alone bear. This allegiance to absence, rather than a passive refusal, is more often an unremitting, active process of deadening potential affective links; a withdrawal from the possibility of what might be new and enlivening, a continuous negation of the potential to create new objects that requires a measure of energy to maintain.

In addition to a lack of representability of absence, there is often the lack of a *framework* within which to create internal representations, and which holds the capability to contain the experience of emptiness in the self (Green 1993). Because of the intensity of fear that separateness evokes, there is no structure, or experience of internal space with which to hold the absence; there is no blank background against which anticipatory fantasy can arise that spans external and internal worlds (Winnicott 1958). Without this framework, one cannot do the psychic work of *imagining* what is absent, instead shielding the self from its knowledge through denial of difference. The patient cannot conceive of the emptiness. She cannot imagine, contain, or give shape to it, so she remains consumed by an undifferentiated state of internal emptiness.

The absent object paradoxically fills up all of the psychic space, pervading all so that nothing new can take root. The potential creativity of internal emptiness is unmanifested as this type of generative space would bring to light the catastrophe of the original experience of absence. The goal of treatment, then, is to begin to give shape to the patient's uniquely experienced internal absence (Gurevich 2008), to symbolize it so that it may be thought about, thus allowing the beginnings of generative emptiness to be experienced in the center of the nothingness, the creative emptiness that is the space from which internal process grows and expands to create increasingly more complex and affectively rich connections.

Absence in treatment

As the traumatic severing of self from other which is being addressed here occurs before the acquisition of language, and is defined by an act of omission rather than commission, there are no words nor any meaningful actions available to the patient with which to represent what is missing. This leads to a daunting technical difficulty: not only is there an attachment to absence, but the absent object is also undeveloped and thus inaccessible to verbal representation. Because of the unformulated, preverbal nature of the absent object, language is an often inadequate vehicle for the communication of meaning between patient and analyst. The ability to utilize language meaningfully is predicated upon the capacity to both experience and symbolize the absence of the object. For this one must be able to tolerate separation (Amir 2013). The acceptance of the ambivalence necessary for the symbolic use of language requires individuation and a tolerance for the work of mourning, as it depends both on a tie to the object as well as the capacity to release it and conjure it within.

With an allegiance to absence, language simultaneously enacts the transmission of meaning and renders it void, cutting off internal linkages and affective resonances in order to protect absent objects. Because of the split that this type of "absent language" maintains (Amir 2017), cutting off the live (absented) internal child object, in favor of giving voice to the deadened adult, one must establish a receptivity to a kind of grammar that stands outside of language, in the most basic register of concrete sensation. Specifically, for patients who have experienced preverbal, catastrophic neglect, experiences of the object primarily occur at the level of sensory experience (Ogden 1989). Furthermore, patients who maintain encapsulated or dissociated experiences of early absence are caught in a "closed, bodily world without room in which to create a distinction between symbol and symbolized" (Ogden 1989, p.131). At this level of object relating, words are experienced as things, sensations that soothe or intrude on the emergent sense of self.

The demand on the analytic relationship is thus either one of total non-engagement or of merger. It requires the work of two psyches, two bodies and minds in communion with each other to "dream up" (Ogden 2007) an absence within the analytic third of psychoanalytic treatment. What is missing must be first experienced on a sensory level, then represented in the treatment so that a deep, primary knowledge of the absence can be symbolized, accepted, and integrated in an organic way that does not call up defenses related to traumatic intrusion. A psychoanalytic patient cannot be told simply with words that he is holding on to an early absence. For an integration to occur, the piece that is missing must be accessed from a more basic register of sensory experience; this more basic register is on the level of the experiencing self, in the mode of perception over apperception (Winnicott 1967). This primary, sensory register bypasses the narrative structure imposed on experience by the higher-order intellectual functioning of the mind, which can be defensive in nature.

This undertaking is one in which what is absent becomes accessible through enactive engagement with internal objects that begin to tell the story of absence, often first coming to be known by the analyst who then makes it available, representable, and thus knowable to both analyst and patient (Grossmark 2012). Communication through words, especially ones that draw attention to the separateness of the patient and analyst, can attenuate the elaboration of the patient's inner experience by arousing his vigilance. As Milner (1969) wrote, "the 'other' has to be created before it can be perceived" (p. 404). The primary attachment, or absence thereof, becomes actualized in treatment in the relationship between patient and analyst, the unique manifestations of which bring to life the absence in the here and now where it can be experienced and transformed. Paradoxically, the absence of connection can transform into the presence-of-absence once represented and symbolized, generating novel psychic significance.

Over the course of their process, the analytic couple comes to represent the lack of representation, the absent object manifesting itself through deep engagement with the other in the process of psychoanalytic treatment. But not only does the absence become lived out between patient and analyst, but so too does the countervalent wish for the reparative *total presence* of the mother (Peltz 1998). This primal wish for merger, amputated at an early age, can be re-experienced in the imaginative space of the analytic frame: as Winnicott's (1971) patient mentioned above told him, "I suppose I want something that never goes away" (p. 23). Thus not only the experience of the original absence "comes to life" in the lived experience of the analytic process, but also the impossible longing for the missing experience of total presence of the maternal figure which can be surrendered to in a fantasy of completeness.

The primary link that has been missing can never be returned, but the integrative psychic work of suffering the pain of this absence can be made possible through the processes of reflection, symbolization, and attribution of meaning. The dissociated state of total dependence and its absence are both conjured up through creative imaginings, dreamed up in the transference–countertransference matrix. The conjunction of the analytic couple who engage in dialogue verbally and non-verbally, in body and in mind, gives meaning to what is being experienced, turning what once felt frighteningly meaningless into a source of meaning itself.

Through this process, the analytic dyad together creates moments of significance in which they relive and give shape to these early experiences. For example, in the vignette described above, in which Jennie described feeling like "a hole," we first felt merged together in an idealized mother/idealized baby transference–countertransference in which there was an implicit promise that our connection could hold her trauma in a way that would last forever—an experience of total presence. Asking a question that pointed to our separateness, the fact that I couldn't read her mind and was aware of the approach of the end of the session ripped us apart into a state of two-ness that left her feeling erased from my mind—an experience of total absence—most likely causing her to retreat into the safety of absence by defensively erasing herself. Points of contact such as these can begin to articulate the presence of absence by connecting up to create a matrix that approximates the missing framework for the creation of meaning.

What follows is a continuation of this case example that illustrates the way a fidelity to a dissociated internal absence was repeatedly enacted in a treatment. The analytic framework encased repeated representations of this motif, each time from a slightly different angle, each time with a slightly different point of view. The theme of absence persistently appeared and disappeared, and was experienced and articulated at differing levels of development and of reality, creating a chain of levels (Hofstadter 1979) that became meaningful through repeated experience of enactment and representation within the therapeutic relationship. This eventually resulted in the internalization of a framework within which to imagine and give meaning to the absent object.

The case of Jennie

When she arrived at my office for our first visit, Jennie immediately struck me as slight, and pale, with her long hair pulled back in a tight bun, and dressed in dark colors that accentuated her pallid complexion, calling to mind the image of a ghost. A 32-year-old freelance journalist, Jennie entered into our meeting with an air of shyness, and approached our relationship tentatively, never seeming to have been asked about her internal experience before, and never having paid much attention to it herself. From the start, she seemed detached, far away, and unreachable, and I felt similarly far away from her myself.

Jennie grew up in a middle-class home in a suburban area with her father, her mother, and a brother three years older than her. She described a neglected childhood in which she felt isolated and unseen, remembering being left alone to play by herself or watch television for extended stretches of time. When Jennie was eight years old her parents divorced. After that, her father moved out of the house along with her older brother. Her father told Jennie that she had to stay behind, so that her mother would not feel abandoned. So Jennie was left alone in the house to accommodate and contend with an erratic mother who was addicted to painkillers and marijuana, depressed and constantly in and out of tumultuous relationships. She was forced to care for herself and her mother, but her most prevalent memory was of spending hours and hours alone in her room with the door shut—isolated and dejected, with her mother similarly barricaded in her own room next door.

Jennie said that she came to therapy because she felt that people seemed to lose interest in her quickly and reasoned that this was because she was "boring." She spent stretches of time following strangers who seemed "interesting" to her through the streets, buying things they bought, tasting things they ate, trying to mimic their behavior in a way that would somehow make her less "forgettable." In her attempts to fit in she emptied herself, "erased herself," as she called it, becoming a chameleon, as she drained herself of her own desires. In her attempts to understand what was missing inside she minutely reconstructed her interactions with people in our sessions, describing conversations with acquaintances, and dealings with professional colleagues at length.

As we started our three-times-a-week treatment, one of the first things she told me was that she tries to distract people by being vivacious and accommodating "over here" (pointing to herself) while what's really going on is "over there on the side" (pointing to the empty place next to her on the couch). She explained that was where there's a part of her that she didn't want anyone to see, the absent part in despair, abject, terrified, and desperate for help. Though she described this other state "over there on the side" to me in a tone devoid of affect, I felt that she was telling me something important about her inner world, and made a mental note of the imperative to keep the existence of this absent part of her alive in my mind as a vital element of our work together.

But even as she described this other, more vulnerable part of herself, Jennie came across as utterly impassive. Especially at first, Jennie appeared to be hesitant and guarded about entering into our relationship. Though the material we talked about always *seemed* rich, and we always *seemed* to be doing good work, Jennie felt far away and detached. At times I was dismayed at how unreachable she seemed, but still tried to allow and make space for what was present on a basic level, challenging her assumptions about her internal sense of badness, putting her feelings into context, and remaining especially sensitive to her unexpressed early needs, attempting to build trust and provide a holding environment in order to facilitate access to these more vulnerable states.

Jennie was both indifferent to my presence and exquisitely sensitive to any intrusion; at times even my gestures and the rhythm of my breath seemed to impinge on her ability to think. As time went on and she began to intermittently experience her affect, Jennie's feelings tended to flood and overwhelm her. She experienced intense somatic symptoms in sessions (for instance, she described a feeling of despair as a burning sensation radiating out of her belly button up into her torso). Remarkably, when these acute experiences arose between us, I felt her intense internal sensations in my viscera too, her descriptions of what was going on inside of her seeming to enter into and change my own internal experience, her words physically transforming and giving shape to my feelings as if they were a pliant lump of clay.

What seemed confounding and unique to me about our work was that, though we made genuine contact in these powerful and painful moments, and though these experiences seemed to erase all distance between us, our link seemed to dissolve in the very moment Jennie left my office. I started to realize that I wasn't thinking of Jennie between sessions, even after we shared intense experiences together. For example, after the session in which we relived the terrifying night of the car accident described above, I did not think of Jennie again till right before our next meeting, when I reviewed my notes, internally wincing as the affective intensity of her story flooded back into my awareness. But instead of thinking of her, I remembered her, with a tinge of guilt in terms of the *lack* of thought I was giving her; I only recalled her in her absence.

I came to see our experiences of deep connection as encapsulated pockets of aliveness—oases surrounded by long stretches of deadness in which the bulk of our meetings lacked affective intensity and the only thing binding us seemed our mutual sense of duty to one another. We were in the midst of one of these long, mutually withdrawn stretches when I started to notice that, as Jennie was speaking, I often situated myself in the same characteristic position I usually find myself in when I'm with my own analyst. Though I think about my analyst when I'm with other patients, it is usually in identification with her position as analyst, as in, "What would my analyst say in this situation?" Now, with Jennie, I realized that instead of identifying with my analyst in her role as analyst, I was identifying with myself as patient, as in, "I miss my analyst. Maybe I should call her and ask for an extra session this week." I started to realize that these musings during our sessions were reflective of my dissociated needs, and perhaps of Jennie's too.

I began to wonder about this, and about what else was absent from our relationship—what aggression, what fears, what desires? Where was the vulnerable part of Jennie in the empty spot next to her on the sofa, "over there, on the side?" And why couldn't I connect to her? A potential space had opened up where it had previously been collapsed, allowing reverie to start to emerge as a symbolizing process between us (Ogden 1997). I became aware that I had been privileging the experiences in which her younger states emerged, using them as proof of our connectedness, and lost my faith in our bond the more time we spent in a state of detachment. It occurred to me that I had been thinking of her withdrawal as a defense against loss rather than the representation of a specific form of object relationship—a tie to an absent mother.

Though nothing between us changed externally, I began to get more in touch with my own loneliness and fears of abandonment, along with a deep wish for closeness with Jennie that I had previously kept out of awareness. Reinvigorated, I began to make a point of thinking about what might be happening inside of Jennie, working to consciously keep her experience in mind, at times even visualizing a live and beating heart inside of her, wondering about the inner workings of a separate subject, with a center of gravity, an intelligence, and an internal spark all her own.

In the week following these realizations, Jennie brought in a dream: *I have this little baby and I'm supposed to feed it, but I keep losing it. I first start to feed it and then I lose it. Then I find it again and feel relieved, but then I lose it again. I keep scrambling to find it and then settle down, but as soon as I relax and start feeding it, it disappears again. It was a frantic dream.* In the discussion that followed, Jennie associated to her recent experiences of losing several of her personal effects. Over the course of two months, she had lost her phone, an expensive pair of sunglasses, and a set of keys—all of which she found again soon after. I was curious about what this losing and finding could represent. Was there some part of her without words that kept getting lost in our work together? Was she attempting to alert us to the possibility that something in her was missing and needed to be found? The urgency of the experience was striking.

Thinking of her dream, I said, "Maybe it feels like there is a piece of you that we keep losing and finding over and over again. A piece that is hungry and needs to be fed." Jennie nodded, then went on to tell me about the bulimic issues with eating that she had long been keeping secret from everyone, including me. She described the way she restricted her food intake for extended periods of time and then compulsively binged on rich foods that filled her up till she made herself sick. She felt ashamed of her problems with eating and connected them to the experience of the infant in the dream that she couldn't keep hold of. Jennie said that, in her core, "there is this small person, my little self. She's not capable—she's too young. It's just me by myself, there's no family and it's without love. It's like a vacuum. It feels like there's hardly air." Jennie's chest started heaving as she spoke, as if gasping for air. "I can't breathe," she said.

Unsettled, I could feel the fragility of the moment but felt unsure of what to say. Eventually, Jennie's breathing began to slow down, but she remained distraught. I could sense that she felt alone with her feelings, as if her words and affect kept ricocheting back at her in an isolated space all her own. She needed something from me, but I was paralyzed, unable to think. Jennie left the session unsoothed. In the following sessions, she felt far away, deadened, intellectually engaged in reflecting on the session, and the feelings that had emerged in it, but emotionally absent from our relationship. There didn't seem to be a way back to the affective experiences of that session.

Dismayed at what felt like a lost opportunity to build on our connection, I thought about Jennie after our session, and brought up what had happened between us in supervision. As my supervisor and I discussed the ways I kept myself from being too involved in Jennie's traumatized states for fear of intruding on or injuring her we came to a pause in our conversation; my attention became unfocused, my mind wandered. In that moment I imagined with great clarity an image of Jennie and me sitting together in my office, an inert body laid out between us. Gray, corpselike, it rested on a block with intravenous (IV) tubes coming out of each of its arms. One of the IVs ran from the prostrate body to Jennie's arm, and the other to mine, each of us connected to this lifeless mass, infusing it with our own blood, each of us feeding it, sustaining it, keeping it on life support in some limbo state between life and death.

When I imagined the corpse coming to life, I became flooded with dread. I realized then that I had been unconsciously invested in keeping something dead between Jennie and me, and that in fact we were both invested in keeping something absent, something immobilized and frozen in ourselves and in our relationship. As I mused about this image and how it reflected what was happening within and between me and Jennie, I connected back to my childhood. I realized that, because of my allegiance to my own internalized absent objects, I had been avoiding stirring up and experiencing certain feelings in our work together. It was an early attachment in which I committed myself to enlivening the dead other and remained dedicated to this impossible task, the structure of which formed the basis of our bond and as such was never meant to change. Jennie and I were holding the emptiness together, both of us committed to maintaining the connection to the absent object and thus keeping our relationship suspended in a liminal purgatory between life and death. We had entered an unconscious pact in which if one of us threatened change in the relationship, attempting to leave behind the deadened object, the other took her up again, asserting her dominion over the interactions between us. Here, because of an overlap in our internal worlds, we shared in an enactment in which we both maintained allegiance to the absent object from the past, holding on to the archaic fear that something alive and spontaneous between us could rupture the strong attachment to the non-present primary object. The unconscious belief that liveliness would betray a primal bond, leading to catastrophic abandonment into an objectless, uncontained, disorganizing explosion of potential aggression and/or desire kept us from allowing a spontaneous, authentic connection to grow between us. Instead, we each maintained our own allegiance to absence, an isolated refuge in a state of nothingness in which no authentic interpersonal contact is allowed to flourish.

This most recent enactment helped me to see more clearly the ways I had been dropping things that came up—on a conscious level I withdrew or smoothed things out to protect Jennie, but I was also unconsciously enacting the role of the absent mother, participating in keeping the deadness alive to guard myself and Jennie from the overwhelming affect that felt certain to arise should the tie to the absent object be challenged. This new awareness of the internal resonances between us freed me to engage in a more lively way with Jennie. I felt more empowered to pursue the meanings and impact of our rupture, to keep the uncomfortable feelings open despite her anxiety and my own fears of being intrusive, and to face what might happen to our link if something new transpired between us.

In our next session, Jennie started out with an air of resignation, recounting how everyone in her office was somehow featured in an article in a local magazine, except for her. I brought up the theme of erasure and connected it to the way I had left her alone in the session when she had experienced the panicked breathing. I had left her alone by not stepping in, I told her, effectively erasing her. She looked surprised, and went back to the stark image in her mind of the little girl at the center of a vast void. As Jennie returned to this image, the feelings of panic began to rise inside of her again, her breath becoming more constricted and her body rocking side to side in an effort to self-soothe. "Jennie," I said determined to stay alive and connected, "when you look at the void, can you see its edges? How far out does it go?" "Yes," she answered, "it's like there's a pool of black but I can also see a shoreline at its edge." "Can you imagine anyone inside the void together with you?" I asked. "No," she answered, "but I guess I can visualize you on the edge of the void, looking in, wanting to join me."

The look of panic in Jennie's wide eyes began to fade, and her breath began to slow as we fell into a deep silence. We had never previously experienced such a silence together, our sessions filled up with many words, whether they were used to communicate or distance. The silence felt profound, weighty, and I found myself imagining a very young Jennie, swaddled up tightly in a blanket, nestled on my chest. Jennie seemed similarly occupied with thoughts of her own, and the silence felt alive, and grew.

In the next session, Jennie told me that being alone was a foundational assumption that she brought into every relationship and this aloneness was what felt most true. Being alone felt like less of a risk, safe, she said, like a refuge. "I can really understand that," I responded, pausing for a moment, "but maybe that's what being mothered feels like to you. Being in a room with the door shut, all by yourself, that was what it was like to be with your mother, and maybe when you start to feel need that's the kind of relationship you go back to." After a moment I continued, "But I wonder what it would have felt like for someone to come knocking on the door back then, or for me to come knocking on it now." "I probably have been wishing for that for a long time," she answered. I could feel our connection growing. We had been enacting the cycle of absence and presence, coming together and ripping apart, losing and finding, and in this moment could meet in a mutual place that suspended this cycle so that it could become a vantage point from which to reflect and a source of significance.

Discussion

Of course, this was not the end of the absence that was and continues to be a main focus of this treatment, but the case illustrates the powerful hold and central place an early bond with absence can take up in the psyche. Jennie had suffered a childhood suffused with absence and neglect, and as such was devoted to maintaining an internal void in order to protect a sense of order and meaning in her life. This powerful tie, which overlapped with one of my own, manifested itself in the ways Jennie and I took turns absenting ourselves from each other throughout our work together, together taking on the task of maintaining the presence of the absent object in the analytic relationship. In this way, we unconsciously entered a pact in which we both pledged our allegiance to absence, placing the safety of non-interaction above the possibilities of the dreaded unknown that constantly threatened to take place between us.

This work with Jennie powerfully brought to light my own unworked-through allegiance to absence. With the new awareness brought forth through the elaboration of reverie and a series of sensory experiences in our work together, I could begin to see the ways I was participating in not allowing anything new to grow in the analytic relationship. The resistance to seeing this created a powerful enactment in which our internal worlds interlocked such that authentic, generative contact between us was forbidden. I had been blind to the presence of the absent object. Coming to see my own allegiance to absence in situ created a platform for observing and understanding these dynamics (rather than remaining mired in and reacting to them), that imbued our enactment with meaning where there had been none before. From this vantage, I could see that not only was there an absence between us, but that we were each invested in maintaining this absence in fidelity to our respective absent and dead objects. This allowed me to conceive of the absence and subsequently access myself in a new way, to integrate and connect with other parts of myself and of Jennie.

The profound dread I experienced during the reverie in which the corpse between Jennie and me came to life revealed the fear of breaking this primal bond to the absent object. It is the force of this fear and the attendant feelings of disorganizing abandonment and overwhelming loss that keep vitality from manifesting interpersonally in an allegiance to absence. As our process unfolded and became more symbolizable, I no longer had to hold on to the primal tie to the absent object to avoid catastrophe; new types of feelings and my own creative process were allowed to emerge in the space between us. This internal experience clued me into a similar investment in absence in Jennie's inner world. Jennie was fearful of allowing anything new to happen between us and remained loyal to the interpersonal nothingness we had both long been nursing. As the absent object became more clearly articulated, we could begin to look at the power of that attachment and the forces that kept it in place, and I could start to challenge the absence by coming to life myself.

Because the type of early absence illustrated here comes about at a time when the difference between self and non-self is still developing, language and other types of communication that clearly define self and other may not be the most useful methods of broaching these early unformulated states. The split between the articulate adult and non-verbal child selves makes it difficult to access such early affective states through verbal communications. Experiences of merger and fusion that blur the delineation between self and other create opportunities to non-intrusively reach split-off parts of the self, so that a wordless or absent state can be understood from *within* that position, while also being moved into a transformative interpersonal relationship. This is similar to Winnicott's (1945) notion that a mother and child "live an experience together" (p. 141) when the pair meet in a moment in which each of their desires temporarily coincide, creating an illusion that blurs the lines between internal and external worlds. Treating an allegiance to absence requires that the story of the black hole in the early care-taking environment be told in a medium that does not require the patient's self-definition.

One medium in which this can occur is through the register of enactment and bodily experience, a recreation of what is missing within the dream-like space of the transferential field. As Bion (1970) wrote, "The analyst must focus his attention on O, the unknown and unknowable … With this the analyst cannot be identified: *he must be it*" (p. 27, italics added). With Jennie, the story of absence was communicated in the register of the enacted (Grossmark 2012), in which the absent object became embodied in and between us through our overlapping identifications. The analyst is receptive to the full range of the patient's communications, on sensory, bodily, as well as affective and intellectual levels, and makes her inner contents available to be used to "become" early objects in an array of different manifestations. In this way, Jennie and I became both the absent mother and the absented child in our work together, such that her early object history could begin to be told between us in the enacted dimension, without words. Specific internal resonances, such as the identifications with absent objects that Jennie and I shared, brought aspects of patient and analyst to the fore in the context of the intersection of two internal worlds. Accordingly, lost parts of the patient's self could be linked up, recognized, and given significance. But this recognition cannot come in externally, by persuasion, force, or coercion; it is conjured organically in the overlap of two lives lived together. This requires the analyst to allow herself to be used in the service of creating the environment in which the patient's early object relationships can come to life.

This process occurs slowly through the process of elaboration of proto-symbolic material in the analyst's reverie and through the intersubjective engagement with the concrete, enactive aspects of psychoanalytic treatment. Interestingly, moments of transformation in Jennie's analysis first emerged in the form of new types of sensory awarenesses; for example, a bodily position that brought about an association to my own analysis, the visualization of a beating heart inside of Jennie, and the vivid reverie in supervision that helped bring to light some of our shared dynamics. Jennie then used the visual image of herself in the void to conjure an affective experience that evoked a powerful bodily experience, and I was able to build on this image to help find the edge of the void in which containment of the absence could become a new possibility.

Communications thus took place in language, but also spoke to more basic parts of the self through utilization of the grammar of the sensory and visual registers that don't require the work of self–other differentiation. As Aulagnier (2001) said, "The cathexis of sensory activity is the very condition of existence of a psychical life, since it is the very condition for the cathexis of the activity of representation" (p. 35). Connecting to the sensory mode of communication and utilizing it to make meaning accesses the most basic building blocks for creating internal representations. Perhaps, with Jennie, non-verbal communications were necessary to first give shape to and symbolize the unique experience of internal absence before more directly challenging the ties that keep it so powerfully in place.

An allegiance to absence is an intense, pervasive bond to a non-present caretaker whose lack leaves a void in her wake. It is important that the process of recognizing, formulating, and giving shape to this inchoate object experience takes place in treatment so that the powerful tie to the absence can be addressed. The different manifestations of absence that arise in the analytic relationship can be linked up to tell the story of each person's unique bond with absence, so that the allegiance that exerts a tight grip on the internal world can begin to be loosened. In this way, what once felt like nothingness can become the generative emptiness from which the internal world can be allowed to expand and grow into a universe filled with possibility.

References

Amir, D. (2013). The psychic organ point of autistic syntax. *J. Child Psychother.*, 39:3–21.

Amir, D. (2017, February). Phantom pains, phantom language: Discussion of Rachel Sopher's paper. Paper presented at the meeting of the Israel Winnicott Center, Tel Aviv, Israel.

Aulagnier, P. (2001). *The Violence of Interpretation, From Pictogram to Statement*, trans. A. Sheridan. London: Brunner-Routledge.

Balint, E. (1963). On being empty of oneself. *Int. J. Psychoanal.*, 44:470–480.

Bion, W.R. (1962). *Learning from Experience*. London: Tavistock.

Bion, W.R. (1970). *Attention and Interpretation: A Scientific Approach to Insight in Psycho-Analysis and Groups*. London: Tavistock.

Emery, E. (2002). The ghost in the mother: Strange attractors and impossible mourning. *Psychoanal. Rev.*, 89:169–194.

Eshel, O. (1998). Black holes, deadness and existing analytically. *Int. J. Psychoanal.*, 79:1115–1130.

Fairbairn, W.D. (1963). Synopsis of an object-relations theory of the personality. *Int. J. Psycho-Anal.*, 44:224–225.

Gerson, S. (2009). When the third is dead: Memory, mourning, and witnessing in the aftermath of the holocaust. *Int. J. Psychoanal.*, 90:1341–1357.

Green, A. (1986). The dead mother. In *On Private Madness*. London: Hogarth Press, pp. 142–173. Translated by Katherine Aubertin from "La mère morte," *Narcissisme de vie, narcissisme de mort*. Éditions de Minuit, 1983.

Green, A. (1988). *On Private Madness,* London: Hogarth Press.

Green, A. (1993). *The Work of the Negative*, trans. A. Weller. London: Free Association Books.

Green, A. (1997). The intuition of the negative in playing and reality. *Int. J. Psycho-Anal.*, 78:1071–1084.

Grossmark, R. (2012). The flow of enactive engagement. *Contemp. Psychoanal.*, 48:287–300.

Gurevich, H. (2008). The language of absence. *Int. J. Psychoanal.*, 89:561–578.

Hofstadter, D. (1979). *Godel, Escher, Bach: An Eternal Golden Braid.* New York: Basic Books.

Lombardi, R. (2015). *Formless Infinity.* New York: Routledge.

Milner, M. (1969). *The Hands of the Living God: An Account of a Psychoanalytic Treatment.* The International Psycho-Analytical Library. London: The Hogarth Press and the Institute of Psycho-Analysis.

Ogden, T.H. (1989). On the concept of an autistic-contiguous position. *Int. J. Psychoanal.*, 70:127–140.

Ogden, T.H. (1997). Reverie and interpretation. *Psychoanal. Q.*, 66:567–595.

Ogden, T.H. (2004). The analytic third: implications for psychoanalytic theory and technique. *Psychoanal. Q.*, 73:167–195.

Ogden, T.H. (2007). On talking-as-dreaming. *Int. J. Psychoanal.*, 88:575–589.

Peltz, R. (1998). The dialectic of presence and absence: Impasses and the retrieval of meaning states. *Psychoanal. Dial.*, 8:385–409.

Reed, G.S. & Baudry, F.D. (2005). Conflict, structure, and absence: André Green on borderline and narcissistic pathology. *Psychoanal. Q.*, 74(1):121–155.

Tustin, F. (1972). *Autism & Childhood Psychosis.* London: Hogarth.

Tustin, F. (1981). *Autistic States in Children.* London: Routledge; revised edition, 1992.

Tustin, F. (1986). *Autistic Barriers in Neurotic Patients.* New Haven: Yale University Press.

Winnicott, D.W. (1945). Primitive emotional development. *Int. J. Psychoanal.*, 26:137–143.

Winnicott, D.W. (1958). Transitional objects and transitional phenomena. In *Collected Papers: Through Pediatrics to Psychoanalysis.* London: Tavistock Publications.

Winnicott, D.W. (1967). Mirror-rôle of mother and family in child development. In *Playing and Reality.* London: Tavistock, pp. 111–118.

Winnicott, D.W. (1971). *Playing and Reality.* London: Tavistock.

Chapter 3

Activating lifeness in the analytic encounter

The ground of being in psychoanalysis

Rachael Peltz

Introduction

This chapter offers a spectrum of ideas about the bringing-to-life dimension of the therapeutic challenge. Those who have participated in the psychoanalytic tradition may be aware of key historical moments in which, not unlike other disciplines, the pendulum necessarily shifts, ushering in a new Kuhnian paradigm. In my estimation, we have embarked on one such crossroad in psychoanalysis as we move from the language of "absences" to "presences"; symbolic to semiotic (pre-symbolic and even non-symbolic); mentalization to the realm of the proto-mental; verbal to non-verbal/sensorial/procedural; receptivity to "emphatic resonances"; interpretive to enactive fields; subjectivity to awakening (from states of de-subjectivization); and word to thing (Peltz, 2018).

The emphasis here is on activating affective, *vitalizing presences* in the field of the analytic relationship—transformation in action—transformation in being, in which we "use all there is to use"[1] to establish emotional contact. When vital contact is made and sustained, thus kick-starting, rebooting, or even "booting" development, the more familiar "dreaming" process can proceed—à la Bion (1965), Ogden (2003), and Ferro (2002a)—or the entry into the sealed-off vault of heretofore unknowable absences, i.e., death objects (Durban, 2017).

I will draw on a beautiful collection of essays about the significance of fiction by James Wood (2015) to elaborate on this phenomenon of *vitalizing presences*. For Wood, fiction "open(s) up abysses" (p. 25), capturing the "details" of a character—the "*magical fusion*" achieved by gathering the "bits of life ... with the writer's literary artifice—which allow(s) that artifice to indeed convert into new life" (pp. 38–39). According to Wood, "details are not lifelike but irreducible: things-in-themselves, what I would call *lifeness* itself" (p. 39).

In this chapter, I will offer a collection of ideas that illustrate the need for the establishment of that lifeness—a "palpable present-intimate," in the words of Henry James (as quoted in Wood, 2015, p. 39) in the therapeutic setting akin to what Wood describes is present in novels. We are speaking here of the "flesh" (Merleau-Ponty, 1968) of intimacy as a felt experience in the therapeutic setting. In our psychoanalytic lexicon, these experiences partake of "bodily reveries" (Civitarese, 2016), the "motor imagination" (Stern, 2010) that drives our connections, those viscerally shared experiences in the field among other shared perceptual, sensory, textual, and so on, experiences. They contain the emergent "whatness" (Alvarez, 2012) or "thisness" (Wood, 2015) or "withness" (Eshel, 2013) of each unique analytic story, such that a "pocket of resistance" (Peltz, 2012a) is established—which, of course, can never be fully captured or described, but holds within it the "lifeness" that is itself necessary in and for life. These fleeting moments of lifeness animate our souls. They make life worth living. They hold the "truth" of our "own-most" fleeting and impossible-to-capture flashes of life—what Wood coins as "life-surplus"—the "punctum" of a photo (Barthes, 1981), the "face" of a painting (Berger, 2001), the "O"-ness of Bion's (1965) O. I am trying to approach vitalizing contact-making" at its core, which could be considered the domain of the soul. Infant researchers describe "action schemas," non-symbolic attentiveness, our operative vs. cultivated languages, and Ogden's (2019) "ontological" domain of being, which I think of as the beginning register of this vitalizing domain.

Wood (2015) says of a story:

> But if the life of a story is in its excess, its surplus, in the riot of things beyond order and form, then it can also be said that the life-surplus of a story lies in its details, for details represent those moments in a story where form is outlived, cancelled, evaded. I think of details as nothing less than bits of life sticking out of the frieze of form, imploring us to touch them.
>
> (p. 38)

Our patients also implore us to touch them. My aim here is to close in on the register of life-surplus as it comes alive in the therapeutic encounter and consider how such lifeness serves in *establishing the ground of being in psychoanalysis.* Only from this ground can we approach our patients' more treacherous death haunts. Where are we when we feel most alive? Or, put another way with regard to our clinical work, what register are we in with our patients when what I am calling a vitalizing exchange occurs? What are we "presencing"? Can we think of these experiences forming the ground for what Cartwright (2008) refers to as "containing states of mind"? The proto-containing states of being? Or, do they live somewhere else?

Before proceeding I find myself looking back over the 35-plus years of doing clinical work. By now, I imagine many of us have found a comfortable "way" of being our analytic selves when we work. I notice myself being more and more of that self—perhaps holding back less or, put it another way, being acutely aware of coming forward more. The worst thing that can happen is that I am wrong in what I have said or done. But I have moved into this *forward-coming stance* because I have decided it is more important that my presence is felt then that I am right. I am hoping for a form of engagement that generates presences in the face of all of life's inevitable absences, not to mention absences associated with the frame of our work (Peltz, 1998; Gurevich, 2008; Chetrit-Vatine, 2014; Goldberg, 2018b,). I also think that we are living in an era in which we are called upon to engage in the *life-affirming dimensions* of our lives, and that it is no accident that this shift is bubbling up in our theories now. Until recently, we have heard more about the "fort" than the "da" part of Freud's game in our meta-theories. I think the tide has shifted—not necessarily because we see more disturbed patients, but because our metaphors are changing—from digging, which used to be the metaphor for what we did to achieve "depth," to keenly recepting, enhancing, amplifying, and actuating what is happening (Ogden, 1999; Alvarez, 2012; Foehl, 2014; Peltz, 2015; Goldberg, 2018a).

Emergent enabling registers (of shared experience)

I think many of us were trained to try to explain our patients and thus we focused on the causal dimensions of our work—the *whys.*

Why is patient *X* so disregulated, so self-critical, so resigned? What are the operative unconscious phantasies, defenses, relational patterns, internal object representations? We have learned to formulate dynamic explanations, based on the stories and internal dynamics we piece together while mostly listening. While these formulations are critical, they have often felt divorced from the emergent demands of the clinical situation—a lament I often hear about in supervision with candidates and trainees. I think we are in the midst of a shift to attending much more closely to the lived experiences of being with our patients—day by day, session by session—cultivating an engaged and more *phenomenological* rather than *explanatory* approach. This underscores what Alvarez (2012) calls the *descriptive and the vitalizing* dimensions of what's happening—the territory Ogden (1999) began charting when he wrote: "the music of what happens in poetry and psychoanalysis," what Stern (2010) refers to as "vitality forms." Rather than seeking explanations and trying to "understand," from more distant and observing positions, this shifting tide in theory and clinical practice is allowing—perhaps is even *demanding* of us—to "enter into" the field of the relationship, to move in close, keeping a second eye on what we have entered and what it stirs in us (Civitarese, 2010).

Furthermore, sometimes we must insert ourselves in very real and embodied ways, again referring to Alvarez's (2012) work and what she calls *vitalizing presences* (see also Gerson, 2013; Schwartz Cooney, 2018). Of course, all child therapists know this. It is often the only way of being with children. One of my claims here is that it is useful that all of us consider ourselves child therapists in relation to the contacting dimension of our work (Peltz, 2018).

What is a vitalizing presence? A vitalizing presence is a presence that momentarily awakens the most rudimentary capacity in a person to feel alive as her/himself. "In each baby," Winnicott remarks, "… is a *vital spark* and this urge towards life and growth and development is part of the baby, something the child is born with and which is carried forward in a way that we do not have to understand" (1964, p, 27).[2] Winnicott (1945) begins with what he calls "personalization"—one's "own-most" sense of oneself in one's body in the world, as "me." *Indwelling* is another term he used—"This is where I live." *Un-integration* is another term—"This is how I (safely) fall apart." As we know full well by now, that sense of *me-ness* begins as a *we-ness*.

For Winnicott, that we-ness begins in the conceptualization of the hyper-attentive mother who houses the infant in and with herself—*Home is where we start from* (Winnicott, 1986). In Goldman's words, "At the heart of Winnicott's work lays an abiding concern for the *urge toward life* and with the deadness that results from failures to create and discover a world that can tolerate one's own aliveness" (Goldman 2012, p. 333).

When we have all had the occasion to meet a patient in the context of their often trauma-filled, chaotic familial and social worlds, we immediately register the direness—the visceral necessity of establishing vital emotional contact. At the same time, we know about the difficulty of doing exactly that. We can find ourselves describing the stages of doing this, beginning with those first months in which we acutely notice, sense, and accompany this person (and ourselves with him/her), speaking simply and directly. We might add that we keep our comments "close to" our "experiences" together. Then we might notice a sudden shift, which we are able to notice out loud. What was happening here? A place is being established—a place for being sensed, steadied, and held—even enveloped (Anzieu, 1987)—gently and firmly, in the manner that our patient can tolerate. I think of the ways we are called upon to reach for our "maternally preoccupied" internal objects—who listen for the baby's breathing, cries, stirrings; who try to figure out the baby's rhythms, spatial preferences, carefully calibrating when to stimulate, when to calm, and when to simply "be." This is a regular yet paradoxically hyper-acute state of mind—a "prehistoric" time and place, in that it is the place of immediate and present cohabitation, of embodied and timeless presence, where everything is what it is—a place before the capacity to inquire (and thus constitute one's presence as a person in time) is attained.

When we are with our patients, yes, we use our words, but fundamentally we are acutely and "attentively" percepting, sensing, recepting in the hope of establishing a place in time—a special time where, despite all that has or has not happened in their lives, a new *place* can be established—a place where what I call the "face" of him or her can show itself (Peltz, 2012a). This state of acute sensitivity and perception we try to reach in ourselves is as desperate as it is ordinary. In the instances in which a child's life was dominated by the absence of a maternally pre-occupied presence, our primary task is to innocuously and unobtrusively establish such a presence in the space that we share with him or her.

As an undergraduate student reading philosophy, I came across a wonderful action phrase that captures the spirit of such a vital personalization. Merleau-Ponty (1962) coined the phrase, "*Je peux du monde!*"[3]—one's experience of "able-ness in the world," a sense of capacity to be and to live in the world, the verb form or action-oriented way of saying "the world is my oyster." Out of Winnicott's embodied psyche-soma comes Merleau-Ponty's experience of "ableness/*pouvoir*," as active engagement in the world. What flows from this rudimentary sense of one's embodied self is everything—depending on the capacities of the environment to meet, or in Wood's terms, to "seriously notice." A vitalizing presence is a presence that allows one to feel alive, in some instances to be "born again." How? Alvarez (2012) might say, "By Mattering!" She calls this the "hey" dimension, as in "hey—you matter!"

In the realm of our meta-theories and the assumptions they are grounded in, we have not caught up with ourselves. We are still used to thinking about exercising "parameters" of the frame—those guilty *extras*—in relation to the degree of pathology present, or in terms of the degree to which a person is capable of symbolic functioning—a harkening back to old debates about the differences between wish and need in Winnicott's terms; or conflict and deficit in Anna Freud's. Even in more contemporary writings, I hear the assumption that the less interpretive responses to pre-verbal or non-verbal unconscious or non-conscious communications necessarily partake of more disturbance or primitive pathology, which may be correct, but not the whole picture. I think we are still rather haunted by the privileged status of representation and the capacity for symbolization, viewing other more direct experiences as lesser and indicative of more disturbance.

Ogden's (1988, 1989) contribution of the autistic-contiguous position and re-visioning of Kleinian stages to a theory that posits not stages but dialectically constituted/decentered states of subjectivity present throughout life helps us move from a logic of linear to a non-linear spiraling process of development also present in non-linear systems theory (Seligman, 2005). In another sphere altogether, infant research—pointing to "the non-symbolic implicit/procedural level" (Beebe, 2004, p. 3)—directs us to the "action dialogues of our non-verbal communication" (p. 5). Ogden (2008) also makes the critical distinction between Winnicott's conception of holding and Bion's of containing—holding pertaining to *being* and containing to *thinking*—and describes the complex relationship between the two, akin perhaps to the *proto-containing dimension* (Cartwright, 2008) of holding. Here, I am trying to home in on the active holding dimension—the hyper-attentive, awakening dimension of environmental holding that sometimes translates into firm handling.

My favorite field theorists, notably Ferro (2002a) and Civitarese (2010), refer to unsaturated interpretations—interpretations that are hearable and usable, that expand what can be felt and clearly don't persecute the person to whom they are addressed. Unsaturated interpretations represent a move toward a more proactive vitalization in the field (Elise, 2019). Such interpretations are "joining" in the sense that they join people where they are in the language that they speak, including no language at all, or rather a language of the non-verbal, the rhythmic, gestural, and expressive. I would add that we are then joining people in a *medium* that engages them.[4] I think we hope to discover the medium that best captures a person's imagination and embodied, vital sensibility in our work. When that medium is not the one we typically rely on ourselves, does that make the person more disturbed? Is formal/symbolic language, or the state of the transference, our primary mode of communication? What about all of the "derivative" forms of communication that exist, particularly those that we would consider "semiological" (Kristeva, 1982), pre-linguistic, embodied, action forms of communication? We seem to hold an implicit hierarchy of communication even though we also know that without the music the words fall flat. In addition, let us not forget that, in response to the call to be seen as oneself by our patients, we are equally called to allow ourselves to come forth, as best we are able under the circumstances—as analysts. One problem is that we, too, have needs for symmetry (Matte Blanco, 1988)—we can privilege our own love of language in interpretation and diminish other forms of expressive communication.

Grotstein (2004) inquires:

> Why is it, then, that a truth exists that we believe we cannot tolerate, yet, when an analyst *properly interprets* this truth to us—employing the *right* timing and dosage—we experience relief? Perhaps the truth embedded in the interpretation is something about which we already had a premonition but were unable, on our own, to bear. But we could bear it when it came from someone with whom we have a unique relationship of dependency, especially mother or analyst ... Our newfound ability to tolerate a Truth after an interpretation suggests that there was more to the interpretation than just the cognitive and emotional message articulated within it. I believe the missing element is the transference itself, but transference considered in a new way—transference as containment ... I believe that the vouchsafing of the safety of an interpretation may constitute the ultimate meaning of containment.
>
> (p. 107)

This is no small task—*the vouchsafing of the safety of an interpretation! This may indeed capture the ground of being in analysis.* Perhaps what precedes that *vouchsafing* are all of the proto-containing, activating, holding/vitalizing, and contact-full dimensions of the transference as containment.[5]

There are many instances scattered throughout our analytic chronicles of spontaneous, often anomalous, encounters that created new and transformational possibilities—vitalizing encounters that often challenged analysts in what they held as "the right way." I am thinking particularly of members of the independent tradition where one can find Milner's (1987) discovery of her child patient's need for a "pliable medium," Bollas's (1989) encounter with a person's "idiom," Kennedy's (1993) freedom to relate, Casement's learning from the patient, and Symington's (1983) "acts of freedom."

These analytic writers and clinicians, among many others, offered examples of breaches between the psychoanalytic ideas they held dear and what was required by the work they were doing with their patients. In that process, they mounted new theories. As we continue moving in the direction of healing those breaches, we, too, are generating new models that restore the body and soul to the mind of our work, what Alvarez (2012) calls the "thinking heart," only I believe this applies to more than work with autistic and severely disturbed children. I would like us to consider "Alvarez for grown-ups," in which we draw on her work and the growing body of literature on the *ground level* of contact making, including the work of infant–parent researchers so as to integrate the ideas coming from multiple directions about how the capacity for *story making* in the first place rests on internalizing *and intertwining with embodied and engaging story-holding presences*. The capacity to weave any kind of narrative is already quite an achievement. I would hold that more than "containment" is happening in that form of contact-making engagement. With that in mind, I would like to focus on the nature of this shifting paradigm, which I believe rests on a different epistemology grounded in what Merleau-Ponty (1968) describes as an *interwining*.

Epistemological shift—a new ground for experiencing and meaning making

One could say that the critique of one-person psychoanalytic models begun by Greenberg and Mitchell (1983) in the 1980s initiated the last great paradigm shift in psychoanalysis. In the time between then and now, the *ground* of inter-subjectivity has been firmly established. Some might say the same regarding our *grounded-ness* in the social world. Nonetheless, many of the tenets contained within modernist thinking—inextricable from the classical theories generated in their time—remain with us even as we shift our thinking and practices.

The new epistemology of which I speak takes issue with the dualistic/binary logic present in established psychoanalytic theories. Reis (1999) has written about the need for "transcending the Cartesian limitations of the classical paradigm" (p. 372). Among them are the dualisms created between mind and body, subject and object, internal (mental) and external (material), to name a few. According to Reis (2010), in the dualism between mind and body, bodily sensation is:

> split from the mental operation(s) that are thought to yield experience and representation ... Such an approach paradoxically elevates

> the representational contents of the mind to a privileged status over perception, making what is in the mind even more "real" than the world as experience, or immediate relations with others.
>
> (p. 696)

Reis adds that even Bion's theory of alpha and beta suffers the limitation of a dualism between psychic representation and raw sense data (p. 696). He argues in favor of a shift from an empiricist intellectualist tradition to a more phenomenological one in which there is no such thing as isolated datum of perception, but rather that "the perception of something is always in the middle of something else, it always forms a part of a '*field*'" (Merleau-Ponty, as quoted in Reis, 2010, p. 697). Reis says, "Even our most rudimentary perceptions are not atomistic, but complex relational events, always identified against a larger field" (p. 697). For Merleau-Ponty (1964), "the world which is given in perception … is the concrete inter-subjectively constituted life-world of immediate experience" (p. xvi). Again quoting Reis (2010), "Within this logic there is no dualistic separation between body and world or body and cognition or cognition and world" (p. 697). Perhaps this is what Winnicott means when he insists on a maternal–infant unit in which the world in and of the mother intertwines with the infant psyche-soma and equally reverses as the world in and of the infant psyche-soma intertwines with the psyche-soma of the mother, who is herself intertwined in her time and place in the world of family, culture, and society. Reis (2010) encourages us to extend the psychoanalytic notion of dreaming by broadening the conception of dreaming from a private, intrapsychic event to one that includes the body and to think how this sort of dreaming may *disclose* the world rather than *represent* it (p. 698).

Let me zoom in closer now. What is the difference between a dream that discloses and one that represents? A dream that discloses illuminates the unconscious dreamer in her world. It simultaneously spans inwards and outward as the dream itself engages the dreamer in the world of the dream and the process of dreaming. We may ask, what is the dream doing? What is the dream saying? Where does it point? A dream that represents explains. It explains what things stand for. It has an endpoint—perhaps a teleology. It points to what things "mean." Merleau-Ponty's dream has no endpoint. It perpetually engages the dreamer to the dawning disclosure of the dream and neither the dreamer nor the dream will ever be the same as a consequence of that engagement. A dream is dreaming-producing, just as Wood's (2015) "story is story-producing" (p. 36).

Wood (2015) quotes Thomas de Quincey: "The mere *understanding*, however useful and indispensable, is the *meanest* faculty in the human mind and the most to be distrusted: and yet the great majority of people trust to nothing else" (p. 79). In asking what things mean, we limit our perspective—what we can see, sense, feel, intuit. When we dream—whether asleep or awake—and then we speak of the dream, we are speaking to dreaming "in its own language—an act of critique that is at the same time a re-voicing" (Wood, 2015, p. 84) *and in that process something new emerges.* Reis (2010) notes that:

> as regards meaning—meanings are not pre-formed, or formed only inside the individual … There is no place that meaning is—meaning is a constant process of becoming and transforming … The emergent properties of these truths and phantasies are the function of the enactive field—which is in constant flux.
>
> (p. 701)

I have been a member of a writing group. In the process of listening to each other's poems, I have learned the difference between a poem that discloses and one that explains. Our leader cautions us over and over again not to explain, to let the words speak for themselves, to take the reader into the world of the poem rather than explaining what it is after or about. So it goes with Merleau-Ponty's intertwining. The dualism between subject and object is replaced by the "third," intertwined subject/object field phenomenon.[6] For Merleau-Ponty the emergent dreaming process is the order of the day in our fundamental and primordial inter-subjectivity in which the social and material world inscribe or interpolate us from the outset. "I am a field!" he declared. Sadly he died in the middle of writing his treatise, *The Visible and Invisible* (Merleau-Ponty, 1968), in which he built on his earlier writings about the primacy and phenomenology of perception—always embodied and intertwining with the objects of perception.

Vitalizing presencing: surplus-life/lifeness; the grace of the punctum; the "face" of a painting; the enigma of beauty; the ground of shared experience—this is more than containment!

This section begins with a dramatic heading, but I don't want to romanticize what I am trying to capture here. Remember, in the earlier quotes of Wood, he describes the surplus-lifeness that is captured in the paragraph of a novel, or the stanza in a poem, or for that matter, in the sound of a sonata, or even the vista from a mountain top as something grounded in the ordinary details of life as we live it—"adventures in the ordinary" (Wood, 2015, p. 58). In the same way, approaching our patients with engaged attentiveness allows the vitalizing yet ordinary details of life with them to emerge. This can feel scary, ponderous, thrilling … I can't resist adding another Wood (2015) quote:

> What do writers do when they seriously notice the world? Perhaps they do nothing less than rescue the life of things from their death—from two deaths, one small and one large: from the "death" that literary form always threatens to impose on life and from actual death. I mean by the latter, the fading reality that besets details as they recede from us—the memories of our childhood, the almost-forgotten pungency of flavors, smells, textures: the slow death that we deal to the world by the sleep of our attention … The writer's task is to rescue the adventure from this slow retreat: to bring meaning, color, and life back to the most ordinary things—to soccer boots and grass, to cranes and trees and airports, and even Gibson guitars and Roland amplifiers and Old Spice and Ajax.
>
> (p. 58)

The medium *is* the message

In this session, the patient brings in two paintings. He calls them "muddied." There is a lovely backdrop of rose and orange that stands out in each painting with what looks like faded peacock feathers. I notice the lovely backdrop of rose and orange and tell him.

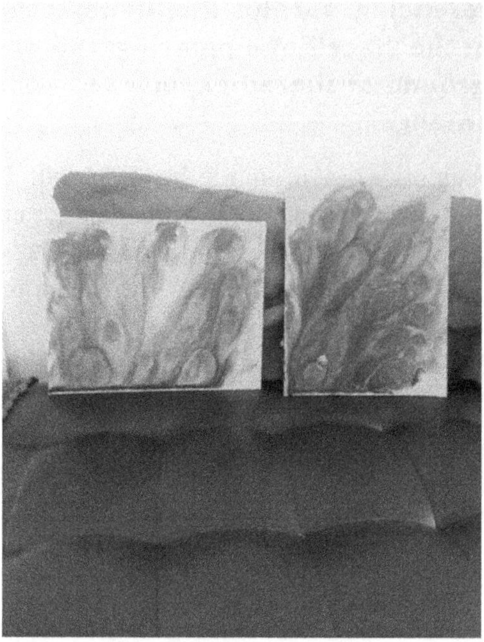

Let me say that it took a substantial amount of time and effort to get to this point. The beginning of the analysis was marked by a strange cloud of paralyzing emptiness that hung over us for long periods of time that cried out for us to discern that *talking alone* was not going to be successful. The essential *non-verbal* dimension of his experience was not coming through. He was terribly frozen and humiliated in his attempts to "*be in*" therapy the way he thought he was *supposed to.* Instead, his paintings have come to function as dreams, but it took us some time to discover this. It also took him quite a while to feel comfortable using the full range of color in his paintings-as-dreams. A spell of stultifying blankness was broken when it became evident that my patient could *come to life in his own way through the medium of painting*, and by bringing his paintings into the consulting room the way one might bring in a dream. A transference such as this about how one is supposed to act and be in therapy or analysis—producing "meaningful" associations, thoughts, and feelings in a manner that has nothing to do with who one is—can clue us into the ways people strain to speak our language, which can feel like a *living death* to them, one that they register as failure. It is also true that the death register has no words most of the time. It feels more like being under the sway of a deathly "spell," that then becomes a persecutory/deathly internal object (Durban, 2017).

I am reminded of Beebe's (2004) research in which there is evidence in what she calls "proto-conversations" of the ways in which babies can struggle to establish a common ground for communicating with their respective parents. Such efforts reveal the subtle and varied forms in which a person inhabits or "indwells" his or her mind–body in communication with an Other. The mutual induction (Goldberg, 2018a) by each member into each other's comfort zone is a complex and potentially fraught process. These are not conscious processes. They refer to what Alvarez (2012) and others call "procedural"—innermost dimensions of our being; memories born of our bodies and the ways we live them and what we hold most precious that we hope can be seen and shared. We are accustomed to thinking about pathological expressions of hallucinosis, but, as Civitarese (2016) reminds us, such events are also modes of early communication in the spirit of Bion's use of projective identification. I have found that in some treatments we must actively lend ourselves to our patients in order to discover the medium, including the use of language, that best suits them. In that sense, the *medium is the message*. It is not a stand-in for something better, or something more necessarily meaningful. It may provide an avenue toward the enrichment of other experiences, but entering into the medium of another person is itself a shared experience—one that cannot be communicated *about* without also being there together.

Returning to the session

After looking at the painting together, the patient announces:

> **Patient**: I have a dream, too. I'm in bed with Jan [now dead] in the afternoon. Intimate. Not erotic. We're in PJs talking. Comfortably talking. We'd like to get out of here, but I suddenly realize we can't because she's dead. Then I think, "You don't know that you're dead and if I don't say anything about it maybe it'll be OK."
>
> **Analyst**: *She won't know she's dead if you don't tell her—so that is one way to live in an illusion and keep her alive.*

Patient: Yes, an illusion. [pause] I'm thinking of a comment you made that stuck with me two weeks ago. You said, "We have to stay in the room." That phrase resonated. I have a huge tendency not to stay in the room. I go blank in therapy a lot of time thinking I should be digging deeper. I go blank with my wife.

Analyst: *In the dream, you don't go blank at all. You think about how to make this illusion feel real. The illusion that Jan is alive when she's dead.*

Patient: Yes, hold on to the illusion by not saying anything. When you hold on to an illusion, the illusion can remain and even become real.

Analyst: *The illusion that people don't die?*

Patient: Not that. More that Jan didn't die. There's still a connection, an illusion about the relationship. I can hold on to it if I don't say anything.

Analyst: *What was the illusion with Jan?*

Patient: In the dream that she was alive. Despite the external evidence. We had a special connection that made all that irrelevant.

She loved peacock feathers. She collected them.

Analyst: *The rose-colored background is perhaps the illusion. Muddied, you said.*

Patient: Wondering what other illusions I'm trying to protect by not being in the room.

Analyst: *Good question.*

Patient: I'm too busy protecting them to come up with what they are. I avert my gaze so as to leave the room.

Analyst: *Is there something in the room you don't want to see?*

Patient: Evidently.

Analyst: *This room?*

Patient: Probably.

Analyst: *You seem to think you're ready now.*

Patient: Maybe, but I'm not seeing it. [Pause.] I like the colors of your blanket running together. I don't like the geometrical pattern of the rug.

Analyst: *You like when things blend, run together—like what we sometimes do?*

Patient: Yeah. [Holds his head.] I'm going back and forth with things running together and things being geometrically precise. Am I needing analysis to make things more geometrically precise?

Analyst: *Even though you are not drawn to the separated lines … you are needing something between us to be more geometrically precise now.*

Patient: Who is it I'm being silent about?—the illusion—so it won't be dissolved. I'm not able to think about it. Open to suggestions. Something's fading.

Analyst: *I am thinking about illusions. Sometimes they just fade away and it feels sad that something so powerful, so full of emotion could just fade away, perhaps something is fading here.*

Patient: [leans back] This is having an effect. This year, I could see people were relating to my new director, not me as the expert. In a year or so I'll be the one who was great but replaced.

Analyst: *You'll feel you've faded, and perhaps so will I.*

Patient: Yeah. Also something else, even more core. The image I have in trying to blend in is that it gets more and more watery and then you disappear into a dull wash.

Analyst: *This is very important. That is how you felt when you first came here—like a person who blended in so completely he lost himself, with nothing to say, awash. I can't help thinking about you as a baby and how the story goes—you blended in so completely you didn't cry when your mother left. Then you were awash, alone and disappeared from yourself—perhaps became even dead to yourself.*

Patient: There's something there.

Analyst: *Yes*

In this session, my patient dreamed his own hallucinosis. That is, he opened himself to the awareness of a psychic truth even if it proved false by the reality of the senses. He dreamed that Jan didn't die despite the fact that she is dead. "I can hold on to it [the relationship with Jan] if I don't say anything." He needed to face the death inside of himself stemming from the mother who died figuratively when she left him alone with strangers after her husband was wounded in the war. It was time to let go of certain past illusions. He needed me to help him track its living form in his less conscious experience in order to disable it and free him to more fully engage in the rest of his life. He needed me to draw clear discernible lines that include his life with me. Lines must be drawn, perhaps as we approach the termination of his analysis and his own aging.

Postscript to the hour

My patient is describing what he calls his "travel anxiety." He simply cannot tolerate traveling. It is excruciating to him. As we sit in silence, I flash on times I have gotten lost and disoriented to the point of having felt rather depersonalized, and then hear myself say, "Everything that is familiar is gone when you travel." He responds, "that phrase does something for me." We both know that he was often left with relatives by his mother when he was an infant and his father was recovering in a military hospital with war wounds. He has multiple "explanations" for his travel terror, but the phrase "everything familiar is gone when you travel" felt somehow different, even new.

I am including this postscript to illustrate the difference between an explanatory, "Your mother left you when you were an infant," rather than a more emergent/descriptive interpretation. This rather innocuous, even obvious, description brought him closer to naming something that feels real and terrifying, to feel alone and unable to locate oneself in the world or any other person, including himself.

In time my patient's therapy came to a close, though it wasn't a definitive termination. He wanted to "take a break" since he felt he needed to establish himself in his new life as a retired person and also felt he was less available or interested in "opening things up." He expressed some disappointment that we hadn't made more of a dent in his travel anxiety as he wished to travel to please his wife, but he simply couldn't do it.

Some time later, I recalled my patient's dream and was struck by having missed an opportunity to address more directly the "death object" (Durban, 2017, p. 20) present in his dream that may have brought us closer to the anxiety he struggled with. An opportunity arose for telephone contact between us, at which time I invited him to meet with me to discuss some of my after-thoughts that I thought he might want to consider. He accepted the invitation. When he arrived, I told him that I thought I had not focused enough on a particular aspect of a dream he once told me that could have been useful to him. I reminded him of his dream about Jan where they were comfortably talking and then realized they couldn't leave because Jan was dead but he thought she didn't know that she was dead, and if he didn't say anything about it, perhaps it would be OK. He remembered the dream. I told him I believe I missed the boat, and that perhaps I left him alone pretending something that had died inside him wasn't dead, but it was imprisoning him. He couldn't travel outside of the closed space in which he and perhaps I might have pretended that something wasn't dead. I had a habit of seeing the "up side" of things, but that perpetuated his belief that no one could survive the down, more deadly, side. He agreed and said he appreciated that about me—seeing the up side.

He was quiet and looked absorbed in thought. I wondered what was going on over there. He prefaced his response by saying he might be deflecting the question but honestly, he wondered, "But will it help my golf game?" I respond that it sounded more like a hit than a deflection. No point pursuing further therapy if it doesn't help his golf game—that is, free him to live more fully with his eye on the ball! He seemed to be asking, "To what end would I be doing this probing?"

He laughed and agreed. He began talking about the ways we had eventually been able to be playful together, but, then, to my surprise, he added:

Patient: If you can be playful but circle back to what's not playful—for whatever—for whatever … I don't think we did as good a job getting back.

Analyst: *You are quite right—what we saw and didn't see—didn't circle back to what you dreamed that night. Yes, that's what I was also thinking.*

Patient: He remembers the state he was in when he first arrived—"logged into that kind of un-playfulness—so it was all there was." He remembered his first therapy and how he judged himself for being and feeling so badly and negative. He was feeling it—not understanding it.

Analyst: *That was your job. You were frozen there, maybe hoping someone could see how lost you were and unable to have access to any of your thoughts or feelings. It was quite deadening. If they saw where you were, you would not have been so alone.*

Patient: I needed to untie the knot of what's there. I feel I need help at finding ways of loosening it up.

Analyst: *Yes, separating the strands—one at a time.*

Patient: Right.

Analyst: *Does it feel like that might be happening now?*

Patient: The knot metaphor breaks down. It's as though it's—I don't have a way to get started into it.

Analyst: *How you loosen the knot.*

Patient: I have to find the spot.

Analyst: *You must fiddle with it.*

Patient: The proper way to fiddle.

Analyst: *You don't trust your impulses.*

Patient: I went for it today. Will it help my golf game? A real shot!

Analyst: *Grabbing the challenge, not passive, not compliant, passionate, playful?*

[Nods]

Analyst: *[Thinking] You look like you're percolating.*

Patient: There's something I want to get to.

Analyst: *Does it have words?*

Patient: It doesn't. There's intensity to it. You used the word playful. It wasn't! There's something un-playful about it.

Analyst: *Oh, now I deflected it.*

[Nods.]

Analyst: *It seems we share something.*

Patient: Our strength and our weakness.

Analyst: *Sometimes you may have to hold my feet to the fire.*

Patient: The harder part might be the other side of that—you holding my feet to the fire.

Analyst: *So, apparently it's hard for both of us.*

Patient: Right! This is not exactly what I expected today.

Analyst: *Why would you?*

[Laughs.]

Analyst: *Something not playful, intense—hard to sustain.*

Patient: The image I'm having—not in touch with it—something very dark—maybe twisted, amorphous. Can't tell if it's a lump of mud [powerful image for me—very empty, listless, dead—no play in sight and no one to play with] or something so tangled you don't know its tangled.

Analyst: *An empty feeling of amorphous lifelessness, knots so knotted they appear as a blob of mud.*

Patient: Don't know. Not willing to look at it up close enough. [A feeling of something uncanny settles in for me—the inertia of a child feeling alone and at a loss, so utterly "blah." I take this as a cue that he needs my active company and perhaps some guidance.]

Analyst: *Perhaps approaching the image and feeling through painting as you have at other times.*

Patient: Yes. How exactly would I do that?

Analyst: *I trust it may be a series.*

Patient: (He gets his phone.) I want to show you something. These are craft paintings. You use a long piece of string, dip it in paint then pull the string out and here is what it can look like. We've been playing with that.

Analyst: *So you know something can come of what appears as nothing.* [This feels like a very poignant moment. "We made something out of nothing" were words spoken by my mother in the aftermath of the war.]

Patient: I'd like to think about all of this and get back to you about whether to resume.

Analyst: *Very good and good to see you again.*

[We shake hands.]

Before closing I will say a few words about what I mean to illustrate in this vignette.

My patient was not able to forge a direct verbal communication of his emotional and psychic states. His "*je peux*"—experience of "ableness" could only begin by bringing in his paintings which both of us responded to—not by inquiring about their (the paintings') meanings, or even his (the painter's) intentions, but by "seriously noticing" according to Wood. We noticed what the paintings brought to mind—what the colors and shapes woke in each of us. We entered the world of the paintings much as we might enter the world of his dreams, and in this session the painting reminded him of a dream. In the conversation that ensued we circled around to the original emotional experience that prompted my patient to seek therapy, that is, his experience of blending in so completely that he had no sense of himself as a distinct entity—a form of psychic death. The dream in which "You don't know that you're dead and if I don't say anything about it maybe it'll be OK" directed us to the challenge that remained between us in his therapy. Could I help him approach the deathly anxiety that overtakes him when "everything that is familiar is gone"—an anxiety that we can surmise speaks to an acute and devastating separation and the visceral effort to not know what has died as a consequence, both in his mother and himself, and the frozen illusion of living life as if nothing had died.

For me, there is a beauty in discovering the medium that ignites another person. Bollas (1989) spoke of idiom. Discovering the face of a person's idiom and allowing ourselves to join them there can be among the most exhilarating or frightening experiences. And sometimes the medium is the message—in itself.

Notes

1 From James Wood (2015).
2 I am grateful to Dodi Goldman for bring this quotation to my attention.
3 See Husserl (1913).
4 Marian Milner (1987)—so ahead of her time—wrote lucidly about the need for a "pliable medium" in the process of discovering that one Matters! Her ideas generated substantial re-visioning of theories regarding symbol formation, the role of illusion and creativity, all of which pre-dated Winnicott's writing.
5 It may also be that, *despite* our interpretations, *because* of the proto-containing dimensions of the transference, our patients put up with the things we tell them when we think we have connected all of the dots in elegant interpretations.
6 I am reminded of Green's (1975) prescient "analytic object."

Bibliography

Alvarez, A. (2012). *The thinking heart: Three levels of psychoanalytic therapy with disturbed children.* Hove: Routledge.
Anzieu, D. (1987). *Psychic envelopes.* London: Karnac Books.
Barthes, R. (1981). *Camera lucida: Reflections of photography.* R. Howard (trans.) New York: Hill and Wang.
Beebe, B. (2004). Faces in relation: A case study. *Psychoanalytic Dialogues,* 14(1): 1–49.
Berger, J. (2001). *The shape of a pocket.* New York: Pantheon Books.
Bion, W.R. (1965). *Transformations.* London: Karnac Books.
Bion, W.R. (1970). *Attention and interpretation.* London: Tavistock.
Bollas, C. (1989). *Forces of destiny: Psychoanalysis and human idiom.* Oxford, England: Free Association Books.
Cartwright, D. (2008). Containing states of mind*: Exploring Bion's "container model" in psychoanalytic psychotherapy.* London: Routledge.
Chetrit-Vatine, V. (2014). *The ethical seduction of the analytic situation: The feminine-maternal origin of responsibility for the other.* London: Routledge.

Civitarese, G. (2010). *The intimate room: Theory and technique of the analytic field.* P. Slotkin (trans.). London: Routledge.

Civitarese, G. (2016). *The truth and the unconscious in psychoanalysis.* London: Routledge.

Durban, J. (2017). Facing the death-object: Unconscious phantasies of relationships with death. In: Erlich-Ganor, M. (Ed.) *Not knowing, knowing, not knowing: Festschrift celebrating the life and work of Shmuel Erlich* (pp. 85–115). New York: International Psychoanalytic Books.

Elise, D. (2019). *Creativity and the erotic dimension of the analytic field.* New York: Routledge.

Eshel, O. (2013). Patient–analyst "withness": On analytic "presencing," passion, and compassion in states of breakdown, despair, and deadness. *Psychoanalytic Quarterly,* 82(4): 925–963.

Ferro, A. (2002a). Some implications of Bion's thoughts: The waking dream and narrative derivatives. *International Journal of Psychoanalysis,* 83(3): 597–607.

Ferro, A. (2002b). In the analyst's consulting room. P. Slotkin (trans.) East Sussex: Brunner-Routledge.

Foehl, J. (2014). The phenomenology of depth. *Psychoanalytic Dialogues,* 24(3): 289–303.

Gerson, S. (2013). Passion in the transference. Unpublished manuscript presented at *The Chicago Psychoanalytic Institute and Society.* September 24, 2013, Chicago, IL.

Goldberg, P. (2018a). Discovering the living world: Discussion of "Life on her own terms: a story of reclemation." *Psychoanalytic Dialogues,* 28: 711–718.

Goldberg, P. (2018b). Reconfiguring the frame as a dynamic structure. In Tylim, I., and Harris, A. (Ed.) *Reconsidering the moveable frame in psychoanalysis: Its function and structure in contemporary psychoanalytic theory.* New York: Routledge, 92–110.

Goldman, D. (2012). Vital sparks and forms of things unknown. In: J. Abram (Ed.) *Donald Winnicott today.* London: Routledge, 2013.

Goldman, D. (2017). *A beholder's share: Essays on Winnicott and the psychoanalytic imagination.* New York: Routledge.

Green, A. (1975). The analyst, symbolization and absence in the analytic setting. *International Journal of Psychoanalysis, 56:* 1–22.

Greenberg, J.R. and Mitchell, S.A. (1983). *Object relations in psychoanalytic theory.* Cambridge, MA: Harvard University Press.

Grotstein, J. (2004). "The light militia of the lower sky": The deeper nature of dreaming and phantasizing. *Psychoanalytic Dialogues,* 14(1): 99–118.

Gurevich, H. (2008). The language of absence. *International Journal of Psychoanalysis,* 89(3): 561–578.

Husserl, E. (1913). *Ideas: General introduction to pure phenomenology*. W.R.B. Gibson (trans.). New York: Macmillan, 1931.

Kennedy, R. (1993). *Freedom to relate: Psychoanalytic expressions.* London: Free Association Books.

Kristeva, J. (1982). *Desire in language: A semiotic approach to literature and art.* New York: Columbia University Press.

Levine, H. (2012). The colourless canvas: Representation, therapeutic action, and the creation of mind. *International Journal of Psychoanalysis, 93:* 606–629.

Matte-Blanco, I. (1988). *Thinking, feeling, being: Clinical reflections on the fundamental antimony of human beings and world.* London: Routledge.

Merleau-Ponty, M. (1962). *Phenomenology of perception.* Smith, C. (trans.). Atlantic Highlands, NJ: The Humanities Press.

Merleau-Ponty, M. (1964). *The primacy of perception and other essays on phenomenological psychology, the philosophy of art, history, and politics.* Evanston, IL: Northwestern University Press.

Merleau-Ponty, M. (1968). *The visible and invisible.* Evanston, IL: Northwestern University Press.

Merleau-Ponty, M. (1973). *The prose of the world.* Evanston, IL: Northwestern University Press.

Merleau-Ponty, M. (2004). *The world of perception.* Davis, O. (trans.) London: Routledge.

Milner, M. (1987). *The suppressed madness of sane men.* London: Routledge.

Ogden, T.H. (1988). On the dialectical structure of experience: Some clinical and theoretical implications. *Contemporary Psychoanalysis*, 24: 17–45.

Ogden, T.H. (1989). On the concept of an autistic-contiguous position. *International Journal of Psychoanalysis,* 70: 127–140.

Ogden, T.H. (1999). The music of what happens in poetry and psychoanalysis. *International Journal of Psychoanalysis,* 80: 979–994.

Ogden, T.H. (2003). On not being able to dream. *International Journal of Psychoanalysis*, 84: 17–30.

Ogden, T.H. (2008). On holding and containing, being and dreaming. *International Journal of Psychoanalysis*, 85: 1349–1364.

Ogden, T.H. (2019). Ontological psychoanalysis or what do you want to be when you grow up? *The Psychoanalytic Quarterly*, 88(3): 399–413.

Peltz, R. (1998). The dialectic of presence and absence: Impasses and the retrieval of meaning states. *Psychoanalytic Dialogues*, 8(3): 385–409.

Peltz, R. (2012a). Ways of hearing: Getting inside psychoanalysis. *Psychoanalytic Dialogues*, 22: 279–290.

Peltz, R. (2012b). Making our hairs stand on end: A call to psychoanalysis to look outside itself. *Psychoanalytic Dialogues*, 22(3): 305–310.

Peltz, R. (2015). What is deep? *Rivistadi Psicoanalisi*, LXI(3): 645–662.

Peltz, R. (2018). Discussion of "Vitalizing enactment: A relational exploration" by Amy Cooney. *Psychoanalytic Dialogues,* 28(3): 361–370.

Reis, B. (1999). Thomas Ogden's phenomenological turn. *Psychoanalytic Dialogues*, 9(3): 371–393.

Reis, B. (2009). Performative and enactive features of psychoanalytic witnessing: The transference as the scene of address. *International Journal of Psychoanalysis,* 90(6): 1359–1372.

Reis, B. (2010). Enactive fields: An approach to interaction in the Kleinian-Bionian model: Commentary on paper by Lawrence Brown. *Psychoanalytic Dialogues,* 20(6): 695–703.

Schwartz Cooney, A. (2018). Vitalizing enactment: A relational exploration. *Psychoanalytic Dialogues,* 21(3): 340–354.

Seligman, S. (2005). Dynamic systems theories as a metaframework for psychoanalysis. *Psychoanalytic Dialogues,* 15(2): 285–319.

Seligman, S. (2018). *Relationships in development: Infancy, intersubjectivity and attachment.* New York: Routledge.

Stern, D.N. (2010). *Forms of vitality: Exploring dynamic experience in psychology, the arts and development.* Oxford: Oxford University Press.

Symington, N. (1983). The analyst's act of freedom as agent of therapeutic change. *International Review of Psychoanalysis,* 10: 283–291.

Winnicott, D.W. (1945). Primitive emotional development. In *Through pediatrics to psycho-analysis.* New York: Basic Books.

Winnicott, D.W. (1964). The baby as a going concern. In *The child, the family and the outside world.* Harmondsworth: Penguin Books.

Winnicott, D.W. (1986). *Home is where we start from: Essays by a psychoanalyst.* New York: W.W. Norton.

Winnicott, D.W. (1989). *Psychoanalytic explorations.* London: Karnac Books; Cambridge, MA: Harvard University Press.

Wood, J. (2015). *The nearest thing to life*. Waltham, MA: Brandeis University Press.

Chapter 4

The generative unconscious and the capacity to be fully alive

Joseph Newirth

In an extremely evocative statement, Grotstein (1995) described individuals who are unable to enter imaginative states of reverie, develop transitional experiences, and utilize symmetrical processes in the waking dream as "Orphans of the Real": people "who fall into a black hole" of unchanging, concrete, and unalterable external reality. These people often appear and describe themselves as depressed, describing their days as pointless, hopelessly going through repetitive, meaningless motions at work and in daily life. Grotstein's concept reflects the well-documented fact that depressed people are extremely realistic, with clear, albeit cynical, views of external reality. I have often thought of T.S. Eliot's poem, "We are the Hollow Men," as expressing the hopeless, meaningless, unthinking experience of being stuck in a never-ending external world of things as they are. In this poem, Eliot evocatively describes this unimaginative, thoughtless state of mind. In describing people as "Orphans of the Real," Grotstein was turning our attention away from their accurate views of external or objective reality, to the lack of capacity for imagination, their inability to use reverie and metaphors in developing a personal world inhabited by new subjective meanings, identities, and hopeful relationships.

Working with patients who have not developed the capacity to use imaginative or metaphorical processes to access their unconscious, or unformulated experience, is a complex experience in which the analyst often becomes unable to think, dulled by the monotonous, repetitive, empty words of the patient, becoming identified with the patient's deadened internal world. In conceptualizing the therapeutic process where the analyst is the container for his/her patient's evacuated, concrete experiences, the analyst often begins to enter into a dissociated state involving disconnected and disjointed associations before becoming able to create meaningful affective images which the patient can join in with and elaborate, creating moments of meeting in a newly developing psychoanalytic play space. This intersubjective imaginative process begins to transform the patient's paranoid concrete thoughts and acts, experienced as unalterable realities, into symbolic, metaphorical experiences through the development of symmetrical symbolic (Matte-Blanco, 1988; Newirth, 2003) metaphorical thought processes. Symington (2007) described this process as the creation of mind, a developmental process through which the patient becomes able to create personal meanings and engage in intimate hopeful relationships, through developing the capacity for imagination, reverie, and dream-like thoughts.

The generative unconscious

Experiences of deadness, of having a meaningless, joyless existence, are frequent complaints of many contemporary patients who feel profound emptiness at their core. How do we, as analysts, understand this terrible lack of relatedness and meaning, this black hole, which is often covered over by depression and addictive behaviors such as being a workaholic, or pursuing constant stimulation and excitement in both the external and virtual worlds of the internet? In this chapter I will illustrate an extreme version of a person's experience of psychic deadness and the problems encountered in my work with such patients. I would like to contextualize both the clinical and conceptual issues within the context of changing views of the unconscious from Freud's (1937) archeological model to Bion's (1965) transformational model and the Generative Unconscious (Newirth, 2003). The transformational model focuses on the development of a sense of aliveness and the capacity for joyful, creative, dream-like process of creating subjective meaning, creating a self. Evolving concepts of the unconscious reflect broad cultural changes, including the movement away from a positivist, mechanistic view of the world which underlies the unconscious in Freudian and ego psychological models, to a constructivist, postmodern approach to the unconscious which emphasizes the creation of meaning and the development of the capacity for intimacy and pleasure.

The traditional psychoanalytic theory of mind, of psychic structure, viewed it as a tripartite hierarchical structure in which the ego acted like an executive decision maker influenced by both the id and superego, attempting to keep unconscious, antisocial forces in check: the ego was thought of as a rider reining in a powerful horse. Freud (1937) analogized the mind to an archeological dig, in which artifacts (memories) found on different levels reflected early-childhood experiences, forgotten through a process of repression. For Freud (1937), the analyst's job was to interpret the repressions, facilitating the patient's ability to remember past events and recover repressed memories. Freud (1937), in recognition of the changing nature of how we understand the world and the psychoanalytic process, suggested that, failing to help the patient remember repressed memories, the analyst would construct a narrative explanation of how the past was being replayed in the present. This change in Freud's goal for psychoanalysis reflected an important shift from the importance of remembering and catharsis to the development of narrative and creation of personal meaning.

Melanie Klein and many other analysts (i.e., Sullivan, Fairbairn) developed different views of the unconscious, not based on repression in which the unconscious was viewed as the underworld, filled with primitive, infantile, destructive, and sexual impulses, but one in keeping with twentieth-century concepts, including attachment, information processing, relationships of mutual influence, and schemas of relating. Klein profoundly shifted the psychoanalytic view of mind from the former hierarchical structures of control to a dialectical structure, the paranoid schizoid and depressive positions, which each process information (experience) differently; perceiving, apprehending, and generating meaning according to different algorithms. Klein developed the concept of projective identification as the central dynamic in her theory; Ogden (1979) suggests that this implies that the Kleinian mind functions as a two-person, intersubjective system and not simply a one-person biological structure analogous to the brain.[1] Klein believed the infant's early experience of affect, particularly painful affects (i.e., hunger, needing to be held, feeling dirty, frustration, anger, etc.), dominates the infant's rudimentary, moment-to-moment sense of awareness which requires the infant to find a way to get rid of these painful experiences through action, demanding attention from a caregiver, or developing early cognitive operations of splitting experience into good and bad, and through projective identification, relocating these painful experiences from inside of me to outside of me. This dual emotional and cognitive process of splitting affect and relocating experience from inside to outside (not me) allowed the infant to experience good affective states inside the self, feeling comfort and safety, and the bad affective states as located outside, projected into the parent, who becomes experienced as a persecutory object.

Third-generation Kleinian theorists (Bion, Winnicott, Ogden, Ferro, Newirth) have further developed the concept of projective identification into a sophisticated intersubjective theory of human relatedness. These theorists view the mind as a developmental structure, integrating two parallel and mutually interacting organizations – the paranoid schizoid and the depressive positions – which each have specific ways of processing experience, creating meaning, and organizing relationships. The contributions of these different theorists have not been integrated into a cohesive theory with a shared language, although they all focus on the developing intersubjective nature of the unconscious as a structure that generates subjective meaning, utilizing the dream-like processes of reverie. Without having developed this capacity the individual is stuck in the paranoid position, feeling like a passive object pushed and pulled by the concrete demands of the external world and feeling victimized by experiences emanating of their body. The paranoid position (Newirth, 2003) is organized around the social dimension of power and control, presenting experience concretely as absolute facts (Segal, 1978), symbolic equations where the word and what it represents are experienced as the same thing. The central question from the perspective of the paranoid-schizoid position is: "do I control you (it) or do you control me (it)?" The depressive position involves the integration of the emotional splits which underlie the process of projective identification allowing the representations of self and other to be experienced symbolically, becoming aware of multiple possibilities, as three-dimensional complex thoughts, feelings, histories, and intentions. In the depressive position the person experiences himself/herself as neither all good nor all bad and is able to acknowledge and take responsibility for having hurt the other, which initiates processes of repair and growth.

Bion (1970) developed the concept of the container-contained as a metaphor to describe the intersubjective process of the developing capacity to transform the painful experiences of the paranoid-schizoid position to the symbolic experiences of the depressive position. In Bion's model the child or patient evacuates or projects the concrete, painful experiences from the self, experienced as absolutely real, into the mother[2] or therapist, unconsciously believing: "I am not bad, you are bad." The mother or therapist needs to be able to tolerate these painful, often accusatory, projections (feelings) and affectively elaborate and amplify these concrete experiences, moving from a state of absolute belief to a state of possibility. Segal (1978) highlights an aspect of this transformational process, noting that thinking in the paranoid-schizoid position involves experiencing something "as if" it is absolutely real, while in the depressive position it is experienced as "what if" this is real, emphasizing the importance of the ability to accept the possibility that a projection may be real; i.e., "what if I am a bad parent, what if I am a bad therapist?" From the intersubjective perspective of the container–contained model, the critical factor is the mother's or therapist's ability to accept, tolerate, and affectively elaborate the child's or patient's conscious and unconscious projections. The parent or therapist who is not able to function as a secure container experiences a great deal of persecutory anxiety, feeling that a difficult moment represents a dangerous crisis, blaming the child or patient in a secondary act of projective identification, accusing the other of being bad, thoughtless, and mean, which often devolves into an oscillating paranoid series of mutual blame–a tragic game of hot potato.

Winnicott (1971), like Bion, presented a radical two-person approach to the mind, emphasizing the importance of the other person, mother or therapist, in the development of intersubjective experiences. Winnicott (1955) illustrates the paradoxical aspects of creating intersubjective meaning with the often-quoted comment: "there is no such thing as a baby." Winnicott differentiates the baby as a biological entity from the baby as a center of psychological experience. Psychologically the baby only comes into existence within the context of the joint fantasies and emotional experiences that link mother and baby into a new, unique intersubjective unit. Winnicott elaborated this intersubjective process, the joint creation of meaning in developing the concept of transitional objects, which becomes elaborated as the individual's capacity to create intersubjective symbolic experiences, relational schemas, and mature transitional experiences, such as religion, art, families, and love affairs. For Winnicott the development of transitional experience involves the movement from the concrete thought of the paranoid-schizoid to the symbolic thought of the depressive position.

Winnicott (1971) describes thinking as occurring in two parallel realms simultaneously: an objective realm where people are objects and a subjective realm in which people become subjects, centers of initiative, feelings, thoughts, and intentions. For Winnicott we live as both objects and subjects, differentiating our being in the external world of things and work from the intersubjective world of affect, meanings, and intimate relationships. Winnicott's view that we are both subjects and objects[3] is similar to Buber's (1970) description of two modes of being in the world, a subjective experience which he describes as "I–Thou" and an experience of self and other as objects, in "I–It" forms of living. Although the difference between being an object and being a subject is implicit in other object relations theories, in making these two experiential realms of experience explicit, Winnicott presents a theory with which to understand the many patients who function extremely well in the objective world of things, business, law, and other professions, while simultaneously being unable to be present in and know intersubjective aspects of life, including their own and others' feelings, inner worlds, intentions, desires, and experiences.

Matte-Blanco (1988), like Winnicott, separated thinking about the external world of objects from the internal world of subjective experience. Knowing the external world of objects involves asymmetrical logic which differentiates experience in terms of person, place, time, and causality. Unconscious experience is organized and generated by symmetrical logic, which identifies and creates similarities, de-differentiating experience in terms of person, place, time, and causality, as in dreams which collapse the dimensions of external reality into a surrealist world of images. Depending on which form of logic we use, the same experience may have different meanings and be understood differently in different realms of experience. A therapist can use either an asymmetrical strategy attempting to differentiate time, person, place, and causality or a symmetrical strategy in which these differences are collapsed, creating poetic-like experiences of similarities and metaphors which provide an intense affective, presentational experience. For example, a therapist who believes that he/she is being experienced as a mother in the transference may say, using an asymmetrical strategy, "I am not your mother," attempting to help differentiate this relationship from the repetition of past expectations and failed behaviors. Alternatively, using a symmetrical strategy, the therapist may say, "I am your mother," highlighting the current emotional reality of the transference–countertransference experience. Both statements are true; however, they each result in different affective and cognitive experiences for patient and therapist. The asymmetrical strategy encourages a differentiation of the therapist from the historical object while the symmetrical strategy encourages the articulation of the affective experience of being a child in a nurturing relationship.

Fonagy and Target's (2007) work can be thought of as a bridge between contemporary Kleinian and relational theory and developmental research. They describes two parallel modes of organizing and representing experience similar to Matte-Blanco's concepts of asymmetrical and symmetrical logic, and the Kleinian concepts of the paranoid-schizoid and depressive positions. The mode of psychic equivalence describes a mental state in which the individual believes that what is in his/her mind is the same as what is in the other's mind and what actually exists in the external world. This is the world of facts, of absolute certainty, of concrete thought, the world that "Orphans of the Real" live in. The second mode of thought is the pretend mode in which the child or adult can imagine possibility, can alter reality to have personal meanings, and develop metaphors in both action and language, like when a child (Fonagy and Target, 2007) turns a chair on its side and pretends that it is an army tank, or when one person tells his beloved that she is the only person in the world. Under positive developmental and therapeutic experiences these two modes of thought are integrated in a third organization, mentalization, in which the focus is on an awareness of others and one's own mental processes of intentionality, desire, and possibility, which involves both reflective thought processes and an intersubjective capacity for mutual play. Fonagy and Target comment on the importance of both child and patient having the opportunity to play with others as a means of developing the capacity to mentalize (symbolize), to co-construct, imaginative states in which meaning is created mutually and does not remain in a dissociated retreat from reality.

Like Fonagy et al.'s (2007) discussion of the importance of mutual play as a critical developmental and therapeutic experience, contemporary Kleinian theorists have emphasized similar imaginative and playful processes in their analytic work with adults. Many of these theorists have focused on the evolution of Bion's theory of thinking, highlighting the idea that dreaming occurs as a constant and parallel experience to waking thoughts. For example, both Ogden (2007) and Ferro (2009) describe the importance of a dream-like process as the heart of the analytic enterprise, of helping patients be able to dream themselves into existence (Ogden, 2004): that is, to be able to generate meaningful and imaginative narratives in their lives. Ferro (2009) believes that the goal of analysis has changed from that of "a psychoanalysis of contents and memories, [to] a psychoanalysis that gives priority to the development of the apparatuses for dreaming, feeling, and thinking (Ferro, 2006, 2008)." Ferro uses metaphors from the movies to illustrate the co-construction of the capacity for imagination. He describes screenplays, film sets, the process of casting characters, and the development of highly saturated visual images which give emotional meaning to movies. His use of visual metaphors to elaborate Bion's concept of the waking dream state is similar to the pretend mode, transitional experiences, and Levenson's (2003) view that the detailed inquiry, the core of interpersonal analytic technique, is largely an experience of re-visualization of earlier experience. Ferro's (2009) more radical suggestion, supported by other contemporary Kleinians, is that when the patient has not developed the capacity for imagination and symbolic thought, the ability to transform proto-emotions and proto-sensations into pictograms (of the waking dream state), the analyst will need to cooperate, perhaps using his own reveries, in the co-construction and development of the patient's capacity to generate intersubjective meaning,

In the following section I will present my work with a patient who experienced a profound sense of psychological deadness, a lack of a sense of having any personal or subjective place or meaning in the world and how the ideas developed by third-generation Kleinian theorists, the Generative Unconscious, are used to enliven this patient's experience and to facilitate the development of his capacity to create meaning, his capacity to use unconscious dream-like processes in enlivening his life. I think of this patient as an "Orphan of the Real," who began therapy because he experienced severe depression and appeared to be in a hopeless state of despair. This clinical vignette illustrates the importance of enlivening individuals who are stuck in an endless, fragmented, and deadened preoccupation with external reality. I believe that an important aspect of the clinical work involves the analyst's ability to tolerate the deadened dissociated states which he/she inevitably experiences, having lost the ability to think and having tolerated the deadness through processes of projective identification that the patient has lived with. The analytic process revolves around the therapist's ability to think, to overcome his dissociation to introduce his/her developing reveries which provide access to the imaginative processes of the Generative Unconscious (Newirth, 2003).

Clinical illustration: working with "Orphans of the Real"

I have been working with Mr. X for almost two years. It is interesting to me that I am calling him Mr. X when in the past I have typically assigned first names to patients that I present in papers. I think this choice reflects my experience of his overwhelming sense of himself as an object, simply an example of what it means to be a human being, no different from the millions of other people populating the earth. Mr. X began to see me several years after he had broken his engagement to a woman who had been the driving force in their relationship. He continued to feel depressed and, although not actively suicidal, expressed his more passive suicidal thoughts through frequent statements that there was no reason to go on living. He described the end of his engagement as having evolved over several months during which time his perception of his fiancée changed dramatically; he began to ruminate about her appearance, he became preoccupied with her physical features, for example her nose which he began to believe was extremely unattractive, and as a result he felt put off her, becoming critical, distant, and hopeless about their life together. As he described his rumination about their relationship, he would project his life into the future, seeing both himself and his fiancée getting progressively older, moving to the suburbs, having children, going through the motions of life, until death finally claimed them. In short, it all felt pointless and hopeless.

This deadened and deadening experience of living was a constant and repetitive way that he spoke of his experiences at work and his very limited social life. It was clear that he had seriously inhibited his sense of desire and ambition; he occasionally and ambivalently talked about his lack of "libido" and interest in women. He diagnosed himself as "depressed," and had seen a psychiatrist who prescribed antidepressant medication (which did not help), and who attempted to motivate him to see the more positive side of his life. Neither of these efforts was fruitful.

Mr. X was a successful software engineer who worked very hard at his job. I thought that Mr. X presented the paradox of many people who I would identify as "Orphans of the Real." He was able to successfully navigate the external world of things and complex, abstract thought, although receiving no pleasure from his apparent success, while personally operating in the mode of psychic equivalence, living in a concrete paranoid world controlled by external events and the impersonal forces of fate and time. Mr. X did not seem to have the capacity to utilize the pretend mode, to use imagination or metaphors to generate new possibilities in his life; all was fixed; he lived and spoke in a passive voice, feeling defeated by the inevitable disappointments when he would attempt to step out of his very limited world. I don't believe that I shared my association that his view of himself, me, and other people was much like watching an ant colony in which we, the ants, each have the same repetitive task, carrying leaves on our backs, marching single file into the ant hill where the leaves are turned into food for the colony.

Mr. X always appeared depressed and lethargic, head hung low, speaking in a slow monotone, presenting his experience as if speaking from a far-away point in outer space. Our sessions often seemed fragmented, dead, and deadening. The sessions were filled with detailed accounts of events in the external world with little thought or self-reflection. As an analyst, I often felt embarrassed, unable to think, filled with guilt, and questioning my competence, working hard to insert a sense of aliveness, while often being distracted by seemingly irrelevant thoughts. I think of my experiences in these sessions with Mr. X as those of being overwhelmed by beta elements, concrete fragments, disconnected descriptions of his life, presented as absolute unbearable facts, which I could not make sense of or interpret. My ability to think and generate images was completely broken. I felt thrown into the chaos of the unsymbolized unconscious, knocked down by wave after wave of transference–countertransference failure. I found myself questioning what I was doing and why Mr. X continued[4] therapy with me.

I have often found Bion's idea of -K which describes experiences of being unable to think as providing the emotional support necessary to tolerate these periods of chaos and inability to think and feel. This theoretical perspective has helped me to feel safe and have faith in following the emerging threads of reverie which possibly lead to the development of proto-symbols which would allow me to develop "pictograms" (Ferro, 2009) that develop into more meaningful experiences of the emerging, unformulated unconscious fantasies which have been created or contained in the analytic field. Mr. X arrived for a session in what seemed like a severe state of dissociation; he was very depressed, he seemed far away, head hung over to the side, speaking in his soft monotone. He began talking about an ongoing problem at work and a frequent theme of his not knowing if he would continue to be employed. He continued, saying that he was not sure if he wanted to be employed and began questioning the point of his work and of working at all. He said that he was hardly eating and continued to question the point of living. He described his daily cycle of getting up, eating, exercising, going to work, coming home, eating, and going to bed, only to repeat this sequence over and over again. I knew that his apartment was barren without any possibility of entertainment or distraction. As Mr. X continued to raise the rhetorical question of why he should continue to live, I became acutely aware of his suicidal preoccupation but afraid of directly interrogating this issue. I was afraid that any explicit discussion of suicide would provide support for his argument of the pointlessness of life. It was as if I also strongly felt the pointlessness of life which left me feeling a sense of hopelessness and shame.

At that moment I could not think of many reasons to go on living – I am not sure if this reflected a part of me or if it represented a complete collapse of the transference–countertransference relationship, a concrete symmetrization of the experience of him and of me as separate subjects. I felt concerned, frightened, and rather impotent as an analyst. As I sat with these feelings an image (pictogram) began to form in my mind. It was like a scene in an old movie, a somewhat disheveled prisoner, in a depressing empty prison cell, was X-ing off the days of the weeks, months, and years, marking off the days of his life, until the end. It was an image of a man unable to alter his fate, only able to count the days until the end of his sentence, of his existence. It was a very clear and persistent image which I decided to describe to Mr. X, explaining to him the reverie that our conversation had stimulated in me. As I write this chapter I did not know if this image was a reflection of me or of Mr. X – which one of us was crossing off the days of his life?

To my surprise, Mr. X responded with more enthusiasm than I had previously seen. In a lively voice he said my image reminded him of the old television series *Gunsmoke*, which he had watched all the time as a boy. He had spent many hours alone in his room watching and rewatching episodes of *Gunsmoke* and other Westerns. He told me that he had never talked about having been so completely involved with Westerns and that they had influenced him a great deal, as he had consciously and unconsciously adapted the role of the heroic and isolated figure in these stories. This session became extremely lively, taken up with the themes and characters from *Gunsmoke* as we each brought forward favorite characters from the show. He identified with the marshall, Matt Dillon, and we talked about how, in this show and other Westerns, the hero never gets the girl but always leaves town having simply gotten rid of the bad guys. As we continued to talk in this excited, mutual way, the conversation about Westerns seemed to function as a metaphor, a waking dream, that we were now creating together. At the end of the session, I remembered the last scene in the movie *Shane*, in which the main character, after having saved the homesteaders from the bad guys, rides out of town while a little boy named Joey is calling: "Shane, Shane, come back, come back, Shane." In retrospect, I think that I was that little boy calling Mr. X, implying that we could play together and perhaps develop a different, less lonely script.

This session highlights the difference between a child who plays alone, which Fonagy and Target (2007) describe as a dissociative state, in contrast to playing with others, which leads to a capacity for the development of mentalization and of being with others in a form of the pretend mode, the capacity to create meaning. This session represented a complex set of experiences in the transference–countertransference. I believe that there was a collapse of our different roles, of the container–contained function, where we each became unable to think, flooded by the impossibility of life, being in a dissociated state in which we each lived in a concrete, barren world, feeling like despised failures. It was only my being able to articulate these hopeless, dead feelings, developing the dream-like image of being a doomed prisoner and articulating this intersubjective experience in the moment that allowed us to move into more playful transitional-like experiences, talking about and being the characters in Westerns. Ogden (2007) presents a similar set of ideas, highlighting that the content of the session, like books, TV shows, or movies, is less important than the mutual intersubjective experience of creating meaning which he describes as talking as dreaming, a symmetrical, metaphoric process through which the patient and analyst are able to create an emotional life, in Ogden's words, to dream himself into existence.

In the following session Mr. X began talking about our mutual reverie about Westerns and said that, when he thought about it, he felt that one of the lessons he took from those experiences was that "he would rather be right than succeed." This statement captured a central value of Mr. X, one that kept him from pursuing more pleasurable and perhaps selfish experiences. I reflected on his wearing the "white hat" of the good guy in the Western, and that I actually liked wearing the "black hat," and how easy it was in the Westerns to know what was right and what was wrong, who was good and who was bad. Although our relationship was becoming more playful and Mr. X was becoming more able to reflect on our process and on other aspects of his life, the overwhelming sense of futility seemed to continue to organize his experience and our sessions. The goal to facilitate Mr. X's ability to use more imaginative and metaphoric processes in developing both intimate relationships and in understanding his own life experiences was still a long way off.

A few months later Mr. X was speaking about the pointlessness of life, seeming resentful of my somewhat optimistic stance as our relationship became warmer as a result of the shared experience of being in the dream world of the Westerns. In response to Mr. X's descriptions of the futility of his life I began to think about the Prisoner's Dilemma game which I had used in my dissertation. Because of his background, I assumed that Mr. X was familiar with the Prisoner's Dilemma, which he affirmed. This is a game in which the object is to see if you can trust the other player not to betray you. If you cannot trust the other player it is to your advantage to try and betray the other player before he or she betrays you. The possible outcomes of the game are that both people trust each other and both can win, both people distrust each other and both lose, or one trusts the other, who betrays the trusting player, and the one who betrays gets a big payoff and the one who trusts incurs a very big loss. This is an interesting paradigm that has been used to understand and study the dynamic issues of trust and betrayal, or competition and cooperation in intersubjective relationships and in organizations.

Having introduced this game into our session I told Mr. X that when computers play this game they become stuck in the position of mutual distrust and mutual loss because the only rational or objective solution is not to trust the other who can potentially screw you – the rational solution is to not trust the other, to not hope for something better. When people play the game they introduce a possibility of hope, success, mutual pleasure, because they take the chance of trusting each other. I said that he seems to "play the game" in an entirely rational (objective) way, always accepting a moderate loss over the possibility of winning. We talked about the different strategies of the Prisoner's Dilemma game and he seemed to be convinced that the only way to play was to not take the chance of losing, of being screwed, and continue in his isolated and hopeless strategy. I felt a bit disheartened at the end of this session as if I had reinforced his belief that it is foolish to hope because inevitably you will lose. Again, it is only in retrospect as I write this chapter that I recognize my identification with the depressed, hopeless aspects of Mr. X and of myself, the sense of being imprisoned both in reflecting on the Prisoner's Dilemma and in my reverie of the prisoner in an old movie, only able to count the days till the end. These experiences reflect both the concept of projective identification and also the breakdown of the container–contained function and the separation of the intersubjective relationship within the transference–countertransference.

Mr. X began the following session seeming more energized than usual and told me that he had seen a trainer and was beginning an exercise program. He said that he asked the trainer, who was a woman, if he began weight training whether that would increase his libido. She reassured him that it would increase his libido and his desire. I felt that this change seemed to reflect a shift in both his capacity to imagine himself as different and to introduce the possibility of sexuality and pleasure into his life and into our sessions. He was beginning to be able to imagine himself, in Ogden's words, "to dream himself into existence," and to metaphorize his body as an alive source of strength and sensual pleasure. I believe that my introduction of the Prisoner's Dilemma game provided a metaphoric experience in which he was able to act, seeing how he chose to "play the game," and to see that he could potentially influence others. This clinical moment also reflected an important element of trust in the process, highlighting that we often do not know how our interventions and relationship affect the patient and the analytic process.

These metaphoric dream-like moments, including my discussion of the Prisoner's Dilemma game, seemed to facilitate Mr. X's beginning to develop the capacity to transform his archaic, concrete experiences of an unalterable reality (fragmented beta elements) into dream-like images, imaginative, symbolic experiences, including the capacity to use imaginative thought processes in creating a possible future involving subjectivity, desire, and pleasure. In a session during this phase of our work in which Mr. X was shifting his way of thinking to include symbolic, symmetrical, metaphoric processes of the waking-dream state, he said that he had been listening to an old favorite song and had been crying uncontrollably. The song was "All my heroes have always been cowboys," which was originally recorded by Weylon Jennings (1976).

When patients mention songs as meaningful association, I think of these songs as forms of a waking dream which represent unconscious structures or phantasies that generate meaning. I always ask my patients to speak/sing as much of the song as they can. Mr. X spoke the lyrics, which I found to be very moving. As we each listened to the words and entered the lonely world of the cowboy, we could feel the transformation from his isolated state of watching Westerns by himself, a daydream-like (Winnicott, 1971) dissociated activity to an emotional meaningful and shared fantasy that we could each feel.

I had not experienced Mr. X to be so present and alive in his life as he was when he spoke the lyrics to this song. He said, after he cried a great deal, that he called his mom and they spoke for a long time in what seemed like a comforting conversation. He also called his ex-fiancée and they had dinner. He seemed to be reaching out to the women in his life, something that he had not done before. We continued to talk about country and western songs which he loved and the session ended with my remembering and talking about Kris Kristofferson's song "Me and Bobby McGee," which describes a contemporary version of a cowboy song in which the central character is remembering a lost love which ironically ends with the powerful, emotional lyric reflecting Mr. X's cowboy ethic, equating freedom with complete emptiness and reprising the loneliness of the song "My heroes have always been cowboys." These lyrics symbolize and transform the pain of loss and desire while simultaneously introducing the possibility of hope as Mr. X moves into a more symbolic, symmetrical state of being.

Concluding comments

This clinical illustration focuses on two interlocking dimensions in the process of enlivening a patient stuck in the deadened and deadening reality of the "Orphans of the Real." The first dimension is the inevitable and necessary impairment of the analyst's capacity to think, enter states of reverie in which symmetrical, poetic, dream-like, presentational process can generate meaningful associations that can be used in the analytic dyad to generate subjective meaning. I think of this process as one of the difficulties in clinical work in which the analyst's capacity to contain the patient's experience breaks down and both members of the analytic dyad are in a concrete, paranoid state overwhelmed by repetitive and meaningless experience. From a contemporary Kleinian perspective we might think of this inability to think as -K and the analytic situation as being flooded with beta elements. The first task is for the analyst to recover his capacity to be a container able to tolerate, accept, and affectively elaborate whatever thoughts occur, even those which reflect his/her own experiences of shame and guilt for being a failure as an analyst. Overcoming the guilt, shame, and hopelessness of being a failed analyst is necessary in order to begin to trust the process, one's self, and one's patient. This does not happen simply as an act of will or an asymmetrical cognitive exercise. Rather this process of repairing the broken container is a complex procedural process in which we must be prepared to feel foolish and frequently fall on our face. At the point that I had the frightening association of being a prisoner in a cell, like in an old movie, "X-ing" off the days of his/my life, I initially wanted to escape from that image, as it suggested hopeless, helpless, suicidal depression. Deciding to tell Mr. X that association felt like it required a kind of courage, perhaps because it was unclear which of us, or perhaps both of us, was actually the doomed prisoner. This represents a difficult moment of recognition, which also reflects a movement from the most concrete thought processes to a possible beginning process of symbolization and the generation of meaning, of becoming alive, of dreaming oneself into existence. I was quite surprised by Mr. X's response and our subsequent lively ability to enter into the transitional play around his earlier fascination with *Gunsmoke* and the Westerns of his childhood.

This moment in which we entered into the world of playing with the Westerns illustrates the second interlocking process, through which Mr. X was able to become enlivened and begin to generate meaning and a more active perspective on his life. Our conversations did more than simply articulate his unconscious fantasies, his unthought known. Through our playing together in this newly generated transitional space, he could become the cowboy that he had previously just been able to observe passively in a dissociated state. He could see how the underlying cowboy values had limited his life and his capacity for pleasure and through the pleasure generated in our sessions he was able to move into a new developmental position which we could understand as the depressive position or that of mentalization being able to integrate the modes of psychic equivalence and the pretend mode. It is important to understand that this is a developmental process, a process of growth, of taking new enlivened perspectives on one's life. I hope these moments from my work with Mr. X. illustrate the transformation from states of deadness, from being stuck in a never-ending world of what is, of being an "Orphan of the Real," to being able to use the enlivening, imaginative, metaphorical processes of the generative unconscious in creating a life, into dreaming oneself into existence.

Notes

1 See Freud (1950) Project in which he attempted to see all mental activity as reflected in brain function.
2 I am using "mother" because Bion assumes that the parent who was engaged in this process was the mother, when in fact it can be any committed caretaker, including a father.
3 In earlier work, Winnicott (1955) described this dual form of being and thinking as the true self and the false self. As Khan (1974) states, these early ideas had a somewhat moralistic tone which the latter concept of object and subject did not have.
4 In reflecting on the dilemma of our relationship, I have thought that Mr. X represented a more hopeful version of my depressed father who I was never able to help and who I had fled from both literally and metaphorically.

References

Bion, W.R. (1965). Transformations: Change from Learning to Growth. London: Tavistock.
Bion, W.R. (1970). Attention and Interpretation, 1–130. London: Tavistock.
Buber, M. (1970). I and Thou. New York: Scribner.
Ferro, A. (2006). Clinical Implications of Bion's Thought. Int. J. Psycho-Anal., 87(4):989–1003.
Ferro, A. (2008). The Patient as the Analyst's Best Colleague: Transformation into a Dream and Narrative Transformations. Ital. Psychoanal. Annu., 2:199–205.
Ferro, A. (2009). Transformations in Dreaming and Characters in the Psychoanalytic Field. Int. J. Psycho-Anal., 90(2):209–230.

Fonagy, P. and Target, M. (2007). Playing with Reality: IV. A Theory of External Reality Rooted in Intersubjectivity. Int. J. Psycho-Anal., 88(4):917–937.

Freud, S. (1937). Constructions in Analysis. The Standard Edition of the Complete Psychological Works of Sigmund Freud, Volume XXIII (1937–1939): Moses and Monotheism, An Outline of Psycho-Analysis and Other Works. London: Hogarth Press, pp. 255–270.

Freud, S. (1950). Project for a Scientific Psychology (1950 [1895]). The Standard Edition of the Complete Psychological Works of Sigmund Freud, Volume I (1886–1899): Pre-Psycho-Analytic Publications and Unpublished Drafts, 281–391.

Grotstein, J. (1995) Orphans of the Real I. Bull. Meninger Clinic, 59(3): 287–311.

Khan, M.M.R. (1974) The Privacy of the Self. Hogarth Press, London.

Levenson, E.A. (2003). On Seeing What is Said: Visual Aids to the Psychoanalytic Process. Contemp. Psychoanal., 39:233–249.

Matte-Blanco, I. (1988). Thinking, Feeling, and Being. New Library of Psycho-Analysis, vol. 5, pp. 1–336. London: Tavistock/Routledge.

Newirth, J. (2003). Between Emotion and Cognition: The Generative Unconscious. New York: Other Press.

Ogden, T.H. (1979). On Projective Identification. Int. J. Psycho-Anal., 60:357–373.

Ogden, T.H. (2004). The Art of Psychoanalysis: Dreaming Undreamt Dreams and Interrupted Cries. Int. J. Psychoanal., 85:857–878.

Ogden, T.H. (2007). On Talking-as-Dreaming. Int. J. Psycho-Anal., 88:575–589.

Segal, H. (1978). On Symbolism. Int. J. Psycho-Anal., 59:315–319.

Symington, N. (2007). A Technique for the Creation of Mind. Int. J. Psychoanal., 88:1409–1422.

Winnicott, D.W. (1955). Metapsychological and Clinical Aspects of Regression Within the Psycho-Analytical Set-Up. Int. J. Psycho-Anal., 36:16–26.

Winnicott, D.W. (1971). Playing and Reality. New York: Tavistock Publications.

Chapter 5

Between Mythos and Logos

Surrender, vitalization and transformation

Boaz Shalgi

By way of introduction, I would like to invite the reader to experience the ideas which I will try to present in this chapter, by quoting, perhaps somewhat at length, what is to me one of the most beautiful paragraphs written in psychoanalytic literature. This paragraph – the opening words of Ogden's *Subjects of Analysis* (1994), is chiefly about vitalization through transformation, at least as I think of it. It might be that I have chosen to open this chapter with these words because they have had a transformative effect on me, i.e., they created an unexpected, intensive, incomprehensible at the time, yet long-lasting change. In accordance with the spirit of these words, and with the ways of thinking which I will try to present in this chapter, one might say that I have modified, vitalized, or re-created the words myself, thus intensifying my experience of transformation:

> It is too late to turn back. Having read the opening words of this book you have already begun to enter into the unsettling experience of finding yourself becoming a subject whom you have not yet met, but nonetheless recognize … You, the reader, must allow me to occupy you, your thoughts, your mind, since I have no voice with which to speak other than yours … This book will not be "understood" by you; you will not simply receive it, incorporate it, digest it, or the like. To the degree that you will have anything at all to do with it, you will transform it … The confrontation with alterity will not let us rest.
>
> (Ogden, 1994, pp. 1–3)

The transformative influence which Ogden tries to capture in these beautiful words, an influence which is straightforward, mutual, subjugating, unexplained, or explained only in retrospect, materializes out of a total, whole, all-out openness towards the alterity of an encounter. It is a kind of change which is created when one courageously confronts otherness, be it the otherness within oneself, the otherness of fellow human beings, or the unavoidable, inescapable otherness of sheer reality—the world "in itself and for itself" (Hegel, 1807, p. 229). This kind of transformative change is not so much about the encounter as such, but more about the unique characteristics of this encounter, in which one allows alterity to penetrate, to occupy one's innermost private experiences, to "let it do things" inside without awareness, introspection, or any sort of control. This is an influence and a change which does not rely on understanding psychic structures or processes, and which does not evolve out of reflection, but out of exposing the soul to the relentless and uncompromised influence of reality upon it, and of itself upon reality, including upon its fellow subject. This is the kind of encounter with the world which Emmanuel Ghent tried to capture with his unique re-invention (1992) of the term "surrender."

Surrender, emphasized Ghent repeatedly, is not an act performed by one psyche *on the other* (like in Winnicott's (1945) "primary maternal pre-occupation"), but a letting go, an acceptance of "what is"—an event, an act between two entities (be they human or non-human) in relationship which penetrate and create each other while freeing themselves to experience, moreover, to *become* whatever is being created among and between them. Referring to Ghent's concept of surrender, Benjamin (2004) writes: "Surrender is not *to* someone … [but] letting go into *being* with them" (p. 8); later (2007) she defines it as: "surrendering to the dyadic mental state" (p. 678). "To me," writes Ghent, "surrender is an act of embracing the unknown, whether in a quiet, meditative, receptive way or in an all-out 'active' assertive way, a 'letting it happen'" (2001, p. 31). As I will try to show shortly, I believe that one surrenders to what Bion calls O, and in the same act, transforms O and infuses it with life.

Ghent sees surrender as the most basic need of the human psyche, which is characterized by expansion, creating oneself and reality in many evolving, propagating forms and shapes. Yet, Ghent reminds us, this most fundamental need is teeming with terrors and anxieties, which sometimes distort the vitalizing "movement of surrender" (Becker and Shalgi, 2013; Shalgi, 2018) into its deadening, petrifying, "ever lookalike" (Ghent, 1990, p. 115) submission. Another crucial point about surrender, emphasizes Ghent, is that it always "catches" us off guard, unprepared, by surprise. Paraphrasing Winnicott's (1971) statement, that "the significant moment is that at which the child surprises himself or herself" (p. 51), one can say that for Ghent the significant moment in psychotherapy, or in life, is that in which the patient and the therapist surprise each other and themselves. Indeed, transformative change is not a consequence of a logical, sequential, reflected-upon process, but of conscious, pre-conscious, and unconscious, sub-symbolic mutual penetration. Thus, as Mitchell and Aron (1999) eloquently put it, "Ghent's psychoanalytic goal is not insight, information, or understanding alone, but, rather, transformation, a radical change in people's nature as they come into contact with the frozen parts of themselves that are yearning to be reached, known, and recognized" (p. 211)—a change which is always a result of interaction.

The term "radical change" requires special attention: It is not entirely in accord with traditional notions of psychoanalysis, in which the concept of change is grounded in gradual, incessant processes, constructed of an accumulation of many moments of self-reflection and self-understanding. But Ghent offers a model for a profoundly different kind of change: immediate, daring, intensive, and, most importantly, logically incomprehensible and interaction-dependent. If classical psychoanalysis sees insight as leading to change in one's inner psychic needs-equilibrium resulting in change in the quality of interactions with one's surroundings, in Ghent's psychoanalysis we can say that interaction leads to transformation, and transformation, in turn, creates new understandings. This is not only a different conceptualization regarding human development, but a totally altered way of thinking about and perceiving change.

While most basic premises of psychoanalytic change were, historically, founded on Logos-based postulations, the concept of change as it emerges from mutual surrender to co-created (intersubjective) reality is founded on Mythos-based suppositions. *Logos and Mythos, as will be elaborated and illuminated in this chapter, are two categorically distinct epistemological and ontological systems of thinking; each presents a way of perceiving and explaining "all there is"—the universe, the human subject, the existence of a God or gods.* Logos is the rational faculty, based on reason, linearity, a sequential concept of time (the Greeks' Chronos), and cause-and-effect laws of explanation. Mythos, on the other hand, is grounded in imagination, intuition, an instantaneous-spontaneous concept of time (the Greeks' Kyros), inspiration and creativity. There is something vital, I believe, in bringing the "language of Mythos" more centrally into psychoanalytic discourse. By the term "Mythos" I do not refer to the use of metaphors, fables, or culture-shaping myths (like Oedipus, Narcissus, or Sisyphus), but to the all-encompassing way Mythos considers and perceives both non-human and human realities. Among the numerous disparities between the "language of Logos" and the "language of Mythos," there are two differences that I would like to focus on that have uniquely contributed to the ideas presented in this chapter: particularity vs. universality, and the nature of influence and impact.

Both Mythos and Logos reflect man's endeavor to provide cohesive, lucid, and meaningful explanations for the vast phenomena that comprise the world, including the inner world of the human psyche. Yet, their methodologies are completely different. Mythos elucidates a *particular phenomenon* by creating a *particular story* about it. In an attempt to explain natural phenomena—the change of seasons, birth, death—or human experiences—love, hope, vanity, intergenerational struggle with its tensions and complexities—Mythos creates a collection of stories and legends about men and gods, about deeds and affairs, to ascribe meaning to these phenomena, to the things we see, feel, and experience. Mythos generates varied stories to explain varied phenomena. Thus, one of the most fundamental characteristics of Mythos is its respect for diversity, multiplicity, and particularity.

This method of understanding stands in clear contrast to Logos' reasoning through logic. Following Aristotle, most philosophers and scholars see Thales' cosmological statement "all is water" as the beginning of Logos-based philosophy. The importance of Thales' contribution does not rest, of course, in its "answer"—all matter is water—but on the question it posits—what is all? It is considered to be the first time in the history of human contemplation that man takes upon himself the challenge of searching for unity, of searching for the fundamental essence that serves as the bedrock for everything else. This is a crucial and awesome revolution: unlike Mythos, Logos-based thinking searches for the Universal, and tries to explain the Particular through the Universal. See, for example, the way Hegel (1805–1806) conceptualized this transformation in human thinking:

> The proposition of Thales, that water is the Absolute … is the beginning of Philosophy, because with it the consciousness is arrived at that essence, truth, that which is alone in and for itself, are one. A departure from what is in our sensuous perception here takes place; man recedes from this immediate existence … the Greeks had considered sun, mountains, earth, sea, rivers, &c., as independent powers, revered them as gods, and elevated them by the imagination to activity, movement, consciousness and will … This wild, endlessly varied imagination of Homer is set at rest by the proposition that existence is water; this conflict of an endless quantity of principles, all these ideas that a particular object is an independent truth, a self-sufficient power over others existing in its own right, are taken away, and it is shown likewise that there is only one universal, the universal self-existent, the simple unimaginative perception, the thought that is one and one alone.
>
> (Hegel, 1805–1806, p. 178)

Thus Logos negates specificity, particularity, and multiplicity, in search of the one, united essence of all things. In contrast, Mythos embraces an assortment of diverse and unique entities, powers, and forces—each exists independently for itself and as itself,

The second difference between Mythos and Logos I would like to shed light upon, which in a sense derives from the above distinction, has to do with the way these two methods of thinking conceptualize and conceive of the nature of change. According to Logos, effect takes place due to causality based on analysis. *A* does not change *B directly*, but an inner and analyzable *component* of *A* changes inner and analyzable *components* of *B*. In order to understand the way an encounter with *A* changes *B*, we need to analyze what parts of *B* were changed, what parts of *A* caused the change, and in what ways. The language of Mythos, on the other hand, does not analyze. *A* acts on *B directly, immediately, and spontaneously.* Change does not occur due to a process whereby certain ingredients of *A* and of *B* influence each other in a logical-analyzable cause-and-effect process; it emerges all at once, without any explicable reason, out of the sheer and pure encounter. Logos explains that a tree grows gradually, because certain components within the seed encounter certain chemicals that reside in the earth, combined with water and the sun—a mixture of elements that when fused with the seed's material cause reactions that lead to the growth of the seedling and later the tree. Alternatively, Mythos tells us that Daphne transformed into a tree, completely and spontaneously, when her father, the river-god Ladon, answered her prayer to escape Apollo's lustful embrace. When one looks at Bernini's astonishing sculpture "Apollo and Daphne" in Villa Borghese, one can see and feel how Daphne transformed, in the blink of an eye, into a tree. This is the amazing impact of the sculpture; this is the amazing power of Mythos. Thus, the most basic category of change according to Logos is a gradual, analyzable, cause-and-effect process; and the most basic category of change according to Mythos is transformation which involves immediate, vitalized, spontaneous interaction.

The characteristics of spontaneity and particularity in the language of Mythos place human beings in a living interactive world, which is constantly evolving and transforming. Logos provides man with reassuring and fortifying feelings of control, a kind of control that derives from order, law, and logical-based causality. Mythos does not offer such consolation. It is not comprised of systematic laws that make the world we live in familiar, predictable, or reliable. The Mythical world has no consistency. It presents a surprising, unexpected, shifting reality, at times even overwhelming and alarming. It has no structures, no "essences," only ever-changing interactive qualities. Ghent (1995) puts it eloquently when he writes:

> *Everything* is in flux, which means that *everything*, living or not, is interactive. When the rate of change—the rate of interaction—is rapid we call it process; when it is very slow, we refer to structures ... We have come to recognize that not only is there no such thing as a baby, there is no such thing as an individual, only matrices of individuals in constant interactive flux.
>
> (p. 481, italics in original)

What, then, does Mythos offer in order to make the world more familiar, more conceivable, more possible to live in? It makes it *personal, and personally meaningful.* In the effort to transform an estranged, indifferent world into a familiar, comfortable, encouraging reality, Mythos tells us a particular, personal story. The most meaningful change a person goes through in his or her encounter with reality is transforming what was foreign, external, threatening, and "*unheimlich*" into a part of oneself, that is, a part of one's own subjective reality. It is a creative experience of transforming "not-mine" into "also-mine," an act of *personal vitalization* of the reality one lives in. By "*personal vitalization of reality*" I mean an act of infusing life into an experience, or even more so, infusing my own utterly unique and distinctive life into reality, thus transforming it, creating it anew,[1] giving life to reality and to myself at the same time. The Oedipus complex might be universal, and thus explained according to the laws of Logos, yet the story that Sophocles tells us is not universal. The play's power does not lie in its generality, but in the fact that it tells a universal story in a particular, personal way.

The therapeutic power of realizing one's Oedipal drives lies in the specific way one re-writes the story as one's own, creates it as a part of one's own childhood, together with one's own parents. If the Oedipus complex has any therapeutic value, it is only insofar as one personally and uniquely re-creates Sophocles' Oedipus, and Freud's Oedipus, and with this act vitalizes Sophocles, Freud, and the self.[2] It is said that myths are universal. Perhaps, but their transformative impact is not due to their universal meanings. Rather, it stems from their amazing ability to infuse the universal with a very particular subjective sense.

I will return shortly to the issue of the particularity of myths, but first I would like to highlight an idea which, to my mind, is of prominent importance: this process, in which the universal becomes personal, in which knowledge becomes personal, in which truth becomes personal, is one of the most transformative processes in life and in psychotherapy. It might seem odd to say that "one's" psychic reality becomes "personal," since, allegedly, one's psychic reality is always a personal reality. But this is not always so. In his journey to clarify the notion of "true self," Winnicott (1960) writes: "In the area that I am examining the instincts are not yet clearly defined as internal to the infant. The instincts can be as much external as can a clap of thunder or a hit" (p. 141). Indeed, patients, people, often experience their psychic realities—be they instincts, needs, internal objects, wishes, or phantasies—as estranged, as alienated, as being forced upon them. This stance is wonderfully described by James Grotstein. In the last chapter of his seminal book *Who is the Dreamer who Dreams the Dream*? (2000), titled "Bion's transformations in O," Grotstein describes a third position, which is beyond Klein's paranoid-schizoid and depressive positions, a position he refers to as "the transcendent position." It is a position which in its essence is a surrender to "what is" (Ghent, 1990, p. 230), to one's being, to what happens in oneself and in the world around, to the mutual influence one experiences with the world. Grotstein writes that the:

> transcendent position account[s] for the state of serenity that accompanies one who finally, after traversing the nightmares of the paranoid-schizoid position and the black holes and mournful inner cathedrals of the depressive position, is able to become reconciled to the experience of pure, unadulterated Being and Happening.
>
> (Grotstein, 2000, p. 282)

This "reconciliation with experience," which characterized Grotstein's transcendent position, has both the qualities of letting go "into" an experience and of owning it for oneself. Thus, the concept of the transcendent position is not unlike Ghent's surrender:

> To me, surrender is an act of embracing the unknown, whether in a quiet, meditative, receptive way or in an all-out "active," assertive way, a "letting it happen" ... in surrender, arguing ceases; there is a feeling of liberation ... there is no trace of complaint or blame; there is acceptance.
>
> (Ghent, 2001, pp. 31–32)

Ghent and Grotstein share this view of freedom experienced in infusing the external world with one's own internal agency. Indeed, Grotstein goes on to describe the transcendent position as the most liberated and vitalized experience one can aspire to:

> Transcendent means having the ability to transcend our defensiveness, our pettiness, our guilt, our shame, our narcissism,

> our need for certainty, our strictures in order to achieve or to become "one with O," which I interpret as becoming one with our *aliveness* (Ogden, 1997) or with our very *being-ness* (our *Dasein*; Heidegger, 1927).
>
> (Grotstein, 2000, p. 300)

The positions Ghent and Grotstein present here need not be conceptualized as bridges to the "transcendental beyond," or as acts of "emerging into O." On the contrary: they describe a process of altering O, altering externality, by re-creating it as one's own, by personalizing it, by linking it to the numerous seemingly unimportant day-to-day idiosyncratic details that comprise our lives. By personalizing O, one infuses it with life, mobilizes it, changes it from a motionless, petrified "thing as itself," an unalterable universal reality, into a particular, ever-changing reality, a vital O that is being created anew every moment, by every human being, by every therapeutic couple:

> O *evolves*; it is always changing. Spontaneous transformation becomes automatic and ineluctable. The problem for the individual in the river of experience is to accept the transformations by personal transformations of these impersonal transformations of O. Thus, for me, the important transformation is from impersonal O to personal (emotional) O.
>
> (Grotstein, 2000, p. 283, italics in original)

This kind of personal transformation of O involves the ability to "face the music," as Ogden (2005, p. 21) puts it, to confront reality with open eyes (Shalgi, 2018), or what Bion called "the human need for truth" (1959, p. 100). When one surrenders to "what is," to reality, one accepts it, takes it in, and in the very act transforms it from a "Logos-reality" into a "Mythos-reality." Yet, this animating transformation cannot be carried out by one person/mind alone. There must always be another person, someone with whom one creates reality together. So here is another paradox: in order to create one's most inner, private, personal reality, in order to transform indifferent reality into experience which carries personal/emotional meaning, one must "join consciousness in companionship" (Trevarthen, 2009; Grossmark, 2016), what Grotstein refers to as "the mutuality of alpha function" (2000, p. 299). Thus, the most subjective and personal approach to reality is by its nature intersubjective.

I would like to tackle this all-important paradox, in which the way to personalize reality, make it one's own, is both subjective and intersubjective by nature by applying Bion's (1963) conceptualization regarding the three dimensions of every psychoanalytic interpretation. In *Elements of Psychoanalysis*, Bion explains that every interpretation, in order to attain its full meaning, in order *to achieve its validity as real human experience*, must contain within it, or have links to, three dimensions of experience: "the domain of sense; the domain of myth; the domain of passion" (p. 11).

I believe that the therapist's pursuit of and surrender to these three dimensions of being and experiencing is what vitalizes the lives of both patient and therapist. It is what transforms the therapeutic couple from estranged and alien life to personal-emotional life, a life that feels worth living, a life one can hate, one can love, one can dread, one can desire. A life one can live. Before turning to a more detailed explanation of Bion's mutually created dimensions of every interpretation and of every meaningful moment in life, I would like to present a short vignette, taken from my therapeutic encounter with Solly.

Solly—an "ordinary" person

Solly, a student in her mid-20s, came to therapy out of a desire to change some important things in her life. Solly is an amazing person—no one doubts this, actually not even she herself doubts it. She is beautiful, smart, amazingly sensitive, loved. However, she has never been in a relationship, and very much wants one. It isn't that she has never been in love—she has been a number of times, but habitually does not give the men she is interested in any sign of this. In her words, she feels very awkward doing this. Instead, she would plunge into rich and varied fantasies about the relationship that could have been. These fantasies gave her immense pleasure, and aside from the sad truth, that the *concept of an apple* (to use Hegel's term), or the *fantasy of an apple* (to use the psychoanalytic term) can't mollify hunger, it seemed she was almost able to satisfy herself with these fantasies. However, of course, these fantasies always carried a trace of melancholy, a flavor of something missing. In the cases when the objects of her love tried to "make a pass" at her, Solly froze, her reactions clumsy and confused, so that the story would end before it ever started. The sullen taste that accompanied her fantasies seeped into other parts of her soul and life.

Although very high functioning—Solly was a brilliant student, worked, and supported herself independently—she felt detached from society, depressed, often that there was no point to life, and infrequently even expressed suicidal thoughts (not with the intensity of real danger, but with a very harsh feeling). Nevertheless, it was apparent that Solly elicited a degree of satisfaction from the emotional/romantic state she was in. It seemed that, to some degree, she had built her identity around this loneliness, the fantasies in her room by herself, the sadness, the dreariness, and the deep and rich emotional and nuanced experiences that accompanied them. With the progress of therapy, we started talking about a sense of uniqueness, of being special, that she derived from her situation. Phrases like "the bitter romantic" or "the sad lone ranger" surfaced.

When Solly first called me to inquire about starting therapy, she mentioned the name of the person who had referred her to me, someone who I very much care for and appreciate. The fact that she mentioned his name felt significant and left me feeling that I had no choice but to accept her as a patient, despite the fact that Solly, a student, immediately clarified that she would not be able to pay my usual fee. I found myself, uncharacteristically, saying over the phone that we would find a solution, that this obstacle would not preclude starting therapy. This choice was triggered by both my very positive attitude towards the person who had referred her, and something in her voice and speech that made me want to meet her and gave me the feeling that I could help her. I did not feel that the decision made at our first encounter—that she would pay a fee significantly lower than the customary one—was forced on me, that I was making it against my will, but rather the opposite. It felt like a pleasant and uninhibited act of generosity and liberation, a release from the need to conform to the rigid rules of the customary setting. I felt rather content with the decision.

One of the central topics that arose during the first few months of therapy was the relationship between Solly and her parents. Solly's parents had separated when she was 14 and her only sister was 10. The two sisters lived with their mother, but most of Solly's emotional energy was directed towards her father. While her attitude towards her mother was characterized by a combination of indifference, a degree of contempt, and a sense that she was always there but did not contribute much to her life, Solly's attitude towards her father was much more complex and intense. On one hand, she consistently tried to appease him, but on the other she was very angry with him due to his strict demands on her. Solly had to satisfy her father with achievements—to excel in high school, be a brilliant student at university—but also had to take care of him in a deeper sense, an emotional one, something that was closer to protecting him. She experienced him very closely, and when he was distressed, sad, or anxious, she would find herself forced to do something to cheer him up or calm him. It seemed she was relentlessly trapped in a role of mollifying, taking on a heavy load of "hauling" her father's emotional world, but also derived pleasure from her ability to soothe, feel her father so closely, and hold his emotional world in such a nuanced way.

The following vignette transpired about eight months after therapy began. The picture as I have described it was already pretty apparent to both of us. Moreover, for a number of weeks, a vague feeling had begun materializing in me, which I had perhaps not yet formulated clearly for myself, that something in our fee arrangement was wrong, was not really appropriate for Solly, or for me.

From the start, Solly felt extremely uncomfortable when there were silences between us. Actually, there were very few, as our conversations were usually quite smooth and interesting. During the few times that there were silences, when I asked Solly what she was feeling, she talked of feeling awkward, that she felt under pressure, that it was hard for her to be looked at by me when we were quiet.

I don't remember what exactly we were discussing in the moments before the one I am about to describe, other than the fact that we had reached a moment of silence. The moment lasted a little longer than usual. We were both uncomfortable. Solly was uncomfortable with the silence while I was anxious about leaving her with it. But, I (at least) had the feeling that we needed to hold this moment, not "get rid" of it quickly, to see what would emerge. Solly looked at me with a speechless gaze that said something like "you know I don't like these silences."

"So what actually happens to you in these moments?" I answered her gaze with a spoken question.

Solly started saying a few things. She spoke about feeling boring, dull, dreary. As she was speaking, a phrase popped into my head: "an ordinary person." I thought that Solly's greatest fear during our silences was that she was becoming just an ordinary person, another patient, one who was quiet, who was uncomfortable with silences. Just one more patient who sometimes has nothing to say, just one more patient who feels uncomfortable about it. I thought about the connection between this phrase and her relation to her father, the special relationship, where she was special, in comparison to her mother who was "just a regular-humdrum person." A thought came to me, that perhaps Solly couldn't be just another girl with a boyfriend: just another girl with another boyfriend. One of many. There are thousands just like her.

I considered saying something about this, but found, to my surprise, that it was very hard for me. "Am I afraid of hurting her? Causing too much pain? How would I feel saying a sentence like that? What do I feel it might destroy? Her? Me? The relationship between us?" The sense started growing in me that this whole relationship was built on the premise that she was not an ordinary patient and I was not an ordinary therapist. I had agreed to see Solly for a reduced fee, because she was not "just one more patient," and in this way perpetuated her fantasy of not being "one more patient," and no less, my not being "one more therapist." I was a special therapist with her, who was willing to "break the rules." For the first time I asked myself why I had never checked with her to see if she could ask her parents to help pay for the sessions, as with many other young people who come to therapy and are not yet able to cover the cost. It seemed we had created a special connection, a pact between an extraordinary patient and an extraordinary therapist who would not ask her, as he would with everyone else, to check funding possibilities, but would volunteer to shape the relationship as something unique and exceptional. The thought of an "ordinary person," that had formed in my mind earlier, took on another form—"an ordinary therapist." Just one more. There are thousands like him.

If we return for a moment to O in the meaning Grotstein affords it, of the simple, present reality of life as it is, then the fact that I was an "ordinary therapist," and that Solly was an "ordinary person," was, at a certain level, clear and known. This was the simple and present reality. There was no doubt about this. But it seems this was a reality it was not so simple to accept.

I said to Solly:

> You know, I think your greatest fear during our silences is that when they happen, you might feel, and I might see, that you are just another person. An ordinary person. Not brilliant, not producing special and interesting thoughts, not extraordinary. We all know how to say that every person is special in their own way, etc., but I don't think that those sayings are relevant for you in this moment. I think that what it is hard for you to be, here, with your father, and in life in general, is an ordinary person. Just an ordinary person.

A propos of ordinary, I realize, of course, that this "interpretation," if we want to call it one, does not say anything special. I didn't say anything that hasn't been said many times in therapeutic sessions. Even Solly's difficulty was not an extraordinary one. An ordinary difficulty. There are thousands just like it. And yet, and this is also a simple fact, for Solly this was not an ordinary statement. She pondered it quite a bit, smiled, and said: "Wow, what a sentence, it's hard for me to think about it." Silence. Something in her presence became very calm. Something in the way she was sitting became relaxed as I had never seen her before.

"It seems to me that there is something liberating in this thought," I said, not entirely sure if I was saying this for myself or for her.

Solly continued to play with the idea, with the words. To me it seemed very clear that she was making the sentence her own. It looked like she was trying to test out what she could do with it. Does she want to choose it for herself? I could tangibly feel Grotstein's words, the way knowing something as foreign to me becomes a knowing of something as mine. It looked to me as if she was managing a negotiation, or as if she was on a first date, with this sentence, asking: Who are you? What are you actually saying? Why am I running away from you all the time? Why is this sentence so trivial to other people and so hard for me?

Sense, myth, and passion: the objective–subjective–intersubjective creation of meaning

With Solly in mind, let us look again at Bion's three domains—the domain of sense, the domain of myth, and the domain of passion—three dimensions of experience and existence through which foreign, strange-to-oneself alienated "psychic material" transforms into an experience which feels like a part of oneself, emotional, personal, intimate, and vitalizing.

Regarding the domain of sense, Bion raises a point which, to my mind, is incredibly important: an interpretation given to a patient must be linked to something real, with an *objective*, palpable certainty, which Bion refers to as "common sense" (Bion, 1963, p. 10), an expression that can be understood both as entailing "common logic"—in that any reasonable person could see and perceive it—and as a "sense which is common," or a communion of senses. He states:

> I propose common sense … namely some "sense" that is common to more than one sense. I shall consider an object to be sensible to psycho-analytic scrutiny if, and only if, it fulfills conditions analogous to the conditions that are fulfilled when a physical object's presence is confirmed by the evidence of two or more senses … I have no doubt that my impression that a man is anxious has the same validity as my impression that a stone, say, is hard. But for my impression to be valid I consider it necessary to feel the stone to satisfy myself of its hardness and at least to look at it to satisfy myself that what I touch is a stone … Put in another way when the analyst gives an interpretation it must be possible for analyst and analysand to see that what he is talking about is something that is either audible, visible, palpable or odoriferous at the time.
>
> (Bion, 1963, pp. 10–12)

It is of vast importance that the "psychic material" we are discussing with our patients be present to some degree, accessible to our senses—not as an abstract idea, but as something which is happening, that we can feel, almost "touch." I believe that the fact that the conversation between Solly and myself about being "an ordinary person" evolved around the moments of silence which felt so palpable between us infused it with an immediate, honest, factual, and genuine power which was invaluable. If we strive to transform what is impersonal, foreign, and alienated into what is personal, into an experience one can own and feel and perceive as part of oneself, as a real part of one's life, it is tremendously important that the interpretation or conversation be linked to a sensual tangible dimension, an objective dimension which pulls the patient and therapist into reality. If the conversation between Solly and myself had evolved around something that took place outside the room, in another time and place, it would have lacked the hue of a realistic, authentic dimension of existence, a dimension which, according to Bion, is crucial to the process of enlivening the parts of the personality that used to be dead and frozen.

The second link is to the dimension of Myth, an element I link to the principles of Mythos described above. Bion writes:

> Suppose that a patient is angry. More meaning is given to a statement to that effect if it is added that his anger is like that of a "child that wanted to hit his nanny because he has been told he is naughty." The statement in quotation marks ... must not be supposed to express a theory that small boys hit their nannies if they are called naughty ... They are not statements of observed fact, or formulations of a theory intended to represent a realization: they are statements of a personal myth.
>
> (Bion, 1963, p. 12)

Bion appears not to be talking about some sort of collective myth, or of myth as a metaphor. Rather, he speaks about the linkage to what can be called "personal myth," i.e., a link to the *subjective* dimension of experience, to the most inner, private, delicate world of the patient. It does not aim towards understanding, but towards an extension of the capacity to feel. Bion emphasizes time and again that he is not talking about theoretical explanation; he does not anchor a particular emotion in a universal understanding, but the exact opposite. He anchors the universal in the particular. Bion does not name this dimension "myth" inadvertently; it is constructed of the very same "language of Mythos" described above, and as opposed to the "language of Logos." Mythos does not intend to carry us towards general-universal dimensions, but transmutes us to a very personal, familiar, intimate experience of our own. Psychological change, Bion suggests here, is not achieved through explanations (Logos), but through emotional/sensual unexplained transformation, which takes place through an instantaneous encounter of the patient with his most private, subjective life. It is the link of one's present experience to one's most personal mythology.

Solly's ability to link her recoiling from being an "ordinary person" to her emotions towards her father, to her finding herself living at home with her fantasies instead of with a boyfriend, was not aimed, essentially, at shedding light on her past, or on her present, but at adding an important dimension to her capacity to feel the expression "ordinary person"—which was created between us and fashioned in my mind—as her own. Among the reasons she could now take such complete ownership of that coming-to-being experience of "ordinariness" was that she felt it "singing [her] life with its words," to quote Roberta Flack's famous and beautiful line. This is not a Logos-based explanation, but a Mythos-like spontaneous, immediate, surprising encounter with long-dissociated life-seeking parts of her psyche.

Furthermore, I believe, the language of Mythos, the language of surrender-to-the-mutually-created transformation acquires its full and upmost meaning in Bion's third dimension, that of passion. In the context of what makes an interpretation valid or meaningful, passion is a strong word to choose, perhaps even somewhat odd. Ferro (2011) regards this dimension as implying "a warm and alive relationship between the analyst's mind and what is being interpreted" (p. 157). While Ferro's explanation is undoubtedly accurate, it seems that there is something else in Bion's formulation.

Bion begins his discussion of the passionate dimension of experience by telling us that when he talks about passion he means something beyond the emotional functions of L, H, and K:

> [by] passion I mean one of the dimensions which L, H or K must possess if it is to be recognized as an element that is present ... That is to say, if the angry tone of the patient is judged to be evidence of hate it must not be assumed that passion has been discerned as a dimension of a psycho-analytic object, H in fact.
>
> (Bion, 1963, p. 13).

When a patient is angry, we can see it, we can hear it, feel it, we can find its evident, objective dimension in the domain of sense. We can also link it to the subjective history of the patient, to the domain of myth. Of course, the presence of L, H, and K is essential for every relationship, of the patient with himself, with his therapist, and with the world he lives in. Yet these emotional functions cannot generate a personal transformation without another dimension, in which two minds create the newfound experiences in a way which never existed before:

> Awareness of passion is not dependent [only] on sense. For senses to be active only one mind is necessary: *passion is evidence that two minds are linked and that there cannot possibly be fewer than two minds if passion is present.*
>
> (Bion, 1963, p. 13, italics mine)

Here we encounter the full paradox of what Ogden (2016) calls "reclaiming unlived life," or, in Bromberg's (2006) words, "turning dissociation into conflict" (p. 13).

For Solly, the experience of being "an ordinary person" was intolerable. It had threatened her most important and invigorating emotional connection, the bond with her father; it thus had to be dissociated from her psyche and from any relationships she might be part of. Every true relationship holds within it, sooner or later, the feelings of ordinariness, of routine, of day-to-day living, at times exciting, at others boring and monotonous. In any true relationship she was bound to find herself, sooner or later, "just her (mundane, ordinary) self." Thus, she had to avoid them altogether, preferring imagined partners over real ones. But this was not even the worst part of it: dissociation inescapably impairs one's psychic movement. When one feels that part of one's psyche must be avoided at any cost, one finds oneself restricting psychic movement to "safe zones," to those areas or self-states in the psyche, in which one feels sheltered and protected from any threat of encountering the dreaded experiences one cannot tolerate. This propensity causes, with time, a more and more limited and constrained range of feelings, thoughts, and experiences (just as our reaction to sharp, acute, unbearable pain in our bodies seriously impairs our ability and willingness to move freely). Thus, the presence of dissociation in the psyche does not only divorce us from those enlivening parts of ourselves which had to be thrown to the "dissociative Gulag," but also robs us of one of our most quintessential characteristics as human beings: our ability, our aptitude, to move freely between and within our experiences, feelings, and sensations. Remember that what brought Solly to therapy wasn't just her difficulty in finding romantic relationships, but also her pervasive and diffuse feelings of depression and emptiness, a direct consequence, I believe, of the impairment of her psychic movement that was a result of her dissociation.

I believe that at the heart of Bion's psychoanalytic conviction, when he added the component of "passion" to the essence of every interpretation, and when he wrote that "*passion is evidence that two minds are linked*" (1963, p. 13), is that every interpretation must aim at resurrecting the patient's psychic movement, especially in the face of his or her most frightening dissociated experiences, and that this psychic movement cannot be attained without a passionate *intersubjective* encounter between patient and therapist.

This passionate encounter, in order to infuse life and rejuvenate the deadened horror-filled areas in the patient's psyche, must to some degree stimulate frozen areas in the therapist's psyche as well. This is the essence of what can be called "passion in the midst of terror," the only kind of passion that can help someone encounter the dreaded parts of his personality, the only kind of passion that could help Solly meet her fears of "being ordinary" without the horror of losing herself and her vitalizing emotional ties. This is the reason that, before approaching Solly's experience, as well as her fear of being "just another patient," I had to encounter my own fear of being "just another therapist" in her eyes, and in my own. I deeply believe that had I not dwelt in my own anxieties concerning ordinariness, had I communicated my realization before surrendering to our mutual effort to work through these fearful self-states, speaking with her about her fears and dissociation from a place of pure Logos would have lacked the dimension of "passion," the intersubjective dimension of experience that must reside alongside the subjective (myth) and the objective (common sense).

Bringing life to the deadened areas within one's soul is one of the hardest and most multi-layered endeavors in psychoanalysis. This process, as I have tried to demonstrate, cannot be conceived in the gradual, analyzable reason-based architecture of Logos, but must take place within the spontaneous, surprising, intersubjective transformation which comprises the "language of Mythos." It is only through the dialectical holding of these three dimensions within the "language of Mythos"[3] that psychic movement can be created anew in the most frozen and deadened areas of the psyche. It is only through these three dimensions that Solly could encounter the fact that she was "just a regular human being" (which, to her surprise and relief, turned out to be so much more than she feared) and begin to realize that "it takes two human beings to make one" (Bion, 1987, p. 222).

Notes

1 As will be clear shortly, what seems here to be a subjective endeavor or movement is actually an intersubjective one.
2 Loewald's "*the waning of the Oedipus complex*" (1979) is a remarkable example of the process described here.
3 In another paper (Shalgi, 2012), I investigate these three dimensions of human existence and experience—objective, subjective, and intersubjective— from both a philosophical and psychoanalytic point of view.

Bibliography

Becker, M., and Shalgi, B. (2013). On being, disappearing and becoming: A journey of surrender. *Psychoanalytic Dialogues*, 23(4), 426–438.

Benjamin, J. (2004). Beyond doer and done-to: An intersubjective view of thirdness. *Psychoanalytic Quarterly,* 73(1), 5–46.

Benjamin, J. (2007). A review of awakening the dreamer: Clinical journeys by Philip M. Bromberg. *Contemporary Psychoanalysis,* 43(4), 666–680.

Bion, W.R. (1959). *Experiences in groups and other papers*. New York, Basic Books.

Bion, W.R. (1963). *Elements of psychoanalysis*. London, Heinemann.

Bion, W.R. (1987). Clinical seminars. In F. Bion (ed.). *Clinical seminars and other works*. London, Karnac.

Bromberg, P.M. (2006). *Awakening the dreamer: Clinical journeys*. New York, Analytic Press.

Ferro, A. (2011). Clinical implications of Bion's thought. In C. Mawson (ed.) *Bion today*. London, Routledge.

Ghent, E. (1990). Masochism, submission, surrender: Masochism as a perversion of surrender. *Contemporary Psychoanalysis,* 26, 108–136.

Ghent, E. (1992). Paradox and process. *Psychoanalytic Dialogues*, 2(2), 135–159.

Ghent, E. (1995). Interaction in the psychoanalytic situation. *Psychoanalytic Dialogues*, 5(3), 479–491.

Ghent, E. (2001). Need, paradox and surrender: Commentary on paper by Adam Phillips. *Psychoanalytic Dialogues* 11(1), 23–41.

Grossmark, R. (2016). Psychoanalytic companioning. *Psychoanalytic Dialogues,* 26(6), 698–712.

Grotstein, J.S. (2000). *Who is the dreamer who dreams the dream: A study in psychic presence.* New York, Analytic Press.

Hegel, G.W.F. (1805–1806). *Lectures on the history of philosophy.* London, Kegan Paul, Trench, Trübner, 1892.

Hegel, G.W.F. (1807). *The Phenomenology of Mind.* London: George Allen & Unwin, 1949.

Loewald, H. (1979). The waning of the Oedipus complex. *Journal of the American Psychoanalytic Association,* 27, 751–775.

Mitchell, S.A., and Aron, L. (1999). Editor introduction to Ghent's: Masochism, submission, surrender: Masochism as a perversion of surrender. In: *Relational psychoanalysis: The emergence of a tradition.* Hillside, NJ, Analytic Press.

Ogden, T.H. (1994). *Subjects of analysis.* London, Karnac.

Ogden, T.H. (2005). What I would not part with. In: *This art of psychoanalysis: Dreaming undreamt dreams and interrupted cries.* London, Routledge, 19–26.

Ogden, T.H. (2016). *Reclaiming unlived life: Experiences in psychoanalysis.* London, Routledge.

Shalgi, B. (2012). The cat ate our tongue – but we got it back: Benjamin's journey from domination to surrender. *Studies in Gender and Sexuality,* 13(4), 277–294.

Shalgi, B. (2018). When time stands still: The non-interactive interaction in the psychoanalytic encounter. *Psychoanalytic Dialogues,* 28(1), 59–68.

Trevarthen, C. (2009). The intersubjective psychobiology of human meaning: Learning of culture depends on interest for co-operative practical work- and affection for the joyful art of good company. *Psychoanalytic Dialogues,* 19(5), 507–518.

Winnicott, D.W. (1945). Primitive emotional development. In: *Through paediatrics to psychoanalysis.* London, Karnac, 145–156.

Winnicott, D.W. (1960). Ego distortions in terms of true and false self. In: *The maturational processes and the facilitating environment.* London, Karnac, 140–152.

Winnicott, D.W. (1971a). Introduction. In: *Playing and Reality.* London, Tavistock, xi–xiii.

Winnicott, D.W. (1971b). Playing: A theoretical statement. In: *Playing and Reality.* London, Tavistock, 38–52.

Chapter 6

Vitalizing engagement

The generative transformation of the project of psychoanalysis

Margaret Black Mitchell

Relational psychoanalysis has redefined our understanding of theory and introduced important reconceptualizations of the analytic process. We have moved from a knowing and authoritative analyst interpreting "the truth" about what, in the patient's mind, is causing psychological distress, to an intersubjective process conceptualized as uniquely co-created together by each patient and analyst. The analyst's "knowledge" no longer refers to an understanding of the contents of what is assumed to constitute the generically configured human mind. The knowledge of the analyst now refers to the ability to use herself in a manner that lends to the activation of the patient's unique capacity for engaging in a vitalizing intersubjective meaning making within the analytic dyad, a process that enlivens, deepens and expands the complexity of the patient's, as well as the analyst's, subjectivity.

Encouraged by relational reconceptualizations we are now fortunate to have access to a wealth of contributions from a variety of sources: from formulations drawing on clinical experience within intensive analytic work, from the findings of infancy research, from energetic debates within the field and from scientific understandings of the workings of the body and mind. Knowledge of a range of theories is essential as there is no singular methodology that creates vitalizing engagement. The clinical process is always a unique creation, necessarily tailored to the needs and experiences of each patient, and expressed within and through the idiosyncratic subjectivity of each analyst. The analyst's ability to offer herself as a vitalizing partner in co-creating this kind of connection with each specific patient is ultimately what becomes "the curative factor" in psychoanalysis. In this chapter I will discuss some of the history relevant to this revolutionary transformation in psychoanalysis and illustrate, in my work, how vitalization was encouraged in two very different kinds of clinical process with two very different patients.

The dynamics of the psychoanalytic process

Regardless of when one enters the field of psychoanalysis, we will each be challenged to engage the daunting questions intrinsic to the efficacy of this profession: how do we sit with someone who is in pain, suffering from problems that are invisible to us, often unknown even to the patient, and craft a useful, hopefully healing, dyadic process? What indications do we look to in determining that this is indeed happening? Freud (1916, 1923) was the first to encounter this challenge, the first to envision invisible dynamic forces within the mind creating psychological distress. Reasonably, he decided he needed something more graphic—a map with discernible markers that articulated these forces and the process of their engagement and transformation. Freud's explicit focus was primarily on the *mind of the patient*. He envisioned a tripartite psyche within the mind, its components operating in specific and coordinated ways. In this model, the primitive sexual and aggressive energy of the id held the potentially vitalizing force of the psychoanalytic process. Its usefulness was realized by encouraging, through free association, a relaxation of the ego's defensive functioning, allowing the analyst to more clearly grasp its primitive intention. Through interpretation the analyst then helped the patient consciously confront the unacceptable gratification it sought. In the patient's ability to reject the wish as shaped by the id, the energy it held became available for conscious redirection towards socially acceptable goals such as satisfying experiences of love and work—for Freud the hallmarks of a successful analytic treatment.

Since all minds were understood to be generally structured by similar desires and conflicts, the well-educated analyst was for the most part considered to be "accurate" in interpreting what was invisibly motivating the neurotic patient's experience. The patient's disagreements with the analyst were thus not seen as potentially meaningful sources of new information but as "resistance," since the analyst was presumed to know the "truth."

Freud's conceptual map (1923) referred primarily to an isolated psyche: that of the patient. From the very beginning, however, it was apparent that Freud sensed additional complexity in the project he had undertaken. From his clinical experience Freud could see there were intrinsic potential connections *between* the minds of patient and analyst that allowed the process to go forward. The patient's inability to form a transference, an *emotional connection with the analyst,* rendered the therapy useless. And, in one of his few direct expressions of clinical advice, Freud instructed that *the analyst* must also be deeply and collaboratively engaged in the process, turning "his own unconscious like a receptive organ towards the transmitting unconscious of the patient" (1912, pp. 115–116). It was left to history, however, and more specifically to explorations within relational thinking, to further investigate the myriad avenues available for this potentially vitalizing psychic connectedness between patient and analyst.

Unfortunately, over time Freud's work became entangled in the politics of our field. Once imported to the United States these problems became particularly intense, threatening to limit his many contributions. Understandably fascinated by a treatment protocol capable of offering tangible help for mental disturbances, and intrigued with the possibility of treating more functional "neurotic" patients who could be seen in one's office and afford intensive treatment, American psychiatrists were eager to claim this promising European process as a "medical specialty." They were intent on possessing and controlling it.

While Freud had developed his own thinking within a broadly engaged intellectual community and had not wanted his work to be isolated and defined in this way, in the United States it became almost impossible for a non-medical professional to obtain psychoanalytic training. Ph.D. psychologists, for example, were allowed to train at the elite "classical" institutes only by signing a waiver agreeing never to *practice* psychoanalysis, but to restrict the application of their training to research pursuits. Social workers were not even a consideration at this point.

More troubling than the excluding limitation of access to training were the constraints on thinking inherent in this medical stranglehold. Freud's evocative and brilliant grasp of the essential role played by out-of-awareness experience in the functioning of human mind and his depiction of aspects of human mentation as facilitated by the often unconscious *collaboration* of minds could have provided a point of access to many newly developing perspectives in the field. But these features were under-emphasized within mainstream American psychoanalysis, backgrounded to a rigid insistence on the "truth" of Freud's then-held *theory*: the experience-distant drive/defense metapsychology that Freud himself questioned and altered during the course of his life became elevated as the singular defining hallmark of a "true" psychoanalytic process.

Glover's (1931) paper on "inexact interpretation," for example, emphasized the unfortunate outcome risked if the analyst's offered interpretation was not "correct." If, "while analyzing anal phantasies" a "genital interpretation alone were given," rendering the intervention "not only incomplete but inexact" (p. 401), the analyst could expect a disrupting increase in the defensive operations of the id. The enormous potential of Freud's brilliant discoveries in the workings of human mind seemed to be devolving, at risk of being collapsed within a one-size-fits-all teachable methodology. Within the literature of psychoanalysis, newer contributors who did not position their work as derivative of Freud's were rejected for publication by the existing psychoanalytic journals.

A rethinking of what it means to "think analytically": the vitalization of the field by relational psychoanalysis

For Stephen Mitchell, who had trained at the non-classical William Alanson White Institute, and whose major pleasure in life included cross-disciplinary reading, deeply pondering new ideas and teaching his students to work at understanding the pivotal thinking that inspired each analytic author—particularly those who held perspectives with which they disagreed—this was an appalling situation. How could young analysts learn to use and value their minds—to intelligently compare differing ideas, to creatively extend them? How could the field continue to develop with this deadening intellectual stranglehold in place?

In the 1980s, greatly inspired by Mitchell's contributions (1979, 1981a, 1981b, 1984a, 1984b, 1986, 1988a, 1988b), the relational perspective began taking hold, gradually encouraging psychoanalysis into becoming a "field of study" exposing students to a wealth of conceptualization drawn from a variety of sources: seasoned clinical observation, infancy research, energetic debate within the field, scientific understandings of the workings of the body and mind were among them. *Object Relations in Psychoanalytic Theory*, Greenberg and Mitchell's book (1983), heralded this revolutionary change. As one of the first major texts to challenge the primacy of drive theory's claim to be the singular "true" expression of thinking within psychoanalysis, the book carried a radical departure from the existing thinking in the field: it respectfully introduced the contributions of *all* the major analytic thinkers of the time *in a single text*, creating, in its very organization, an analytic "meeting of minds." *Psychoanalytic Dialogues*, the journal Mitchell founded in 1991, served as another powerful vehicle for the emerging relational perspective. Again, structured to model how a *field of study* would function, the journal published discussions by analysts of differing perspectives, welcomed articles that drew on diverse sources and eliminated the required demonstration of a loyalty pledge (to any particular theory) that had stifled so many voices. New authors were published and the relational conversation proliferated, expanding understandings and challenging practitioners to use their minds not simply to learn *how to do it* but inviting them *to think*, from their own perspective, about the value of any particular contribution to *their particular ability* to better conduct a generative therapeutic process with their patients.

When introduced, in an effort to begin to create space and legitimacy for other, non-classical, perspectives, the relational perspective stressed human connectedness and socio-cultural context, not internally arising drives, in the shaping of personal self. However the fundamental intent of relational understanding was not to eliminate classic thinking but to redefine *all* analytic theories as *metaphoric organizations of experience* that needed to be thought about, rather than competing "truths" needing singular allegiance. Important changes in larger philosophical understandings have had resonance with this shift within psychoanalysis. The essentialist perspective's valorization of "truth" as intrinsic to human experience gave way to a growing appreciation of the broad implications of personal subjectivity. Within psychoanalysis, experience was no longer regarded as a "truth" we simply "run into": we each create our own subjective version of what we have experienced. An analytic process whose goal had been the patient's acceptance of "the truth" of the analyst's largely predetermined vision of the patient's inner experience became intellectually anachronistic as each mind was now understood as developing within a necessarily idiosyncratic social milieu of family, gender, race, sexual orientation, place in history, etc.

These fundamental changes in our understandings of human nature have led to a shift in emphasis in psychoanalysis from a working through of repetitive, old patterns to the creation of new relational possibilities within the therapeutic relationship. As in the times of Freud, contemporary patients continue to seek treatment for help with their jobs and personal relationships, but in addition frequently emphasize a troubling sense of feeling "dead" or "empty." They describe an absence of joy, feeling they are "going nowhere" in a meaningless experience of being alive.

As a concept, vitalization has been afforded a place in our theorizing. Defined as "the state of being filled with life—to make vital or alive or endow with meaning," the task of how this crucial experience is achieved has fallen to authors in our field. Fortunately, supported by the relational shift, a more broadly defined theoretical inclusivity now allows us, as Ester Thelen notes, to take advantage of "the many rich ... and important contributions to our understanding of the human mind" which "help us more comfortably occupy the space we need to enter as we focus on the essential issue of vitalization" (Thelen, 2005, p. 255) and consider its disruption and clinical repair. What follows are descriptions of clinical work illustrating how I engaged imagery from two different theoretical sources that I feel are highly relevant to the issue of vitalization.

Contributions to the study of vitality in psychoanalysis: the Boston Change Process Study Group

We might reasonably begin with contributions that concern the most foundational forms of perceived subjective aliveness: those articulated in infancy research. Daniel Stern, with his colleagues in the Boston Change Process Study Group (BCPSG), was another theorist who challenged Freud's vision of energized human motivation as fueled by the expression of intrinsically arising unconscious psychic forces. In his final book, *Forms of Vitality* (2010), Stern explained that human vitality (for him a term that serves for human energy in a subjectively experienced sense of aliveness and expressed in personally motivated intentionality) is not a *mental* creation but an *embodied* expression: mind and body are inseparable, an understanding he feels was seriously undermined by Freud's decidedly singular focus on invisible psychic operations taking place inside the mind and requiring translation into language to be clinically useful (Freud, 1914). Movement, offers Stern, not understanding, is the primary manifestation of being animate and is what provides the subjective sense of aliveness.

While it is beyond the scope of this paper to fully represent their extensive research on early infancy, for the BCPSG (2002, 2005, 2007, 2008), early forms of attachment consolidate without the conflict or defense envisioned by Fairbairn (1941, 1958) and Winnicott (1965, 1980). Forms of connectedness are simply non-verbal procedural practices, "ways of being with others" that emerge adaptively from the process of "fitting together" within the intersubjective matrix that operates from the time we are born (BCPSG, 2002, p. 1051). This process takes shape with the mother's making a continuing attempt to apprehend the infant's current subjective reality (his affect, current desired goal and level of understanding) as well as trying to devise a response that acknowledges and elaborates on that subjective state. Here movement is not understood as simply physical but as represented in the myriad forms of expression of personal intentionality: in personal feeling states, levels of understanding and desire.

When applied to work with adults, the focus of the therapy is decidedly *not* on interpretation but on attempting to revive this earliest form of generative energy. In its co-constructed choreography, the analyst's participation, like that of the early mother, involves an emphasis on grasping and supporting the patient's internally arising subjective intentionality. The analyst yields to the patient's perceived lead, paying close attention to and supporting initiatives expressed in affect, verbal rhythm and perceived goal, privileging these expressions over any specific *content* of discussions. Meaning is determined by the revival and engagement, between patient and analyst, of a non-linear "messy" process of "fitting together" and "moving along" that emerges within the co-created journey unique to each clinical pair. Ultimately, vitalizing change comes not from the patient's "knowing information" but from *small changes in interactions* between patient and analyst that open up new ways of being without their necessarily being interpretively understood, or even necessarily explicitly noted (BCPSG 2005).

Gerald: the early disruption of vitalizing fitting together

Gerald's therapy highlights the disastrous consequences when recognition and engagement of personal intention are severely compromised by early maternal misattunement, thereby disrupting a generative intersubjective process that expands personal subjectivity. Gerald's sense of self had been severely distorted and thwarted by an intrusive, controlling, profoundly confusing mother who had methodically sabotaged her son's expressing and receiving recognition for his own experience. Rather than supporting her son's initiatives as the Boston Group recommends (BCPSG, 2002), the mother frequently concluded that, "unfortunately," whatever Gerald wanted to do was "too hard" for him; he should abandon any effort in order to protect himself from the humiliating failure his mother knowingly anticipated. Gerald was confused when homework was returned with written commentary, unsure to whom it was directed; as his mother had been so "helpful" he could not decide who had written the paper. When he would finally express himself by exploding in desperation and frustration, his mother would collapse in tears, begging for her son's sympathy, as she was only "trying to be the best mother."

As we worked together on these issues, Gerald started a session by describing, in a flat but pressured way, how his brother Frank, who had been fired several months earlier, was still out of work. Then Gerald stopped speaking, announcing he had nothing more to say. After some time, sensing he was upset, I wondered aloud about the pressure that was evident to me in his speech. Gerald became quite defensive and felt I was criticizing him. In a collaborative effort we came to understand that he experienced my question as actually masking *my* underlying feeling of criticism—that I did not really *have* a question but rather held an already confident opinion that he should have done more to help Frank. I told him I regretted that however I had spoken felt critical to him, as I did not feel he should do more; in fact I had been very aware of and moved by all the different ways he had already involved himself in trying to support and help Frank.

Gerald relaxed. Eventually he told me that beneath his initial pressured commentary and emotional flatness *was* something else—not a sense that *I* felt he should do more but a sense that *he* felt he should do more for Frank. Gerald described a new and emotion-filled awareness that the confusing and undermining circumstances of his early life had made it impossible for him to respond to the emotional needs of his neglected younger sibling. At this moment, letting himself tolerate feeling guilty without feeling defensive allowed him to also feel what was perhaps his more basic affective experience. Gerald described his love for his brother as something "deep inside" him that had been impossible to contact as long as he was so engaged in warding off expected external criticism.

We can see here how a more natural space was opening up, one that had been flattened by Gerald's mother's asking him "questions" without any recognition of his separate mind and personal subjectivity. In "already knowing" the answer Gerald's mother recognized only her own mind, eliminating any possibility of a two-minded potentially generative intersubjective experience.

Later in our work, a few minutes into our session, I sensed there was something brewing in our connection. Rather than try to give it shape (i.e. opting to try to *follow* him and not lead) I shared this feeling with Gerald and wondered if there was something else he wanted—maybe something I could have said when the session began that would have felt closer to what he really needed. Gerald responded with clear enthusiasm, the first time I had heard this kind of energy in his voice. Somewhat shyly he said he wished I had known "how many different things were going on" in his mind today—and wished that I would have helped him with that complexity—maybe by saying something about it, like, "Wow, Gerald, there are so many ideas you have today—let's talk about them together and see what they all are." Here we can see Gerald's increasing awareness of the particular initiatives of his own mind and his sense of the newly opened space between us that allowed him to let them be known to both of us. The changes for Gerald were not primarily about new understandings: they concerned the way our relationship was changing. He could imagine a generative response from me that would further enliven his subjective experience of having a "full of ideas" mind. He energetically shared his desire of *wanting my interest* in appreciating what was in his mind *and my help* in managing all this newly felt excitement.

From a relational perspective, my clinical approach was informed by trying to imagine, given the specifics of his history and my own sense in being with him, what kind of engagement would allow Gerald to feel, and then feel safe to express, his own thoughts and intentions. As a consequence of the contorted relationship with his mother, I knew Gerald was not sure he could be seen, could easily question whether anyone else could "feel" his presence and expected others to blindly run over him. I knew these problems could only be affected by new relational experience that we could co-create together: "explanations" per se would not reach him, and strongly introducing my own subjectivity was likely to overwhelm him. I had to let him live new relational experiences that privileged his experience and let him feel my genuine interest in his mind.

Such considerations led me to work with Gerald in ways that are in many ways resonant with the approach outlined by the Boston group. Acknowledging my felt impact on him, as I did when I apologized, openly recognizing what I see about him, being alert and generally deferring to any "sense" I had of his inclinations, while certainly being open to and calmly surviving his criticisms carried the relational intention of my wish to create experience where his needs for connection could bring him recognition and support for his subjective reality. I would agree with the Boston Group that the change between us did not come from knowing information learned from verbal interpretation. I would want to emphasize, however, that the "small changes in interactions" that they credit with therapeutically opening up new ways of being are frequently made possible by how we communicate with our patients at critical junctures.

Relational approaches appreciate an expanded understanding of the importance of language beyond its classically identified function of carrying information. In tone, timing, rhythm and choice of words, language has powerful social meanings that can create transformative relational experience between patient and analyst. Changes in interactions in the therapy are frequently the result of *internal* changes in the patient's increased sense of safety, his sense of being felt, genuinely engaged and accurately recognized, changes that frequently occur within the vitalizing intersubjective impact of verbal communication.

The generative co-creation of meaning: vitalization through intersubjective relating

In being seen and tabulated, research findings can offer valuable support for particular ways of understanding and working clinically. They cannot, however, offer us "the only way" nor establish that this documentation of infancy continues to exclusively define any particular area of human experience over the course of one's life. Within relational thinking, an openness to sensing the unseen unconscious channels of dyadic communication operating as we work, an area recognized so long ago by Freud (1912), has allowed us to articulate a wide range of imagery relevant to potential dyadic vitalization. In being aware of and able to imagine myriad channels of conscious and out-of-awareness connection between patient and analyst, i.e. in grasping the inevitability—and importance—of the co-creation of the analytic process (Aron, 1996), in noting the interactional pull of relational configurations that encourage us to learn more by "accepting the patient's invitation to dance" (Mitchell, 1988a, p. 293), in a recognition of enactments (Bass, 2003; Black, 2003; Bromberg, 1994; Stern, 2004; Stern et al. 1998), in finding, in ourselves, versions of the bad objects that haunt the patient (Davies, 2004) and in understanding that in order for new experience to develop both patient and analyst must change (Slavin and Kreigman, 1998) we are in a position to more comfortably open ourselves to and make better use of the often invisible intersubjective processes that infuse clinical experience. Sometimes, as with Gerald, this results in our consciously thinking, imaginatively sensing what is missing in the patient's experience that keeps him closed off from generative engagement. Sometimes, as in the case that follows, such understanding begins to activate our feeling that something is missing but offers no conscious imagery to suggest a direction for its repair. Our knowledge of possible channels of connection, however, allows us to better tolerate the resulting sense of confusion and anxiety, feeling more confident that a meeting of minds is taking place despite our being unable to immediately articulate it.

Within clinical psychoanalysis the awareness of dyadic generativity has led to the conceptualization of the Third, envisioned as a space wherein patient and analyst can co-create new meaning neither could have achieved alone (Aron, 2006; Benjamin, 1990, 2004; Gerson, 2004;

Green, 2004; Ogden, 1994, 2004). Some clinical approaches aim to provide more receptivity for this mind-to-mind potential. Christoper Bollas draws on Winnicott's 1971 paper in advising that "the analyst needs to play with the patient, to put forth an idea as an object that exists in that potential space between the patient and the analyst, an object that is meant to be passed back and forth between the two" (1983, p. 6). He encourages intentionally de-emphasizing power differentials between patient and analyst, framing interventions within the patient's subjective experience rather than asserting authority over him. For example, he suggests leading with comments like "what occurs to me" or "I have a hunch about something" (Bollas, 1983, p. 7), implicitly inviting the patient to join him in adding thoughts to a co-created process.

The area of thinking about generativity as co-created between human minds defines an essential aspect of contemporary psychoanalysis. This idea inspired early relational thinkers to actively seek a "meeting of minds" rather than accepting a singular "truth" about human psychology. It encouraged infancy researchers to study earliest human interactions, extending our thinking beyond attachment to considerations of how the humanity of our minds develops in relationship. According to Edward Tronick, our mind is never really our own. From the moment we are born, virtually everything we think and feel takes form in a process of mutual influence with another mind. "New capacities that result from neurological maturation are included," he notes, "as they require an interactive intersubjective environment to be realized." (Tronick, 2007, p. 406) "We have come to understand," he continues, "that the *fundamental motivational force* in human experience is not gratification—nor is it simply relations with others but the very engagement between minds that enables the development of personal subjectivity. Minds seek other minds so this can happen," he concludes, "That's what they do" (Tronick, 2007, p. 422).

In its earliest form, researchers have identified the mother's recognition of the infant's nascent initiative as fundamental to human vitalization. While seeking other minds may indeed initially provide the fundamental human motivational force, with time and trauma this "seeking" can take on increasing complexity. Areas of mind can lose this essential capacity, becoming psychically deadened or infused with a rigidity immune to transformation.

The impairment of the capacity for intersubjective relating is currently a topic of great interest among psychoanalysts. Schwartz Cooney (2018) has emphasized, for example, that enactments have potential for engaging both patient and analyst in vitalizing, progressive energy that can bring submerged or unborn experience to life, sometimes reviving aspects of this functioning. Thomas Ogden (2004) feels that the specifics of the analytic engagement involve the minds of patient and analyst in unique ways. To this end our best understanding would encourage us to no longer think of analyst and patient as "separate subjects who take one another as objects" but consider that within the process of psychoanalysis there is a "jointly created unconscious life of the analytic pair." Ogden refers to this as the "analytic third" (pp. 167, 168).

While Tronick's focus emphasizes the generative potential of the more social connection between minds, Ogden examines dimensions of mental functioning, distinguishing among specific operational capacities that he feels greatly impact the potential within any analytic encounter. In defining these differences Ogden investigates what he refers to as the varieties inherent in "what work we do psychically with our lived experience" (2010, pp. 316, 317). He delineates three forms of thinking that he feels exist in all of us, always in varying degrees and in dialectical tension with one another (Ogden, 2010, p. 317). He has carefully described these features of human thinking as he feels they contribute to—or interfere with—the potentially vitalizing experiences of intersubjective relating that enrich and deepen our personal feelings of aliveness. I would like to draw on his work, to lend what feels to be useful imagery relevant to the issue of vitalization, to the clinical process, with one of my patients.

Ogden's first category, *magical thinking*, is defined as a way of organizing thinking which has the sole purpose of avoiding facing the truth of one's internal and external experience. It requires the creation of a state of mind in which the individual believes in the singular "truth" of his experience: he *creates the reality* in which he and others live. He feels that, whatever he says, his words "have the power to substitute a newly created reality for a reality that is no longer convenient" (p. 321). To create this illusion, omnipotent fantasy holds that one is not subject to the laws that apply to others, including the laws of nature, the irreversibility of death, and so on. Within this mode of thinking one cannot *reflect* on experience, as whatever is experienced is immediately understood to be simply the truth. While such a person may feel confident and even powerful, fundamentally, he cannot learn and cannot change. The second category of *dream thinking*, to be illustrated in the clinical vignette that follows, provides a bridge out of this isolated state of mind, and lends itself to the potential for an increase in Ogden's third form of thinking, *transformative thinking*, a generative intersubjective engagement allowing for growth and change.

Michael: vitalization constrained by defenses against early trauma

Michael, a 30-year-old contract lawyer, was becoming my favorite patient. He had come into treatment because his marriage was falling apart. His wife Jessie had discovered his friendship with Sara whom Michael sought out after Jessie began to seem "less available," a problem they had never discussed. Jessie left Michael and moved back in with her parents, taking their two young sons along with her. Michael felt undone and unfairly treated.

I liked working with Michael. He wanted to make things right. He was direct, thoughtful and seemed to try very hard to be honest even when it was uncomfortable. He prided himself on being a "good" person and I admired the way he pulled himself out of a difficult early life. His father, a salesman for a publishing company, had divorced his mother when Michael was a young teen. An awkward kid, Michael had clear memories of sports he enjoyed but "drew a blank" when thinking back on family life, having "no memories" of his parents' interactions or of personal moments with either of them. He did remember his father's narcissistic self-promotion and self-involved obsession with model trains: the basement in their small house had been transformed into a railroad empire into which his father would disappear for hours.

After the divorce, Michael's father rarely visited. Child support came episodically. Michael had powerful emotional responses to these experiences. He vowed he would become highly successful, depend on no one, and that he would *never* be the kind of man his father was. He became an excellent student, attended law school on scholarship and, as he began treatment, was in high demand for his legal expertise.

Michael engaged the analytic process as though we were two intelligent adults, discussing any snag we could both calmly observe. His depiction of his relationship with Jessie emphasized his thoughtful and attentive traits. As the discussion of the marital difficulties deepened, however, Michael seemed increasingly stymied. Admired for his competence in dealing with "tough" legal tangles, he seemed at a loss in navigating angry differences of opinion with his wife. In his descriptions of their social life he and Jessie had often spent their weekends socializing with other families, "dropping in for a while" at one location, then moving on to the next of many additional destinations, all in one day. Off-handedly he told me of Jessie's comment that she felt he was "never really there."

As we proceeded, Michael became less measured, more unsure and intensely interested in everything I said, eventually seeming to hang on my words as though hoping to import them wholesale into his conversations with Jessie. As I encouraged him to notice his own experience, he felt "surprised" but intrigued to find sadness and anger, and a feeling that "no one was concerned" about him.

Dream thinking enters the process

As therapy continued Michael's professional obligations became more pressing; he was a central figure in high-power contract negotiations in Washington. He missed some sessions, always alerting me in advance. He ended one session surprised at becoming aware of a disturbing dream—"something about rooms," he offered vaguely. Then his absences increased; I received text messages the morning of the session informing me he would be absent. He apologized profusely. He was under a great deal of pressure with his work. He mentioned something about getting up in the morning and not knowing what he had to do that day until he checked his schedule. I was puzzled. We were delving into increasingly difficult territory, but I experienced us as still connecting well emotionally. Now I began to feel uncertain: was he connecting with me as I thought? Or was his meeting with me simply a generic appointment he needed to remind himself to keep?

The following two sessions were missed with no word from Michael.

When we met the following week Michael started by referring to what he had said to me "last week" as though there had been no break in our contact. At this point I was feeling as though I was walking through a dream, unable to find its edges, while Michael seemed to be acting as though nothing of note was happening. Despite years of working in the field and working with many challenging and dismissive patients, I was struck by how powerful the experiences with Michael felt to me. When I raised the issue of his frequent absences and his lack of memory of when we had last met Michael was deeply apologetic and understanding, stressing the pressure he was under and assuring me this would "not last forever."

His assurances did not, however, alter my growing sense of destabilization. I felt an increasing uncertainty about my experience with him: I didn't know what was going on. I felt my general mood dropping, my sense of clarity fractured. Had I misjudged our connection? I wrestled with feeling dismissed and unimportant. Perhaps I could not trust my perception of people's feelings about me. Michael's apparent obliviousness to what was happening made me feel even less able to pursue it with him. I could see I was thinking in a strange way—as though if I didn't mention the problems, they would just go away. When Michael was present he continued to seem engaged and thoughtful about what we were discussing. I, however, was somewhere else.

Memories of waiting endlessly for my emotionally unreliable mother to pick me up after school began floating into my mind—she sometimes worked unpredictable hours. I could picture the parking lot emptying, my classmates disappearing into waiting cars, the winter daylight fading. It infuriated me and was the kind of experience that contributed to my early pattern of determined self-sufficiency.

At this point I knew Michael and I were in something together but my resistance to entering this space with him was palpable. I had to *will* myself back into the room with him, reminding myself of his early trauma and trying to recall my warm feelings for him. Finally I was able to begin reflecting on what I was experiencing, thinking about early loss, disappointments, feeling invisible to someone else who was very important to me. These were emotional experiences that I knew must be part of Michael's history, but that he had never been able to describe in words; experiences that were now painfully, almost overwhelmingly, alive in my mind.

I told Michael that I wasn't sure what was happening, but it felt like he was trying to communicate something to me in his actions—something important that might be hard to put into words. "When you are here," I began, "you and I seem to have a good connection, but somehow it doesn't seem to hold as a reality for you over time." Michael looked almost scared. I felt a heightened urgency to reconnect and not frighten him away. Hoping to accomplish this by lightening the conversation, I playfully shared an image that had just entered my mind. "Sometimes," I said with a wry smile, "I feel like I'm working with a traveling salesman."

Michael's face paled: he looked horrified. "I can't believe you said that," he said in a deadened tone. To my astonishment he then shared something I had no memory of having known before that point: his father did not just sell books, but was indeed a *traveling salesman* who sold books. Michael began haltingly describing how his father regularly left the family "for work" with little or no notice and no shared plan for his return, missing his son's important swimming competitions, never acknowledging that anything noteworthy was going on with his erratic and disturbing coming and going "so it seemed almost as if it weren't happening."

On not knowing what is happening

I had somehow found Michael's father in our enacted behavior, feeling his odd and implicitly hurtful disregard for our experience as he played out an unacknowledged pattern of thoughtless detachment, which evoked resonant personal experience for me. And I had found something of Michael's *experience* of his father within myself—in my destabilizing sense of unreality and growing uncertainty about our connection. Michael then remembered the rest of the dream he had referred to just as his absences from our sessions began increasing: he was running through rooms, empty rooms but he couldn't stop to look. He had to keep moving or he would be trapped—something was terrifying. Then it changed: he became invisible; he was floating but now not so scared; no one could find him.

Out of our awareness Michael and I were joined in Ogden's intersubjectively generated analytic Third, enacting emotionally resonant disowned experience, dividing it up between us as we grappled with our shared pain. Within Ogden's formulations, we were also joining in an early expression of *dream thinking* as we worked together, a process

Ogden regards as the most encompassing, penetrating and creative form of thinking. Existing without order or sequence, dream thinking offers itself to the analyst and patient to creatively engage as a source of psychic vitalization. Within this form, we unconsciously view our lived experience from a multiplicity of vantage points simultaneously, which allows us to enter into a rich, non-linear set of unconscious conversations with ourselves as we engage primary and secondary process—mature and infantile—magical and real, psychotic and non-psychotic perspectives, becoming the projector and recipient of projected identifications (Ogden, 1995).

Ogden sees this often confusing process as intrinsic to psychic health, reminding us of the psychological importance of the earliest mind-to-mind communication as the mother accepts the infant's unthinkable thoughts and unbearable feelings, "holding" them until the infant is more able to dream on his own. He feels every individual is, to varying degrees, limited in his personal capacity to subject aspects of his lived experience to dream thinking. "[i]t takes (at least) two people," he concludes, "to dream one's most disturbing experience" (Ogden, 2010, p. 328).

Michael and I, our minds working silently together, had engaged some of his and some of my most disturbing experiences, co-creating vitalizing linkages between aspects of our individual minds that had, for us both, been rigidly detached and strongly defended against. His absent father and Michael's efforts to remain untouched by the pain of that relationship had clearly resonated with similar aspects of my psyche.

Ogden has noted that in participating in this process we "create ourselves in and through the other-who-is-not-fully-other; at the same time we unconsciously allow ourselves to serve as the vehicle through which the other (who-is-not-fully-other) creates himself as a subject through us" (Ogden, 2010, p. 190). Michael's bringing in a dream reflected a stirring of his connection with his disavowed internal life. Ultimately the dream thoughts were too difficult to express, giving expression, as they did, to his wish to flee the terrifying experienced emptiness of his paternal attachment that our process was stirring up in him (Sopher, 2018). His behavior, however, was not simply avoidant. As though we were playing charades, while his verbal report of the dream abruptly ended, Michael acted out with me his experiences of his father's erratic and hurtful behavior, a pivotal aspect of his history that had remained unrepresented in our verbal process. With my emotional connection to him I was open to taking him in—intuitively wanting, like the early mother with her infant, to hold his experience; but when this non-verbalized process became too experientially real, stirring up my own resonant and unwanted pain, it became destabilizing. Being able to bear it involved reaching, as Ogden describes it, for the capacity to "observe"—which allowed me to think it rather than just feel it and thereby to reflect on what was happening. I could then hold this piece of him—and me—and return it to him, letting him know the disowned experience had become thinkable between us.

There are many issues to consider here: certainly Michael's history holds evidence of developmental disruptions in the area of narcissism, his father depriving him of needed personal recognition while also failing him miserably as an idealizable early object. Unlike Kohut's descriptions of such patients' actively demanding the missed mirroring experience, Michael had tried to bury any awareness of this need, emphasizing his ability to rise above painful losses and, without help from anyone, become his own "perfect" man. Unfortunately this "perfect man" seemed to have been developed in a manner that was largely uninformed by Michael's awareness of himself as a "real" person in his own right. Consciously avoiding being swept into some version of his father's unquenchable narcissism, Michael intentionally limited his actual consideration of what "felt good" to him, concentrating on being a "good person" rather than being guided by a felt awareness of what he wanted or needed. His aggressive feelings were intolerable in this arrangement, tainted by their connection with his experience of his "bad" father. His sadness was risky as it stirred up unwanted feelings of need. Evoking Fairbairn's (1958, p. 381) emphasis on the child's necessarily taking in whatever is available, however, Michael's powerful need for a connection with his father was not to be dismissed. Evoking descriptions of the silent intergenerational transmission of trauma (Bromberg, 2008; Pistole, 1995), outside of Michael's awareness he had taken in his troubled and troubling father, identifying with him internally as he blindly lived out his father's obvious anxieties about connections and modeled his father's chronic defensiveness against engaged contact.

Ultimately Michael became another version of this rejected "traveling salesman" who used the obligations of work as the self-blinding regulating excuse keeping him always on the move, protecting him from the anxieties of connections with others. Michael was seriously crippled in his ability to engage intersubjectively with those around him. He was a "good man," but to those closest to him he often seemed "never really there," hampered by the psychic fragmentation resulting from internalizing a father he unknowingly longed for yet consciously rejected.

Ogden feels that it is from the kinds of analytic experiences I am describing between Michael and myself that his third kind of thinking, *transformative thinking*, can—over time—emerge. *Transformative thinking* involves recognizing the limitations of the categories of meaning currently thought to be the only categories that exist (I must be perfect, do everything on my own, need nothing from anyone else, etc.) and generating, from newly developing experience, types of feeling, forms of object relatedness and qualities of aliveness that had previously been unimaginable.

Clearly much work needs to be done to enable this kind of personal transformation. One relevant obstacle concerns the workings of narcissism in both patient and analyst. Self-states formed within an emphasis on the denial of needs, grandiose self-sufficiency and defensive isolation from others ask the analyst to be particularly mindful of unspoken enacted dimensions of the analytic process where exploration is avoided and meaning is left unarticulated. To engage these potentially rich experiences in our patient, however, we must often tolerate our own painfully defended-against self-states that are activated in resonance. After being immersed in the pain of feeling cast aside by both Michael *and* my mother, for example, I could feel my enraged narcissistically offended isolation taking root and the tempting allure of *magical thinking* encouraging me to simply "not notice" what was clearly taking place between us, thereby "substituting a newly created reality for a reality that is no longer convenient" (Ogden, 2010, p. 321).

By asking myself to reflect on what was happening and refinding my actual feelings for Michael I was able to more confidently access the image we both wanted to avoid: the experience of being parented by a seemingly unconcerned and implicitly abandoning "traveling salesperson." Sharing this image gave implicit comfort to us both. It gave evidence of our emerging emotional connection. Michael spoke of feeling "real for the first time," and began what he termed "experiments in feeling," gingerly exploring the sadness and anger he had ignored for so many years. And sitting with him I could feel he *was* really there!

This kind of vitalization is not accessed through a process of privileging the patient's intentions: it requires the surrender of both patient and analyst to an often unconscious process of available psychic connectedness. For someone like Michael this process can occur when, despite aspects of self that remain deeply defended against, enough trust has been established in the therapy that other aspects of the patient begin to feel hopeful of the possibility of a generative connection. This was reflected in Michael's allowing himself to report part of a dream, then quickly devolving into an earlier form of communication. Still holding the potential intersubjective generativity between us, nonverbally Michael let me feel what he was feeling. I was able to hold it and return it to him in a form that felt safer to him because we were in it together.

With a patient like Michael, the clinical process required an active engaging and holding experience that did *not,* for long periods of time, seem to "fit together." Often this kind of experience represents fragments of defensively dissociated self-states that have been unthinkable and that, in their defensive rigidity, greatly interfere with the vitalizing mind-to-mind engagement that eventuates in the further development of personal subjectivity. Our capacity to empathically and creatively participate in a process of emotionally connecting with our patient through the challenges of this process can lend itself to the potential repair of the crucial vitalizing channel.

Conclusion

As analysts we are facing an ever more complex field: we know more, we are asked to hold more, our lens is broadening to include more. Our field's early emphasis on maintaining objectivity as we draw on the "correct theory" to offer perfectly worded interpretations has yielded to our contemporary mission of wading into the messiness of intersubjective confusion in the service of co-creating a vitalizing and generative connection between the necessarily idiosyncratic aspects of the minds of analyst and patient.

There is no singular theory that will help us—no one "way to do it." There is only the way that each of us embodies, digests and makes thoughtful use of the theories we learn—and how these organizations of thought resonate with our personal experience of our patients and ourselves, emboldening parts of ourselves, refining others, activating aspects that have lain dormant or that have been defensively walled off. Relational thinking offers a revised set of clinical concerns: we now pay less attention to the specific destination and put greater emphasis on a personalized journey, one which aims to activate the psychic vitalization made possible by the meaning-making collaboration between the minds of our patient and ourselves.

Bibliography

Aron, L. (1996). *A Meeting of Minds: Mutuality in Psychoanalysis*. Hillsdale, NJ: The Analytic Press.

Aron, L. (2006). Analytic Impasse and the Third: Clinical Implications of Intersubjectivity Theory. *Int. J. Psycho-Anal.*, 87(2):349–368.

Bass, A. (2003). "E" Enactments in Psychoanalysis: Another Medium, Another Message. *Psychoanal. Dial.*, 13(5):657–675.

Benjamin, J. (1990). An Outline of Intersubjectivity: The Development of Recognition. *Psychoanal. Psychol.*, 7S(Supplement):33–46.

Benjamin, J. (2004). Beyond Doer and Done to: An Intersubjective View of Thirdness. *Psychoanal. Q.*, 73(1):5–46.

Black, M. (2003). Enactment: Analytic: Musings on Energy, Language, and Personal Growth. *Psychoanal. Dial.*, 13(5):633–665.

Bollas, C. (1983). Expressive Uses of the Countertransference: Notes to the Patient from Oneself. *Contemp. Psychoanal.*, 19:1–33.

Boston Change Process Study Group (2002). Explicating the Implicit: The Local Level and the Microprocess of Change in the Analytic Situation. *Int. J. Psycho-Anal.*, 83(5):1051–1062.

Boston Change Process Study Group (2005). The "Something More" than Interpretation Revisited: Sloppiness and Co-Creativity in the Psychoanalytic Encounter. *J. Am. Psych. Assn.*, 533(3):693–729.

Boston Change Process Study Group (BCPSG) (2007). The Foundational Level of Psychodynamic Meaning: Implicit Process in Relation to Conflict, Defense and the Dynamic Unconscious. *Int. J. Psycho-Anal.*, 88(4):843–860.

Boston Change Process Study Group (2008). Forms of Relational Meaning: Issues in the Relations Between the Implicit and Reflective-Verbal Domains. *Psychoanal. Dial.*, 18(2):125–148.

Bromberg, P.M. (1994). "Speak! That I May See You": Some Reflections on Dissociation, Reality, and Psychoanalytic Listening. *Psychoanal. Dial.*, 4(4):517–547.

Bromberg, P.M. (2008). Shrinking the Tsunami: Affect Regulation, Dissociation, and the Shadow of the Flood. *Contemp. Psychoanal.*, 44(3):329–350.

Davies, J.M. (2004). Whose Bad Objects Are We Anyway? Repetition and Our Elusive Love Affair with Evil. *Psychoanal. Dial.*, 14(6):711–732.

Fairbairn, W.R. (1941). A Revised Psychopathology of the Psychoses and Psychoneuroses. *Int. J. Psycho-Anal.*, 22:250–279.

Fairbairn, W.D. (1958). On the Nature and Aims of Psycho-Analytical Treatment. *Int. J. Psycho-Anal.*, 39:374–385.

Fonagy, P., Gergely, G., Jurist, E., and Target, M. (2002). *Affect Regulation, Mentalization, and the Development of the Self.* New York City: Other Press.

Freud, S. (1912). *Recommendations to Physicians Practising Psychoanalysis.* Standard Edition, Vol. XII. London: Hogarth Press.

Freud, S. (1914). Remembering, Repeating and Working-Through (Further Recommendations on the Technique of Psycho-Analysis II). *The Standard Edition of the Complete Psychological Works of Sigmund Freud,* Volume XII (1911–1913): *The Case of Schreber, Papers on Technique and Other Works* (pp. 145–156). London: Hogarth Press.

Freud, S. (1916). Introductory Lectures on Psycho-Analysis. *The Standard Edition of the Complete Psychological Works of Sigmund Freud,* Volume XV (1915–1916): *Introductory Lectures on Psycho-analysis* (Parts I and II) (pp. 1–240). London: Hogarth Press.

Freud, S. (1923). The Ego and the Id. Standard Edition of the Complete Psychological Works of Sigmund Freud, Volume XIX (1923–1925): *The Ego and the Id and Other Works* (pp. 1–66). London: Hogarth Press.

Gerson, S. (2004). The Relational Unconscious: A Core Element of Intersubjectivity, Thirdness and Clinical Process. *Psychoanal. Q.*, 73(1):63–98.

Glover, E. (1931). The Therapeutic Effect of Inexact Interpretation: A Contribution to the Theory of Suggestion. *Int. J. Psycho-Anal.*, 12:397–411.

Green, A. (2004). Thirdness and Psychoanalytic Concepts. *Psychoanal. Q.*, 73(1):99–135.

Greenberg, J. and Mitchell, S. (1983). *Object Relations in Psychoanalytic Thinking*. Cambridge, MA: Harvard University Press.

Mitchell, S.A. (1979). Twilight of the Idols: Change and Preservation in the Writings of Heinz Kohut. *Contemp. Psychoanal.*, 15:170–189.

Mitchell, S.A. (1981a). The Origin and Nature of the "Object" in the Theories of Klein and Fairbairn. *Contemp. Psychoanal.*, 17:374–398.

Mitchell, S.A. (1981b). The Psychoanalytic Treatment of Homosexuality: Some Technical Considerations. *Int. Rev. Psycho-Anal.*, 8:63–80.

Mitchell, S.A. (1984a). Object Relations Theories and the Developmental Tilt. *Contemp. Psychoanal.*, 20:473–499.

Mitchell, S. (1984b). The Problem of the Will. *Contemp. Psychoanal.*, 20:257–265.

Mitchell, S.A. (1986). The Wings of Icarus: Illusion and the Problem of Narcissism. *Contemp. Psychoanal.*, 22:107–132.

Mitchell, S.A. (1988a). *Relational Concepts in Psychoanalysis: An Integration.* Cambridge, MA: Harvard University Press.

Mitchell, S.A. (1988b). The Intrapsychic and the Interpersonal: Different Theories, Different Domains, or Historical Artifacts? *Psychoanal. Inq.*, 8(4):472–496.

Ogden, T.H. (1994). The Analytic Third: Working with Intersubjective Clinical Facts. *Int. J. Psycho-Anal.*, 75:3–19.

Ogden, T.H. (1995). Analyzing forms of Aliveness and Deadness in the Transference–Countertransference. *Int. J. Psycho-Anal.*, 76: 695–709.

Ogden, T.H. (2004). The Analytic Third: Implications for Psychoanalytic Theory and Technique. *Psychoanal. Q.*, 73(1):167–195.

Ogden, T.H. (2010). On Three Forms of Thinking: Magical Thinking, Dream Thinking, and Transformative Thinking. *Psychoanal. Q.*, 79(2):317–347.

Pistole, M. (1995). Adult Attachment Style and Narcissistic Vulnerability. *Psychoanal. Psychol.*, 12:115–126.

Schwartz Cooney, A. (2018). Vitalizing Enactment: A Relational Exploration, *Psychoanal. Dial.*, 28(3):340–354.

Slavin, M.O. and Kreigman, D. (1998). Why the Analyst Needs to Change: Toward a Theory of Conflict, Negotiation, and Mutual Influence in the Therapeutic Process. *Psychoanal. Dial.*, 8(2):247–284.

Sopher, R. (2018). An Allegiance to Absence: Fidelity to the Internal Void. *Psychoanal. Q.*, LXXXVII(4):729–751.

Stern, D.B. (2004). The Eye Sees Itself: Dissociation, Enactment and the Achievement of Conflict. *Contemp. Psychoanal.*, 40(2):197–237.

Stern, D. (2010). *Forms of Vitality: Exploring Dynamic Experience in Psychology and the Arts.* New York: Oxford University Press.

Stern, D., Sander, L., Nahum, J., Harrison, A., Lyons-Ruth, K., Morgan, A., Bruschweiler-Stern, N. and Tronick, E. (1998). Non-Interpretive

Mechanisms in Psychoanalytic Therapy: The "Something More" Than Interpretation. *International Journal of Psycho-Analysis*, 79:903–921.

Thelen, E. (2005). Dynamic Systems Theory and the Complexity of Change. *Psychoanal. Dial.*, 15(2):255–283.

Tronick, E.Z. (1998). Dyadically Expanded States of Consciousness and the Process of Therapeutic Change. *Infant Mental Health J.*, 19(3):290–299.

Tronick, E.Z. (2002). A Model of Infant Mood States and Sandarian Affective Waves. *Psychoanal. Dial.*, 12(1):73–99.

Tronick, E.Z. (2005). Why is Connection with Others so Critical? The Formation of Dyadic States of Consciousness and the Expansion of Individuals' States of Consciousness: Coherence Governed Selection and the Co-creation of Meaning out of Messy Meaning Making. In J. Nadel & D. Muir (Eds.), *Emotional Development: Recent Research Advances* (pp. 293–315). Oxford, England: Oxford University Press.

Tronick, E.Z. (2007) *The Neurobiological and Social-Emotional Development of Infant and Children*. New York: W.W. Norton.

Winnicott, D.W. (1953). Transitional Objects and Transitional Phenomena—A Study of the First Not-Me Possession. *Int. J. Psycho-Anal.*, 34:89–97.

Winnicott, D.W. (1965). The Maturational Processes and the Facilitating Environment: Studies in the Theory of Emotional Development. *The International Psycho-Analytical Library*, vol. 64 (pp. 1–276). London: The Hogarth Press and the Institute of Psycho-Analysis.

Winnicott, D.W. (1971). *Playing and Reality*. Middlesex, England: Penguin.

Winnicott, D.W. (1980). The Piggle: An Account of the Psychoanalytic Treatment of a Little Girl Edited by Ishak Ramzy. *The International Psycho-Analytical Library* (pp. 107–201). London: The Hogarth Press and the Institute of Psycho-Analysis.

Part II

The analyst's vitalizing use of self

Love, play and provision

Chapter 7

Reawakening desire

Shame, analytic love, and psychoanalytic imagination

Jody Messler Davies

In this chapter I will attempt to explore the relationship between shame, desire, and what we have come to call "analytic love." From our use of language we have, I believe, grown used to thinking that the opposite of shame is pride. But from my own work with particularly shame-riddled patients, those who have suffered the extremes of parental abuse and neglect, I have come to believe that the clinically meaningful dialectic is between shame and desire. That in order to live fully, to engage in life most deeply, we oftentimes have to reawaken a patient's willingness to "want," to trust life and the people who populate that life, sufficiently to feel hopeful that at least some of what one yearns for will be provided. It has become my heartfelt conviction that instrumental to awakening this desire in the therapeutic encounter is the shared experience of what I will call and later define as "analytic love." When such love is provided a fertile ground in the hypothetical "would that I could" realm of a mutually constructed "psychoanalytic fantasy," that love can flourish without threat to appropriate therapeutic boundaries and can help us walk the ever treacherous boundary between analytic withholding and analytic seduction. Walking such a line is always our challenge. But unless we accept that challenge, the kind of vitalization or reawakening of desire that is the subject of this book will not occur.

Shame is perhaps the most dreaded, most soul-sucking, most psychically deadening experience within the panoply of potential human emotions. How does it arise? What kind of relatedness potentiates it? Why are some people resilient in the face of shame while others collapse under its weight? What place does shame have within psychoanalytic theory? Have we attended to it sufficiently? How do we help our patients to engage with their own shame and heal from it without actually re-enacting that shame within a transference–countertransference impasse or stalemate? And, ultimately, what of our own shame? How do we as analysts deal with the kind of shame that can arise within us in the heat of an intense psychoanalytic treatment? Can we engage it sufficiently to avoid our own dissociation, and bring that shame into the foreground of our work, making it an essential part of the analytic process (Davies, 2005)?

Freud (1905) at first considered shame to be a defensive response to exhibitionistic impulses within the patient. In subsequent formulations (Freud, 1933), he added that shame was related to the ego ideal and to the patient's perceived deficits in living up to that ideal. Building on this, but changing its emphasis, self psychologists focused on the relationship between shame and compensatory grandiosity. Morrison (1989) suggests that shame occurs when the ego is overwhelmed by the grandiose expectations of the narcissistic self, essentially saying, "I feel so bad about myself to begin with that I establish an utterly impossible compensatory standard to live up to," whereas the compensatory grandiose self is saying, "And I am ashamed that I can never reach this self-imposed standard." In all of these formulations shame is defensive, but why the experience of inadequacy to begin with? Why the need for a compensatory standard? What can a relational psychoanalysis contribute to our understanding of this dreaded experience?

It is often said that, while guilt is a response to something we have actively done, shame has its roots in a passive helplessness in the face of something we are. I ask you all to try an experiment with me. Close your eyes, and try, for a moment, to think of an intensely shameful experience in your life. We all have them. They rattle around inside of us ready to pounce and we call upon them at times to convince ourselves of our own internal badness. So call upon one of them now. As you remember the particular event, I ask you to focus on your body. I would imagine, based on my own experiences, and what has been reported to me by so many patients who I engage in this same experiment, that there is an intense physicality to this experience—a kind of nausea in the stomach, an aching in and around the heart, a slight difficulty in breathing, and a burning sensation in the face. The eyes want to close, to prevent the other from looking and seeing inside us; to prevent us from seeing our dreaded reflection in the eyes of the other. We want to fall through the floor and disappear.

For all of these reasons I would suggest to you that shame begins as a physical response. It is a primitive, visceral reaction that begins in the body before it is mentalized and assumes a psychic significance. I have come to believe that the propensity towards shame begins in the very earliest of infant–parent interactions. That the propensity toward shame takes hold when a child's desires are unmet, or erratically met, or met in a way that over-stimulates and terrifies. It arises when the child cannot establish what Benjamin (2002) has called a rhythmicity in his/her earliest relationships, what I have described in earlier papers (Davies, 2016) as the ability to "confidently anticipate" that needs and desires will be lovingly and appropriately met. It is this experience of having one's needs met with some expectable regularity and appropriate modulation that creates a safe enough space for the child to want, long for, yearn for, and desire. When a child's needs go unmet, or when they are met in such a way that the responsiveness cannot be confidently anticipated and taken in, that child learns not to hate the significant others who cannot meet his/her needs because he remains dependent on them for survival. In Fairbairn's words (1943), he eats the poison pudding, becoming toxic himself. He learns to hate the things he needs, and the self-states within him that are "needy" rather than hating those who cannot meet those needs. He begins to see himself as insatiable, or greedy, or "too much." Shame, to my mind, lies in the "too"—too needy, too dependent, too anxious, too sexual. The "too-ness" that comes from yearnings that a parent cannot meet and from a self that would rather accept blame and experience shame over wanting "too much," than see the parent as unreliable. That shame is also exacerbated and made more toxic by a parent who explicitly or implicitly blames her child for "wanting" what she—the parent—cannot provide, thus creating a primitive boundary violation and confusion over who needs what from whom. When a parent cannot accept responsibility for what she is unable to give, or does not want to give, and blames her child for wanting "too much," this boundary violation itself creates more shame along with the terror of boundary dissolution and collapse. Here terror and shame exist in a downwardly spiraling negative synergy that can threaten psychic integration and survival (see Davies, 2005). Desire is defensively shut down, encased in a deadened self-state for whom any form of emotional sustenance can also come to imply psychic penetration and violation. A precocious self-sufficiency and counter-dependency takes hold. Keeping others out while blaming them for not meeting our needs becomes the best protection against a psychotic dissolution into deadened hopelessness and resignation.

Of late, there has been interesting discussion, within the psychoanalytic literature, about the concept of "analytic love." What is analytic love? How is it different from other forms of love? And is there a relationship between the way we use ourselves generatively and proactively in the analytic work and our understanding of what constitutes and what emerges as a consequence of that particular love? In the context of the present discussion I would also like to consider whether there is a relationship between analytic love and shame. To my own way of thinking (see Davies, in press) analytic love is a love that is co-created by patient and analyst together, a love that is uniquely defined within each dyad, a love—and this is most important—that takes into account and metabolizes the best and the worst that we can be for each other. I would suggest that what is unique about the analyst's love for her patient is that it must include discovering, drawing out, and coming to love, through developmentally contextualizing and thus understanding, the patient's most injured, most traumatized and most vulnerable, and shame-riddled self-states. Such vulnerability survives only within a self-constructed psychic fortress designed to keep potentially dangerous others at bay. Whether this fortress is one that disengages with others, or bores others, or attacks and rejects others; whether it is one that keeps things so good that those other self-states never emerge; whatever the nature of the fortress, it is designed to protect the part of the self that survives only through disappointment and isolation. Analytic love includes, as well, the patient's introduction to and acceptance of the analyst's vulnerabilities and flaws as they emerge in the work together. Clinically, the overriding question is whether analytic love, so defined, might be a love that has the capacity to meet enough of the patient's "too muchness," to reawaken desire, facilitate mourning, and mitigate the kind of shame that has been described. The challenge to us is how we can express this love in a way that is appropriately bounded, not over-stimulating, and not inappropriate to analytic work. I ask these questions in this context because I have come to believe that shame-riddled self-states and analytic love are inextricably intertwined forces that involve a deep mutual recognition and acceptance of each other's vulnerabilities, as we encounter our multiple and ever-shifting self-states, within the immediacy of our most intimate encounters.

There is enormous variability in how smoothly a patient can accept and integrate that which we offer. Some of our patients will respond well to an empathic recognition of their need states and a well-modulated provision of that which we can give as analysts. Those long-dissociated desires will begin to unfold and a new hopefulness in relation to the future can be revived. But for many the journey toward self-acceptance and hope is far more complex, and can depend upon how much of a patient's experience is encased within deeply shame-riddled self-states. Is it a few toxic experiences that need to be engaged and worked through? Or are so many of the patient's selves saturated with this kind of shame that an imagined future of hope and aliveness has been crushed under the weight of dissociated yearning, longing, and desire? For those of our patients for whom deprivation, erratic provision, and over-stimulation have been predominant, the question of what psychoanalysis can provide becomes more problematic. How do we reawaken desire and the hope that emerges from appropriately met desires without promising too much, violating the boundaries of an analytic frame, overwhelming the patient with a sense of our aliveness that creates only envy and prevents internalization? Can we live with our own shame-saturated selves who will inevitably be called out and attacked, rejected, or found wanting, in the projective-introjective miasma of the analytic work?

If only it were possible to offer a good and reliable breast and awaken the sleeping baby. But patients who have suffered histories of profound neglect and/or over-stimulation present at least three problems with that solution. First, the analyst's attempts to be a "good object" and provide for the patient what she hasn't had before awaken both the rage against and the need to protect the attachment to the original unreliable or over-stimulating object. The patient's stability has for quite a while resided within that attachment to the original bad object and giving up and mourning that traumatic bond is no easy matter. Second, the analyst's attempt to meet the patient with reliability and provision and generosity can elicit a reaction of intense envy in the patient who does not feel capable of such generosity of spirit. In this sense the analyst's attempts to provide paradoxically end up shaming the patient even more. It is as if the therapist is saying, "Look how good I am being despite your provocations; look how generous I am despite your remaining rejecting and ungrateful" (Davies, in press). And lastly, where projection by the parent has led to the confusion of boundaries, discussed earlier—the situation in which it is unclear who needs what from whom—any attempt to emotionally touch the patient can be experienced as a psychic boundary violation. The analyst's attempts to reach out and nourish, in a way that awakens hope and desire, can be experienced by the patient as an over-stimulating psychic penetration in which she feels hopelessly and inexorably drawn into the terrifying psychotic world of the parent's unconscious. Here her sanity depends upon rejecting the analyst's offering of the very thing she craves most, and via projective identification, awakening the analyst's own shame-riddled self-states. The patient ends up hating the analyst for offering and hating herself even more for rejecting that offer in a way that feels imperative but also incomprehensible and disorienting. The analyst ends up struggling with her own shame and hopefully not re-projecting that shame on to the patient.

Theoretically we tend to view the kind of repression and dissociation that give rise to psychic conflict as a defensive strategy to deal with early, past traumatic events and relationships. We focus on helping patients to work through these traumas, we try to provide the support and containment necessary, we struggle with how to metabolize these early toxic introjects. However, of late, I have noticed another trend in our theoretical writings. It is not new. It has been there almost from the beginning, but only as a mere whisper, which has seemed to grow in force and insistence in recent work. This is the question of what we actually provide for patients—provide, in a proactive way, that can help to reopen previously foreclosed areas of functioning. Having long railed against and shunned

Alexander's prescriptive notion of reparenting, it is only of late that psychoanalysts have found the courage and fortitude to reopen this question and to contemplate it from a more nuanced and complex perspective. A host of writers (Alvarez, 1992; Aron, 1996; Aron and Atlas, 2015; Bass, 2015; Burton, 2012; Cooper, 2018; Director, 2016; Hoffman, 2009; Schwartz Cooney, 2018; Stern, 2015) have written about what we provide for patients proactively in the future tense—enlivening objects, hope, vitalizing enactments, relational freedom, enlivening enactments. I, myself, have written in past papers about what I called generative interventions, i.e., interventions that open up a symbolic space between patient and analyst that has never existed before—a kind of intervention that calls upon what I have come to think of as our psychoanalytic imaginations.

Clinical vignette

Let me describe my work with a patient I will call Salina. Salina came to treatment riddled with shame, convinced that she would overwhelm anyone who got near her with her insatiable demands. "I will destroy us with my neediness," she promised me in our first session.

Salina was referred to me by a good friend of mine. "You are going to love her," he told me. "She is an incredibly special person." Since Salina was a history graduate student my friend convinced me to see her for a slightly reduced fee. "You won't regret it," he assured me. Well—it proved true that Salina was brilliant, and beautiful, and presented herself initially with a pathos and humor that were charming and incredibly endearing. But Salina also entered treatment like a tropical hurricane, disruptive, intense, threatening, stormy, and relentless. I felt quickly drawn up into the swirling vortex of what felt like her insatiable demands for contact, love, and reassurance. "Do you love me?" she asked in our second session. "I just met you." I replied. "I hope I will grow to love you as we get to know each other." "That means you don't love me," she said, her sigh descending into deep sobs. "If you were going to love me you would love me now, already. It won't happen." At other times: "Why can't you be my mother?" "How would that be for us?" I asked her. "Noooooo," she cried. "No therapy questions … I want you to *be* my mother, really, truly my mother, not symbolically, not in that therapist way. Why can't you be my mother for real ... true life?" And then, one day, early on:

> I can't do this twice-a-week thing. I need to talk to you between sessions. I need to talk to you every day ... maybe a few times a day. I'm very needy (I'm too needy ... too needy for anyone). I'm sorry about that, but I need a real mother and I need her to be with me all the time!

Endearing Salina and insatiable Salina both occupied our sessions in those early days, fighting for dominance, oscillating in and out of the foreground from moment to moment. When endearing Salina appeared I felt utterly charmed and engaged, with "she's special ... you won't regret it" echoing in my ears. Endearing Salina lit up the room with her smile and her unique creativity. Did I mention she was an artist? She brought me pictures of wide-mouthed monsters eating children—monster and child merged, their boundaries fluid and permeable. She cuddled under a blanket on my couch, a vulnerable child in need of warmth and protection. Insatiable Salina could not be nourished. Her mental state only as good as her last feed. Any disappointment brought on paroxysms of rage, accusation, and a relentless rejection of anything I tried to offer. My caring wasn't genuine enough, frequent enough, intense enough. I could be there sometimes, she admitted, but not when she really needed me. Where was I when she was sick? When she had a bad dream? When she was frightened or overwhelmed? Why couldn't I come to her house to take care of her like a real mother would? Why couldn't I adopt her? For real. It wasn't against the law; I could adopt her if I really cared! At such times the vulnerable little girl became inconsolable and unreachable. The blanket she would cuddle up in became a suit of armor and she would hide under it, silently fuming, refusing to talk, for silent session after silent session. I remind you that Salina was highly functional and successful in many areas of her life. And yet the words she spoke were not metaphorical, not meant to be symbolic or illusory. Insatiable Salina wanted what she wanted and she wanted it now!

Suffice to say I cursed my referring colleague many times in that first year! No regrets—huh! If we presume, as I do, that the co-creation of analytic love is a vital component of any kind of therapeutic success, figuring out how to authentically love Salina and to do so in a way that she could accept and take in was no simple matter. Clearly we had encountered the worst of who we could each be with each other, but the struggle to find a form of love that would be genuine without being a seductive false promise or a boundary violation was more elusive. My expressions of caring and concern, though expressed as directly as I could, were found to be inadequate and thus enraging. When I did from time to time seem able to emotionally touch Salina, and make contact with those younger, and more vulnerable, self-states we could have a brief respite, a moment of shared warmth and connection. But always, always, at those times, raging, unlovable Salina had to prove that my love was false, superficial, unequal to the task of loving *her*! And some enactment would ensue. I would find myself caught up in it before I knew what was happening and inevitably, inexorably, I would fail her yet again. Fail her with my own admixture of disappointment, frustration, shame, and rage. And so it went.

Because of these raging storms, fluctuating self-states, and long periods of silence, Salina's story emerged slowly. Even today, years later, some of the details remain hazy. Salina's mother, a victim of spousal abuse, took Salina (age 2) and left her father, flying away to live with her own family in a distant country. Salina was sent to her father, flying unaccompanied, every summer, for the whole summer, until she was 12, at which point she simply refused to go. Her mother seemed not to wonder, or care, whether the husband who had so terrified and physically abused her could actually care for and not be violent with their young daughter. Dissociation, indifference, neglect—one wonders. Salina's summers with her father and father's family remain a series of tableaus, a collage of vague memories that emerge slowly over our time together. I hear about a little girl, dependent upon a clearly psychotic father. There is a large family estate on which she is left to wander unattended, not sure where her father is or which adults are around. She has older cousins with whom she plays, horses she rides, animals she loves, but she also spends nights sleeping under a tree, with no blanket or pillow, dressed only in the bathing suit she wore during the day, locked out of the house. Is her father away, is she alone, is he in the house with a woman, locking Salina out? Pictures emerge in her art work; not memories, but pictures. We look at them together, we speculate about what they might suggest. Interspersed are more demands, more failures, more rages, more stony silence. Our progress is slow. We are both exhausted, often disheartened, often ashamed by the primitive hate and disappointment that can flare. How to love Salina? Not just the injured, vulnerable, soulful parts, but the parts that stand guard, around that vulnerable self, the parts that pounce, rage, accuse, reject. How to accept the parts of myself that feel tired, rejecting, and ashamed of at times hating Salina for rejecting what I feel to be the best of me that I can offer her?

Then one day Salina tells me something that impacts me in a way I do not totally understand. She describes a memory of being very little, three or four years old, and her father takes her on a walk, a long walk to a huge meadow. The grass is overhead, and all she can see is miles and miles of this yellow grass, waving back and forth all around her. Suddenly she turns around and her father is nowhere to be seen. She turns and she turns, getting dizzy, calling out for him, but all she hears is the sound of her own voice echoing. He is nowhere. She is alone. He has left her there. Abandoned her without food, water, clothing, or any way to get herself home.

"That's why you always want to know where I am, why you feel you need me right next to you all the time," I say. Salina nods quietly, crying quietly, not raging, wild hysterics, but quiet heartfelt, healing tears.

Something changes inside me after that. Why then, why that image and not any of the myriad other awful images of neglect and maltreatment, I do not know. Something about the simple and achingly horrific memory of Salina, in that moment *my* Salina, abandoned like that penetrates me to my core. The demands—be with me, be there when I'm sick, be my real mother, do more, give more, love me more, love me like a real mother loves, nourishes, protects her real daughter—those pieces begin to fall into place, evoking not the monstrous mouth consuming its babies but a forlorn and terrified child left and lost in the wild grasses of her psychotic father's homeland. How to co-create love with Salina, how to feed the devouring monster and rescue the child whose head lies between its jaws in terrifying proximity to the belly of the beast?

I have wondered often how to nourish and care for Salina. The relentlessness of her demands feels as if it leaves no room for anything I can spontaneously and genuinely offer up from my own heart. I am also aware that she has had two previous psychoanalytic attempts that have not worked—the first a treatment that was too classical and depriving to accomplish much of anything at all. It lasted only a short while. In the second attempt her more relationally identified analyst attempted to mother Salina, but she got caught up in the inevitable enactment of trying to prove her love. The boundaries collapsed. Salina visited at the analyst's house, met her children, had constant phone conversations and emergency sessions. Although I'm sure that Salina did derive much that was good from this analyst's heartfelt attempts to mother her, the boundaries eventually collapsed when the monster pounced and the enraged analyst collapsed under the weight of her own unappreciated attempts to care. "That's it, this has gone too far. No more calls, no more emergency sessions. We meet in my office, and that's it. You live with those rules or we are finished." They were finished. How to create a loving connection with "too needy" Salina?

I am sitting with Salina on a rainy afternoon. This time the storm is outside. We are quiet. She is curled up on my couch under a blanket. "I wish you could come sit here on the couch with me and I could put my head on your shoulder and you could stroke my hair." Her voice is dreamy. "That would be so lovely," I say to her. My voice is dreamy too as I hear it come from my mouth. For some reason, Salina does not up the ante today, demanding to know why I can't do that for real. She smiles; "it's nice," she says. We have entered a dream space together. "I'm imagining it too," I say, "I can feel your breathing slowing down, I can feel the weight of your head on my shoulder; you may even be falling asleep." Something seems to be opening here, but I am cautious. Can Salina live with me in a dream space without becoming disorganized and more fragmented? "Let's imagine this together," I say.

We sit quietly together, the rain soothing against the window, both I believe lost in this shared dream. "Why can't you be my real mother? Why can't this be real?," she says. Here it comes, I think, but this time instead of commiserating with her regret, something different emerges from me—I believe from within this dreamspace we are in.

"I know I can't be your real true-life mother but I so wish you could let me be your mother in my heart," I say to her.

Silence. And then a younger, happier, more excited voice: "You would be my heart mother!" Salina cries.

"Yes," I say, having no idea what exactly that means or where this is leading us.

"Then that means I would be your heart daughter?" Salina meets me again.

"I guess that's what it means," I respond, both of us with a sense of wonder as if we have stumbled together upon some hidden, fertile garden that neither of us has noticed before.

From that day forward Salina called me "HM," and I would refer to her as "HD." We had some conversations about what it meant to be a heart mother and heart daughter. We agreed that it meant that I really really wished I could be her true-life mother and give her all of the things she had been denied, and remove all of the trauma and pain she had suffered, but it also meant that we both acknowledged that I could never be that or do that. "But it's not real," she would say at times, registering the disappointment with which we were both so familiar. "It's not real that I am your mother, but the feelings that I hold for you and you hold for me, in our hearts, those are very very real," I would respond. And I would mean it. Slowly, over time, her belief in my genuine desire to mother her came to be more important than the concrete reality that she had always clung to so tenaciously and defensively. There seemed to be a nascent wedge inserting itself between the concrete and the symbolic.

I have come to believe that there is a level of interaction within psychoanalytic work that is not quite solely interpretive and not quite solely empathic. I consider that realm of our work to be generative, perhaps even poetic (see Hoffman, 1998). Although it derives from a powerful empathic bond, and requires a deep understanding of the patient's unconscious experience, it also creates something new and different between patient and analyst that has never quite existed before. It opens up a metaphoric space in which a new emotional experience can unfold and with it a kind of symbolization and internalization that has not been possible to this point. But the maddening thing about this kind of generative space is that one can't prescribe it or intentionally bring it about. It is something that must be co-created between patient and analyst in a deeply mutual unfolding, like a spontaneous choreography, a *pas de deux* of point and counterpoint.

I believe that what we have of late been calling "analytic love" connotes this mutual journey undertaken between patient and analyst together, that leads them from repetitive enactment into the realm of generative creativity. It is the mutual commitment we make to not turn away when we begin to hate, or grow bored, or experience shame and despair, the commitment we make to see our way through encountering each other's worst selves on our way towards making something different, something better, something entirely new, happen between us. It is an engagement between emergent selves, those of patient and analyst, selves born within the treatment process, who strive to integrate the best and worst we can each be and to love with full acknowledgment and recognition of both.

As heart mother and heart daughter, Salina and I struggled on. Our connection with each other seemed sturdier, not quite as relentlessly stormy. Endearing Salina and insatiable Salina seemed less distinct, more present simultaneously. We weathered more storms and the storms themselves became just noticeably less intense. Then one day before a planned separation, Salina sighed, "I wish there was some place we could go together. Some place I could see you when we were going to be apart. I don't like being apart."

"You mean a place we could each hold in mind when were weren't together, that would make us feel like in a way we were together because we were holding it in mind at the same time?" I countered.

"Yes! Exactly! Salina said. "Like a little house that was just ours."

"Like a cottage surrounded by wild flowers and a beautiful flowing stream," I added.

"And we would have all kinds of art materials inside so we could do projects, and a kitchen so you could bake me cookies when you had to go away; you could leave them for me."

"I could leave them for you with a glass of milk and a note with a funny drawing on it," I said.

Salina laughed, giggled. "Yeah," she sighed.

Together, brick by brick, Salina and I built our cottage refuge. In my mind the cottage existed in a field of tall grass, a haven in the territory of profound abandonment. I don't know if Salina had that same image in mind as she placed her bricks, but place them she did, as you can see in my much-abbreviated account of our initial interaction. Over time, Salina and I played in our cottage. We knocked it down, built it up again, huddled there against particularly cold days, went swimming together in the swimming hole we dug out of the brook that ran alongside. I baked many cookies there that I would leave for Salina. We argued about whether she could have chocolate milk with her cookies or whether that was too much sugar for her. I was after all her heart mother, and I wanted to—and she expected me to—leave her healthy snacks, even when the chocolate was more enticing.

Of course, amidst these conversations Salina and I did some more typical kinds of psychotherapeutic work, but our mutually constructed shared world was never far away. It contained us, and allowed us to broach areas that we had been unable to navigate before: the severity of her neglect, the emotional experience of terror in abandonment after abandonment. I often wondered if we had taken it too far. But Salina grew stronger, our work together more resilient. She did better at work and at school and with her family. This work did not end our breakdown into cycles of mutual shame and despair. It did not end the frustration we both felt about the limitations of what we could provide for each other: Salina's shame over the insatiability of her demands and the limitations of reality that she could not be born again and born anew; my limitations stemming from the awareness that I was after all her heart mother—her analyst—and not her real mother.

So, I wondered to myself, exactly what was happening here? What was it that was changing and evolving? As way of partial explanation—at least one that I have given myself—let's return to the question I posed earlier. The way in which our traditional analytic focus on the past, even on the intersubjective meeting of the patient's past with our own past, has begun to include, as well, that question of what we can provide—provide proactively—for our patients. The question of how the intersubjective mix of the patient's internal world and our own internal world can also open up something about our futures, especially our shared futures.

From a theoretical perspective we have always thought of repression and/or dissociation as a protection against past traumatic events and early traumatic relationships—in this case, Salina's traumatic attachment to a profoundly neglectful mother and an (abusive) psychotic father. But why assume that we only repress and dissociate memories of terrible past events and people? I would like to suggest here, that where shame has succeeded in obliterating or totally saturating desire, it is not only the past that is repressed and dissociated, but any capacity for an imagined future that embodies hope and generativity in human relationship. Where the capacity to desire is shut down by overwhelming shame, it is this highly significant aspect of an imagined and longed-for future of nourishment, gratification, and recognition that can become defensively foreclosed. In this sense our analytic task of "making the unconscious conscious" involves just the kind of future focus as a counterpoint to exploration of the past that I have described as the leading edge of relational theorizing. And so the impossible question becomes: how to awaken a patient's foreclosed capacity to long for and desire without overstepping appropriate boundaries and retraumatizing rather than reawakening?

In his book *Influence and Autonomy in Psychoanalysis*, Steve Mitchell (1997) suggested that psychopathology was always in some sense a failure of imagination. Today I wonder whether a reawakening of imagination can in some instances provide us with a pathway to the future. Perhaps what we have come to regard as intrapsychic fantasy that is based on iconic organizing experiences of the past also has a futuristic perspective. Perhaps each of us has a capacity for emergent fantasy, and perhaps that emergent fantasy holds the reawakened hope that what we seek from others need not be suffused with emptiness, excess, and shame. Bion (1963) suggests that it is only within the parent–child dyad that certain things can be symbolized and thought about without overwhelming anxiety and fragmentation. We have grown used to the therapeutic extension of this perspective, that often it is only within the containing dyad of patient and analyst that certain overwhelming experiences can be symbolized and spoken of for the first time. So I would suggest to you that some of those Bionian beta fragments are not only experiences of the past, but our hopes and dreams for the future that have been defensively fragmented, foreclosed, and made unthinkable by overwhelming anxiety and shame. Here what Bion calls the alpha dreamwork embodies our reawakened dreams for what our future might yet become.

I am aware that our use of a mutual imagination involves walking a very fine line. Imagination can be filled with wonder and vitality, but it can also be experienced as overwhelming and seductive, a promise that can never be fulfilled. In the erotic realm it can be particularly overwhelming, and I would not attempt it. As relational analysts we are aware that no one solution works for every dyad. But here I am suggesting that imagination and emergent fantasy do for some have the capacity to contain that delicate balance between gratification and disappointment; between provision and mourning. I am not Salina's mother; I am her heart mother. We can have our cottage, but we are both aware that said cottage is a figment; we don't need to say that to each other but it is clear that we both know. I cannot give Salina everything she needs and deserves, but I can give her some things that are precious to both of us. She can be disappointed in me without a psychic destruction of both of us.

Let me close on a note of hope, and what I consider a note of wonder. Over these years of my work with Salina my couch had grown shabby and threadbare. I knew how deeply attached Salina was to it, and so I spoke gently to her about the fact that someday soon I would have to replace it. Salina was inconsolable. She could not part with the couch upon which she had lain, hidden herself, buried herself—I had to keep it. I couldn't do that to her, she cried. I stalled. I put off the inevitable. I delayed a new purchase. But eventually other patients began to notice the state of my couch. Prospective new patients seemed to be (at least in my mind) eyeing the stuffing that was coming out of the worn material. Finally I bit the bullet, and bought a new couch, informing Salina that the couch would be delivered in two weeks' time. For two weeks Salina, cried, begged, and pleaded with me to keep the couch. I offered to let her take one of the small pillows home with her when it was time to have the couch removed. But this wasn't enough. Nothing would ever be the same. All safety would vanish with the couch. I felt despair as well. Was all of the progress we had made going to evaporate with the concrete removal of my, by now, dilapidated couch? Was this progress my own wish and not reality? Was I deluding myself into thinking that Salina and I had accomplished some very real therapeutic gains?

And then on the night before the couch was to be replaced, and following a particularly heart-wrenching session, I got a text from Salina. It read:

> HM! The most amazing thing has happened. It is too wonderful for words! The couch … Somehow it has appeared in the cottage. It is right there in front of the window and I am sitting on it right now! Isn't that incredible??

"It is amazing," I replied. "But it sounds like the absolutely perfect place for the couch. Let's keep it right there so we can sit on it together and look out the window at the wild flowers," I texted back to her.

Acknowledgment

I would like to dedicate this paper to Salina for her incredible courage and creativity, and for accompanying me on this most extraordinary journey.

Bibliography

Alvarez, A. (1992) Live Company: Psychoanalytic Psychotherapy with Autistic, Borderline, Deprived and Abused Children. London: Tavistock/Routledge.

Aron, L. (1996) A Meeting of Minds: Mutuality in Psychoanalysis. Hillsdale, NJ: The Analytic Press.

Aron, L. and Atlas, G. (2015) Generative enactment: Memories from the future. *Psychoanalytic Dialogues, 25,* 309–324.

Bass, A. (2015) The dialogue of unconsciouses, mutual and the uses of the self in contemporary relational psychoanalysis. *Psychoanalytic Dialogues,* 25, 2–17.

Benjamin, J. (2002). The rhythm of recognition: Comments on the work of Louis Sander, *Psychoanalytic Dialogues*, 12, 43–53.

Bion, W.R. (1963) Elements of Psychoanalysis. London: Heinemann.

Burton, N. (2012) Getting personal: Thoughts on therapeutic action through the interplay of intimacy, affect, and consciousness. *Psychoanalytic Dialogues,* 22, 662–678.

Cooper, S. (2000) Objects of Hope: Exploring Possibility and Limit in Psychoanalysis. Hillsdale, NJ: The Analytic Press.

Davies, J.M. (2005) Whose bad objects are we anyway? Repetition and our elusive love affair with evil. *Psychoanalytic Dialogues,* 14, 711–732.

Davies, J.M. (2006) The times we sizzle and the times we sigh: The multiple erotics of arousal, anticipation and release. *Psychoanalytic Dialogues,* 16(6), 665–686.

Davies, J.M. (2018) The "once and future" focus of a relational psychoanalysis: Discussion of Amy Schwartz-Cooney. *Psychoanalytic Dialogues,* 28(3), 355–360.

Davies, J.M. (2019) The "rituals" of relational psychoanalysis. *Psychoanalytic Dialogues,* 28(6), 651–669.

Davies, J.M. (in press) “How do we love thee?” *Psychoanalytic Dialogues.* A paper presented at the November, 2016 meeting of The Stephen Mitchell Center for Relational Studies, New York.

Director, L. (2016) The analyst as catalyst: Cultivating mind in the shadow of neglect. *Psychoanalytic Dialogues,* 26, 685–697.

Fairbairn, R.W. (1943) The repression and return of bad objects (with special reference to the war neuroses). *British Journal of Medical Psychology,* 19, 327–341.

Freud, S. (1905) Three essays on the theory of sexuality. *Standard Edition* 7, 125–243. London: Hogarth Press, 1953.

Freud, S. (1933) New introductory lectures on psychoanalysis. *Standard Edition* 22, 3–183. London: Hogarth Press, 1964.

Hoffman, I.Z. (1998) Poetic transformations of erotic experience: Commentary on paper by Jody Messler Davies. *Psychoanalytic Dialogues,* 8(6), 791–804.

Hoffman, I.Z. (2009) Therapeutic passion in the countertransference. *Psychoanalytic Dialogues,* 617–639.

Levine, L. (2016) A mutual survival of destructiveness and its creative potential for agency and desire. *Psychoanalytic Dialogues,* 26, 36–49.

Mitchell, S.A. (1997) Influence and Autonomy in Psychoanalysis. Hillside, NJ: The Analytic Press.

Morrison, A. (1989) Shame: The Underside of Narcissism. Hillsdale, NJ: The Analytic Press.

Schwartz Cooney, A. (2018) Vitalizing enactment: A relational exploration. *Psychoanalytic Dialogues,* 28(3), 340–354.

Stern, D. (2015) Relational Freedom: Emergent Properties of the Interpersonal Field. London: Routledge.

Chapter 8

Moving from within the maternal

The choreography of analytic eroticism[1]

Dianne Elise

In this chapter I describe the clinician's analytic activity as akin to that found in choreography, where the structuring of a dance or of a session each expresses an inner impulse brought into narrative form. The embodied art of dance is linked to the clinician's creative vitality in contributing to the shaping of the movement of a session within the analytic field. We know that the dance of psychoanalysis is not the creative product of the patient's mind alone. Clinical work invites—*requires*—a choreographic engagement by the clinician in interplay with that of the patient. The capacity for this interplay derives originally from *maternal eroticism* (Kristeva, 2014)—mother–child erotic reciprocity—the dance of the semiotic *chora.* A parallel engagement within the analytic dyad is conceptualized as *analytic eroticism* (Elise, 2017). The erotic is an important ingredient in vitalizing the clinical situation, a stimulus fueling the creative self of both the analyst and the patient.

I put forth the premise that psychoanalysis is an erotic project and propose that a creative aesthetic can provide a clinical container for the engagement and exploration of erotic life within the analytic field of each treatment (Elise, 2019). An atmosphere of libidinal energy is seen as a crucial aspect in enlivening the intersubjective field. When fully articulated as an energy potential in both participants, *analytic eroticism* can offer libidinal engagement within an ethical frame as a stimulus to emotionally embodied thinking—linking—that can lead to transformations in many dimensions, including the erotic. Maternal eroticism, as the libidinal vitality and investment that a mother brings to her fully embodied engagement with her child, is developed as a metaphor for clinical process. The analyst holds, contains, *and stimulates*; each of these capacities is mobilized in the service of a patient's growth. An intertwining of the erotic and the creative in the embodied, affective interaction of the analytic dyad allows for deepening contact with an authentic sense of being. In this chapter I offer extended case material from analytic work with a female patient who suffered from a deficiency of maternal eroticism.

The Eros of vitality

Foregoing the original professional aspiration to "scientific" objectivity, analysts recognize the unique unfolding of each treatment. Current conceptualizations of the analyst's role stress that an analyst is a co-participant in the creative unfolding of a dyadic conversation meant to further the development of the patient's capacities of mind toward increasing elaboration of personal meaning: "The patient's experience of *being creative* in the act of communicating is an essential part of the process … coming into being in a way that is uniquely his own" (Ogden, 2018, p. 401; see also Ferro and Civitarese, 2015). The analyst as well must engage in these acts of creativity. I believe our ability to do so is greatly served by a connection with our libidinal, embodied energies. This creative unfolding is each dyad's "work of art"—the aesthetic dimension (De Cortinas, 2009) of the therapeutic process—taking place within an analytic field.

Levine (2012) wrote that analysts must actively lend our abilities for creative linking to the co-construction of narrative meaning, giving imaginative form to that which a patient may not yet have access: "that form will only be shaped as a result of our analytic efforts" (p. 608). Such "acts of spontaneous, intuitive, internal emotional resonance and/or expression (feeling or imagining what the patient may not yet clearly feel or know)" (p. 613) "must first be created by a work that begins in the analyst's psyche and is then offered and inscribed in the psyche of the patient as part of an interactive, intersubjective relationship and process" (p. 626).

As Ogden, Ferro, and Civitarese each compellingly illustrate throughout their prolific work, the creative capacities of the analytic pair to imaginatively co-construct an aesthetic form give shape and meaning to personal experience. I emphasize that this analytic process is not solely to *contain*, as in the modulation and tolerance of affect, but to *elaborate* the symbolic capacities of the patient's mind that in the analytic setting will most often unfold in a narrative-building process. Analytic process can transform painful affect not primarily by naming, but through *the enlivening experience of creating that, in itself, promotes healing* and is thus an essential element of therapeutic progress.

Although interpretation can be a very powerful agent of psychic change, psychoanalysis is primarily about *invitation*—an invitation to a vital exchange and a meaningful narration of the self. Psychoanalysis is more than ameliorating distress; it is an ongoing process of expansion of the personality in many respects toward greater sense of personal vitality. Each analyst hopefully attempts to embody in a personal analytic style an approach to analytic process that catalyzes the healing potential of shared creation. By moving into a potential space of poetic ambiguity, creative imagination, and erotic vitality, we play with, and within, time and space in our relationship with each patient.

In thinking of my own clinical approach as a Winnicottian field theory (Elise, 2018, 2019), I am including in this model my specific emphasis on the erotic dimension of the psyche as the motive force by which creative potential is vitalized. Erotic vitality is a stimulus to creative expression that is itself further stimulating. *Erotic as the adjective of Eros* can be used to refer to embodied affective energies initially derived from the sexual impulse that include libidinal vitality, tempestuous passions, unruly urges, vigor, ardor, and a stimulating, vibrant frame of mind. Hopefully, a skillful, fluent, and creative inhabiting of what I conceptualize as *analytic eroticism* will expand the clinical container for the erotic as both a subject of analytic theorizing and as an experience within the treatment dyad. I emphasize that an invitation is issued to an embodied experience of maternal eroticism (Kristeva, 2014), where libidinal energy is enlivening—"vitalizing" (Alvarez, 2012)—the analytic field.

In the development of a child, a father's libidinal energy is certainly an important component (see Thomson-Salo & Paul, 2017). Males, like females, would internalize maternal eroticism and ideally would embody this quality within a masculine sense of self in their parenting and elsewhere. I am concentrating on the stimulus to the development of the child's libidinal self by being enveloped in an embodied, erotic relation with each parent, including in non-traditional parenting configurations. I am bringing attention to the *healthy* contribution of parental eroticism to a child's development, with pathology resulting from *deficiencies* in the parental erotic matrix.

Providing a calm, secure atmosphere ("holding") and modulating distress ("containing") are crucial parental capacities, yet in order to thrive, children also need stimulating engagements. I emphasize that the marked affect of parental response needed for the development of mentalization (Fonagy, 2008) rests upon libidinal energy in caretakers for a certain level of excited response to a child's excitement. Although I am highlighting the vitality and creativity stimulated through parent–infant erotic interplay, much regularly can and does go awry in parenting, as the vast psychoanalytic literature attests. My attention is to the advantages of ample maternal eroticism and to the problems stemming from a deficit—a deficit that cannot conceptually be reduced to a uniform expression but that must be understood to take form in an extensive range of manifestations that undermine the potential vitality of the child.

I suggest that Kristeva's concept of maternal eroticism is on a par in heuristic and clinical value with Winnicott's concept of maternal holding and with Bion's concept of maternal containment, both in understanding development in the early mother–infant relation and in the relevance that each of these formulations has for the technical approach of the analyst (Elise, 2019). Holding and containing are each highly developed metaphors conceptualizing the functioning of the analyst within the clinical process. I believe that similar theoretical work can be done in employing the concept of maternal eroticism to delineate an additional, equally salient capacity in the analyst within the analytic field: the analyst stimulates development. Maternal eroticism offers a metaphor for technique that can incorporate an analytic eroticism.

As Kristeva (2014) theorized, the semiotic *chora* may be understood as representing a space with potential, with the erotic as the "fuel" to personal creativity and aesthetic living. This potential is embodied and affectively lived through the mother–child dance of development that creates the aesthetic foundation. The semiotics of analytic eroticism permeated with libidinal energy and creative imagination provide an essential foundation in work with patients in whom early trauma has foreclosed or frozen the development of symbolic capacity. Certainly, the analyst's creative energies are not to be a substitute for the absence of such in a patient, but an enlivening contribution to the analytic encounter, even if, paradoxically, to narrate deadness and de-vitalization.

The dance of maternal eroticism

Just as photography captures and preserves a series of images, choreography creates and preserves a series of images of the human body in motion, infused with the vitality of libidinal energies. Clinically, when the creation of a symbolic narrative moves into the verbal while retaining this embodied, affective component, transformation of psychic pain is possible. The aesthetic capacity to keep this embodied vitality alive in the analytic relationship is the quality I refer to as analytic eroticism. In order to elaborate this formulation, I take up the concept of maternal eroticism presented by Kristeva (2014).

Kristeva (2014) offers an evocative pairing: "Reliance, or maternal eroticism." An intimate equivalence is suggested. The relationship between the two intrigues. Yet, *who* is it that relies on maternal eroticism? Kristeva indicates that a mother relies on her eroticism in mothering her child, but also that the child relies on the mother's eroticism in developing a vibrant sense of self. The encounter with the mother as erotic being brings into being the child's erotic self, both in the specifically sexual and in the most general sense: vitality in living, a curious and creative engagement with life—*eros*, rather than functional adaptation. We as a species rely on our inheritance of maternal eroticism as crucial to our humanity—a generational transmission of tantalizing tenderness and fierce passions in an embodied relationship with mother, with self, and with the world. This bequest is, I suggest, what we as clinicians—women and men—may hope to help each patient access and elaborate, as well as, necessarily, to contact in ourselves. In Kristeva's conceptualization of maternal eroticism, we find hints of an expanded understanding of what might be encompassed within the erotic life of the analytic couple.

Kristeva (2014) emphasizes that reliance does not mean maternal omnipresence, but is instead concerned with releasing "another living subject to the world" (p. 76) while "accompanying the living" (p. 78). The mother–infant dyad relies on circulating eroticism within their pairing—a force of life, a rhythmic pulsing that brings them together and sends them apart. A mother relies on her eroticism to *invest* in her baby and in its development *and* to turn her in directions of desire other than her child, setting a limit, a line between the two, allowing for a state of *emergence* from the stasis of a closed unit, and thus supporting the child's unique unfolding *as well as her own*. This dynamic pairing would ideally form the foundation for an experience of a couple relation that breathes—connecting in, releasing out, oscillating, but sustaining over time. Maternal capacity in this regard rests on an internalization of erotic vitality from her own mother (and father) that forwards her own unique trajectories in multiple directions.

As Kristeva states, the mother *holds*; she is not a passive by-stander; she stands by her child; she is committed. Without abandoning, she also needs to release any "hold" that would grip, constrict. Contact with her erotic self supports each of these activities that can seem to be opposing but are each essential to life—hers, the baby's, the couple's, the species'. The parental sexual couple must also be kept in view; maternal eroticism is not solely in relation to the child, for the child, but an aspect of a woman as a sexual being in fullness.

In this chapter, I hold to the *erotic* in maternal eroticism, which is not typically what comes to mind when thinking of an ethic of responsible care and concern. My focus is on the potentiating capacities of eroticism for the analytic dyad. Psychoanalytic theorizing seems to find it easier to stay with themes of tender attachment, violent attack, or the abject. We quickly lose any erotic rooting. In thinking about what maternal eroticism might mean for us as clinicians, we need to be able to envision how maternal eroticism materializes—in what ways it matters—between an actual mother and her child, and then between an analyst and patient.

As Kristeva so provocatively elaborates, an *erotic* environment exists between mother and baby. In these developmental beginnings, the relation with the mother provides a sensuous matrix—an aesthetic birthplace of movement, meaning, and shaping of the self. I have described the nursing couple as engaged in the first, primal act of intercourse, with breast-feeding sexually stimulating for infants of both sexes, as well as for the mother (Elise, 1998). In my work on maternal desire, I include the *mother's* desire and desire *for* the mother (Elise, 2002, 2015, 2019). Encountering the erotic beauty of the mother, the infant experiences an aesthetic world pulsating with energy and feels, with excitement, the resonating vibrations of its own psychesoma. Bodily movement is emotional life now given visible form in a mutual dance of desire.

Maternal eroticism is the affective atmosphere, the embodied vitality of this psychic space that, in Winnicottian (1971) terms, might be thought of as the "environmental mother," but is here conceptualized as alive with the erotic. An impulse to move rhythmically derives from maternal eroticism that libidinally energizes the mother–infant duet. Their sensual dance becomes the infant's first choreography, in the repetition and patterning of these expressive movements. This dancing already partakes of the mother's adult sexuality, albeit enigmatically (Laplanche, 1992), and is, for the infant, a full-bodied, nude embrace with excitation to every part of the mind and body, including genitally (Freud, 1905), that will form the template for the adult dance of sex.

As envisioned by Kristeva (2014), maternal eroticism is both a libidinal energy and a creative surround. This semiotic *chora* is a space for mutual creation within the maternal matrix, "womb," where the sensually embodied mother–infant interaction can be shaped reciprocally and given increasing symbolic form. This primary maternal preoccupation—the mother's preoccupation with the infant, as well as the infant's with the mother—should not be viewed reductively as a "symbiotic" relationship, but as a complex, mutual engagement leading to increasing individuation. Moving from within the maternal, a child eventually takes its first steps into the symbolic, a realm that is most meaningfully expressive when enlivened by semiotic motility.

I propose dance as paradigmatic of the semiotic and choreography as exemplifying a symbolic communication that retains its bodily, affective force. Dance gives shape to affective expression through embodied motion, e-motion. When patterned and available for recollection and reiteration, dance becomes choreography—an embodied narrative of emotional experience. Choreography is uniquely expressive of the transformations of the semiotics of dance into symbolic representation, where the link to affective embodiment remains intact: dance becomes symbolic narration without losing the libidinal energies of bodily motility alive in the *chora*.

I underscore that dance, with its primal beginnings, both pre- and postnatal, is the *most fully embodied* form of art, giving shape to affective life through movement. Each human starts out prenatally with mother as dance partner. Held in the embrace of the mother's swaying body, the prenatal infant is waltzed around the womb, set in motion, always accompanied by the rhythmic beat of the mother's heart, the song of her voice, even when she is not actually singing. The fetus eventually responds with a solo—a first kick, so exciting to the mother (and to the fetus?). Surely there must be, in this mother–infant duet, continuity from womb to the rocking embrace of mother's arms and lap, with nursing returning the baby to proximity with the musical beat of the mother's heart emanating from the depths of her body.

Torsti (2000) describes this "dance":

> At four months, the infant seems to begin a dreamy movement of the hand during breastfeeding,
>
> (p. 289)

> … In some children, this movement develops into an extensive plastic motion of the hand, dreamily and with a wide sweep … *As the infant grows, this movement may take on a dance-like form* … In my view, *in these movements the infant expresses its own, separately experienced kinesthetic image of itself; … The sweeping, dance-like movement forms a space for self-definition and draws the outline of the self.*
>
> (p. 290, emphasis added)

I am putting forth that this mother–infant dance *is* maternal eroticism, and that when maternal eroticism is foreclosed, the dance is as well. In contrast, when a *pas de deux* flourishes, these movements of the body-self evolve throughout development into increasingly complex "choreographies" that express personal creativity in the shaping of the self. Such dances unfold and gather form in repeated sequences—choreographies unique to that pairing, available for recall and to give meaning in a symbolic realm that expands beyond the verbal.

Choreography as artistic expression and as metaphor for clinical process

Dance as a creative art form is a lyrical language that uses the body to speak—a communication uniquely shaped to express deep feeling. In dance, one listens attentively to the music, actual or internal, and to how it moves you to move. A feeling is evoked by the music along with a wish to convey this feeling in bodily movement. Dance is an emotional process—a transference, one might say, to the music. From an internal impulse, one responds with a particular gesture and then another and another, out of the myriad of ways the human body can move, the multitude of possible steps. Finding certain movements that "fit" with an inner feeling in response to a registering of the particular qualities of the music, one develops these steps choreographically into recognizable, but varying, and increasingly complex, patterns.

Going beyond improvisation, in choreography one is conscious of building up a narrative, placing chosen steps in a refrain that can be recalled and revisited. We listen to each musical phrase repeatedly (as we each listen attentively to the "notes" of our patients), and gradually find and develop the movements that most express what we want to say with our body. An emotionally expressive communication is being shaped that can be made use of over time, returned to for further reflection; the process is like composing a symphony or crafting a poem, *and* it is like the narrative-building process of psychoanalysis.

With writing, one arranges words on paper in order to convey a compelling theme. As with writing, a "topic" suggested in dance by a piece of music engages us in a personal way and we find our theme to express in a structured sequence. Each of these creative expressions differs from improvising in that one will take much time to choreograph an intricate pattern—a creative sequencing of emotionally salient themes—that can be held in mind. A choreographed dance sequence gives creative expression to an emotional truth and is itself beauty. As with any art form, there is a mastered technique underlying the aesthetic expression of dance choreography.

Psychoanalysis has a richly developing literature on musical or dramatic improvisation as a metaphor for a clinical process. Such clinical exchanges of creative spontaneity in intersubjective engagement might be thought of as various artistic forms of a squiggle game (Winnicott,

1971). Adding to, and extending from, this literature, I make use of choreography specifically, rather than improvisation alone, as a metaphor for the psychoanalytic process of *creating symbolic narratives*.

As introduced above, my focus on the transformation of psychic pain through a dyadic capacity for narrative building and creative use of metaphor draws upon the work of Ogden (1997) and Civitarese and Ferro (2013), as well as upon the psychoanalytic theorizing of unrepresented states and deficits in the capacity to symbolize (Levine, Reed, & Scarfone, 2013). I bring my Winnicottian field theory approach to bear on my engagement with Kristeva's (2014) conceptualization of the erotic within the mother–infant relationship.

I specifically underscore the erotic as an important ingredient of the clinical situation—a lively spontaneity that partakes of the analyst's as well as the patient's creative self. In my emphasis on meaningful sequencing derived from two-person spontaneous improvising, I most especially want to retain, as is the case in dance, the connection to the erotic vitality that derives from maternal eroticism—embodied, and *moving*—both physically and emotionally. This perspective has implications for the psychoanalytic process, especially in the qualities of the activity of the analyst, as reflected in the analyst's person, presence, and personal creativity.

I suggest that a choreographic process takes place in productive clinical work, both in individual sessions and in the overall treatment arc. Our clinical narratives become verbal choreographies that need to retain affective resonance with bodies in motion. This "dance" of psychoanalysis derives from a choreographic engagement by the clinician in concert with that of the patient. A clinician cannot do this creative work without embodied responsiveness to the patient's "music"—the patient's verbal and non-verbal communications—and personal repertoire of "steps."

Even more challenging is the situation of working with a patient who is without music or movement—someone for whom maternal eroticism has failed and where the mother–infant dance has not developed. With such patients in whom symbolic representation is restricted or foreclosed, analytic eroticism is a crucial element in awakening both the analyst's and the patient's capacity for narrative meaning making. De Cortinas (2009) refers to this capacity for creative symbolization as the aesthetic dimension of the mind: "This dimension enlightens the crossroads between psychoanalysis, art and myth" (p. xxiii).

Clinical illustration: a still and arid landscape

When Sue, single and in her mid-30s, first sat across from me, my immediate reaction was a registering of a profound asexuality. I was quite surprised by this palpable feeling, as I do not tend to consciously assess people on a scale of sexuality. I tried to account for my reaction in her very bland appearance: pale coloring without make-up or jewelry, drab, shapeless clothing with skirts just below the knees; sitting with both feet planted squarely on the floor, Sue seemed neutral to the point of neutered. I had the image of someone a century ago from a farm in a "Great Plains" state. Yet clearly this visual image was the tip of the iceberg; something was wrong at a much deeper level, creating a feeling that something human was missing, frozen out, as if a lizard was coolly regarding me.

Sue reported that her childhood in a small town seemed "normal, uneventful; nothing much happened." Both parents had been accountants, as Sue now was; an older brother, a physicist, remains unmarried. Sue did not date during high school; descriptions of sex with a current boyfriend sounded mechanical, transactional. When exploring what had brought her to see me, she had difficulty getting affective hold of anything meaningful and vaguely offered, "something doesn't seem right … I want to get married." She seemed a female Mr. Spock (*Star Trek*) looking with perplexity at the emotional tribulations of the humans around her. Diagnostically, I thought in terms of schizoid mechanisms and the anti-libidinal self (Fairbairn, 1944).

Sue had recently seen another analyst for a few months, whom she described as "accounting for my childhood with a lot of ideas, but nothing came of it." Her word choice conveyed the absence of reciprocal stimulation, nothing consummated, coming alive. Sue experienced the analytic relationship as an intellectualized exchange between disembodied talking heads, accounting for things in a way that "didn't match up," reminiscent of her accountant parents who tallied numbers, but were not accountable for emotional engagement and bodily relation.

Over the next year or so, Sue reported details of her life as an accountant, describing problems at work, "numbers not lining up," in a deadening delivery that matched the content. Never have I been more challenged clinically to stay alert and engaged, recruiting my own vitality in what felt like a monumental effort on my part to enliven any of the material. I watched the clock inching along in five-minute increments, during what would seem like an infinity of time. Nevertheless, I did manage in most sessions to pull something together from this void of material, linking her recitation to what felt to me to be a more affectively enlivening connection, between thoughts, and between Sue and me. I was feeling both relieved, and a bit amazed, that this could be accomplished and fairly pleased with my ability to make something of her flat, arid presentation.

Then, at one point, things came to a complete dead halt and I asked Sue how she was feeling with me. She responded in a very direct and matter-of-fact way: "You seem quite depressed." I was quite stunned by this pronouncement and rendered speechless for a few moments until I managed to ask gently what her ideas were about the source of my depression.

Sue: (silent for several moments) "Maybe you lost a child."

After another pause, I inquired: "Lost?" and Sue replied: "You know, … dead." We were both quiet for several minutes, taking in this exchange. I then softly commented: "There is a dead baby and a depressed mother; it's not clear which happened first." Sue was quiet for the last few moments of this session. The next day she went back to describing the challenges of accounting.

I palpably feel that I am an analyst, woman, mother who cannot keep her baby alive. I start to have an image of the couch on which Sue is lying as a sterile, metal incubator, almost a cage, where conditions would meet requirements for maintaining life support, but nothing more. Nothing soft or warm is provided that would meet or awaken sensual needs. There is no mother, no nursing couple, no erotic duet that would ever lead to a full-bodied dance of adult sexuality. I too am hard and sterile, inanimate, no flesh, no breasts, no sexuality. I experience myself as the "wire mother monkey" so familiar to those in our field from the Harlow (1959) studies. Clinically, I realize that I need to inhabit this transference–countertransference situation of deadness and dehumanization, *while at the same time holding on to my analytic eroticism as a latent capacity in my embodied, feeling self.* I will need to wait for an opportunity where I can call up this aspect of my person and of my analytic presence in order to introduce it to my patient in a manner that she might be able to register and digest.

Feeling that a scientific study might pique her interest, I ask Sue if she has heard of the Harlow monkey study. She reads a science journal and I think that she might have come across a reference to it. She replies: "Maybe, but I don't recall."

Proceeding quite slowly, gently, with the cadence and tones of telling a story to a latency-age child, I relate the set-up of the study where the baby monkey, in a cage, is presented with both a wire mesh "mother" with a bottle of milk attached and with a cloth "mother" with no milk.

> Analyst: What do you imagine the baby monkey did?
> Patient: I don't know; I've never had a pet before ... Well it would need the milk, but it probably wouldn't know what to do with that other one.

In her phrasing, "I've never had a pet *before"* is an intimation that I have just given Sue her *first* pet, and with it the chance to mother and be mothered, to pet and be petted, with such petting as foreplay to adult sexuality. She had never had a pet, or a pat, from her mother; she was not petted; no breast mother exists. In giving her a pet, I am introducing maternal erotic energies—mine and the potential for hers—in the experience of touching and being touched, emotionally as well as physically. In my feeling tone and rhythm of telling the "story," the poignancy of the baby monkey's plight is brought to life, as in a ballet. I now begin to feel that in the patient I have a human infant—one who needs an intravenous drip of maternal eroticism, an infusion of vitality into an infant who does not yet know what to do with the flesh-and-blood mother holding her. Previously I had been either the wire mother with my intellectual "formula," or the cloth mother who did not have any recognizable "food."

In my introducing a "baby" for the two of us—"our pet"—and a symbolic blanket for the couch, the incubator cage and wire mother begin to transform; something starts moving; our bodily selves engage.

Ours is not just a story creation *about* (missing) maternal eroticism, but an experience developing from within the analyst's own expression *of* maternal eroticism—"the medium as the message," matching and enlivening the content. Now relational space opens for us to develop our dance of embodied relation to one another, supporting our continuing quest for affective meaning. Although the verbal content of our exchanges is the easier to identify and report, much is taking place kinesthetically in our unfolding relationship.

Time passes and one day Sue is describing a film:

> Patient: It had a lesbian sex scene …
> Analyst: Your reactions?
> Patient: (long pause) Lots of breasts.

This rather odd statement gives rise in my mind to Picasso-esque images of disjointed female figures. I am not sure if "lots of breasts" represents a positive or negative image for the patient. In exploring her feelings, Sue becomes able to articulate a feeling that she has not previously "encountered" breasts: "I don't think of my mother as having breasts. I don't relate to having breasts myself; what are they there for? They seem in the way, extraneous." Her mother's sexual body is seen in dislocated, confusing images, where human parts are not assembled in any recognizable manner; sexuality does not "come together." There is an acute sense of not being of the human species—not *mammalian*—that conveys the absence of eroticism from the outset in relation to her mother's psyche-soma and her own.

In contrast, in the film scene, the sexual engagement of two women allows for the opportunity to both suck and to be suckled, an erotic mouth–nipple contact which is genitally stimulating to each partner, unfolding into a full sexual experience—a coming together. As Sue and I absorb the images of this scene, and attune to them over time in our verbal and non-verbal communication, a space opens for a sexual sense of self. In our dyad, this development was not expressed as conscious erotic desire *for* the other (as in traditional conceptualizations of erotic transference–countertransference), but as two women who can each embody erotic vitality individually and in a more lively engagement with one another. Sue starts to come alive as a woman who has breasts.

Her analyst begins to take form as an erotic woman with breasts and a sexuality—a woman whose erotic connection with her baby will not only keep the baby alive, but ensure that she thrives and can mate/matter/mother.

> Patient: You have breasts.
> Analyst: Does that seem to offer any possibilities?
> Patient: I think so; I'm not sure about it.

Paradoxically, our dance of maternal deprivation shapes the beginning of our connection, offering an invitation to vitality, an "*invitalization*" of the analytic relationship. This vitalization (Alvarez, 2012) of the clinical situation—a libidinal force field—constitutes the expanded meaning of erotic transference–countertransference that I have in mind, where both patient and analyst engage their erotic energies and where this engagement is not specific to (though it may include) erotic desire for the other. While becoming more erotically alive with one another, Sue and I choreograph, slowly with much repetition, an embodied narrative of missing mothers and deadened babies.

What I had, in the initial months of the analysis, hoped to inject into the analytic atmosphere had gone unrecognized by Sue: my libidinal energy was accessible to me, but she had no "receptor sites." I begin to name the problem in my introducing the character of the motherless monkey. My affective telling of the study eventually leads to the possibility of an intercourse between us as suggested in the lesbian sex scene; breasts make an appearance in the patient's psychic life. We are now warm-blooded mammals who can become hot-blooded sexual beings. Gradually Sue develops the awareness regarding her relational beginnings with her mother that "something was probably left out—skipped." Things are warming up for us on the dance floor.

Over the next many months, small steps are taken by Sue that show up in timid changes in her appearance, with spots of color appearing both in clothing and in make-up, reflective of a brightening of her personality. One day she comes in looking very appealing, pretty even, in a lively print skirt that is now above the knee and swirling with movement, as is her now longer, curlier hair. Viewing this transformation is like watching a withered branch that suddenly springs to life in a profusion of blooms after a long winter. Something is budding: Sue announces that she is going to a salsa class.

Ours is a small choreography—a minuet—carefully danced, and tentative, though not tepid. Although our duet shows no signs of turning into a torrid tango or a passionate *pas de deux*, it is emotionally meaningful to the two of us, full of poignant, painful feeling about missed opportunities, in a way that previously could not be narrated or even known. I certainly do feel more of the energies of my own creative activity in my engagements with other patients and more rewarded by the intricacies of other duets and the opportunities afforded therein. With Sue I do not experience the thrill of a more intricately choreographed sequence possible with other patients who, even with areas of symbolic failure, bring much more of their own liveliness and creativity to our encounter.

Yet, it is especially with deadened patients that analytic eroticism is so vital an element, breathing life and dimensionality into a flat landscape. With Sue, I initially had the experience of approaching a woman who was more wall than wall-flower. Something was in need of being brought into life—to become animate, before animated—in order to even invite her out on to the dance floor. Kristeva (2014) emphasizes that maternal eroticism involves libidinal stamina to stand by one's commitment to another—"a refusal to collapse" (p. 77) in one's concern for and "care of the living" (p. 77) and heretical in its claim as ethical care. I propose a parallel heresy within the clinical situation.

Analytic ardor: the heretical ethics of the analyst's eroticism

The Harlow (1959) studies on attachment demonstrated that, in a choice between provisions of food or softness, sensuality wins out. The long-term import of being without the erotic presence of a live mother is not apparent until it is noted that none of these monkeys at maturity could mate. I underscore that the babies could not "mate," matter, with their actual mothers as a nursing couple in a full-bodied, skin-to-skin, "dance." We note the shared root of the words *mater*, matter, and mate, yet can lose that maternal erotic connection in a desexualized understanding of attachment and early object relations, with sexuality sequestered in the province of the oedipal. In the actuality of the mother–infant bond, the infant's erotic body is "mapped" (Laplanche, 1992) by the sensuous care of the mother, derived from her own embodied eroticism and sexuality (Freud, 1905).

For Sue, instead of *enigmatic* signifiers (Laplanche, 1992), the signifiers were *absent* and there was no encounter with the enigma of human sexuality as presented in the maternal matrix. As an adult, Sue, like her brother, was having trouble mating. Psychoanalytic theorizing has been having trouble mating sexuality with early object relations (Elise, 2019); clinicians may themselves be walled off from the "enigma variations" of the erotic that encompass the evolutions of both the semiotic and the symbolic, the preoedipal and the oedipal. I believe that Kristeva's (2014) perspective, building on Freud and Laplanche, illuminates the infusion of the erotic throughout development and into what is seemingly other than sexual: "It falls to us to create new metapsychological concepts in order to develop—by paying attention to the sexuality of the lover—the elucidation and support of maternal eroticism, in all its specificity" (p. 82).

In working with Sue, I could not rely solely on my intellectual knowledge of child development gone awry, using analytic theory to form interpretations; we would have remained at a *stale*-mate where intellects cannot create anything alive to break up the deadness of the non-interchange. The situation was not one of *re*vitalizing, but of newly vitalizing. An absence of the analyst's erotically embodied vitality as the core, *chora*, of analytic activity would undermine the potential to create together a symbolic narrative with emotional salience. I needed to actively contribute my own creative sensibilities to the effort to symbolize a narrative choreography with the patient that could speak to her unnamed, and as yet unnamable, problem.

I believe that this type of energy with its erotic substrate is what analysts frequently call upon in clinical work; otherwise, less progress would be made. My intent is to *make this erotic, energic component explicit in theorizing a clinical technique*, rather than left as tabooed, neglected, or cordoned off into a narrow conceptualization "erotic countertransference." Maternal eroticism is introduced clinically through the aesthetic overture of analytic eroticism. This sensory/semiotic dance evolves into a choreographic capacity for symbolic expression, not as dry abstraction, but as genuine emotional experience embedded in embodied eroticism. If it seems heretical to claim an erotic component in ethical analytic presence, *why* is this the case? Can we speak of an analytic ardor?

Kristeva's (2014) conceptualization of maternal eroticism led her to posit a heretical ethics of maternal care: "To live and to think the maternal as *erotic*, wouldn't that be as provocative as infantile sexuality?" (p. 69). Yet, I believe that Kristeva's culminating choice of descriptors—such as "care," "concern," "love," and "tenderness"—will likely be settled upon by readers who wish to comfortably retreat from the provocation of the erotic. Paraphrasing Kristeva, I propose in parallel formation: to live and to think the *analytic* as erotic, wouldn't *that* be provocative?

If we could overcome obstacles to analytic eroticism, we might then consider in what ways psychoanalysis is *itself* an erotic project. We are besieged with lamentable examples of the destructive aspects of erotic desire in the treatment relationship—sexual boundary violations—leading, I believe, to a heightened sense of fear in clinicians about engaging the erotic, their patients' and their own (Elise, 2019). Keeping Kristeva's sensibilities near, how might we think of eroticism as constructive to a treatment? Can analytic eroticism actually "hold" the clinical couple?

Analysts tend to focus predominantly on the patient's libidinal attachment to the analyst in the transference. Yet what of the analyst's excitement, not altruism or duty, in contributing to the development of a person—the clinician's libidinal investment in that unique patient, in that analysis? An analysis cannot rest on the patient's libidinal energies alone. We might, instead, think of erotic energy as circulating in multiple directions in the intersubjective field of an analysis—a libidinally alive matrix. Often viewed *solely* as problematic countertransference (which it certainly can be), the analyst's erotic energy has the potential to be a healing ingredient necessary for the analytic process. A clinical situation of vibrancy can foster patients' increased libidinal investments in *themselves,* not just in the analyst. If our creative self, imbued with our libidinal being, is not actively contributing to the unfolding of the clinical process and narrative, the analysis is deprived of the life force of the erotic.

How might an ongoing reflection on, and self-inquiry into, our erotic life effect a subtle shift in the self we each bring to the consulting room? Can we allow for more of the full palette of *our* psyche within the clinical venture rather than being restricted to a pale version of one's self? The "blank screen" is itself a "colourless canvas"—the metaphor used by Levine (2012) to describe the psychic emptiness of patients suffering from failures in symbolic representation. Both images—screen and canvas—convey a two-dimensional flatness, stasis, and neutral shading. In offering a conceptualization of an analytic eroticism, I am speaking of *analytic vitality*, rather than neutrality. I want to shift the metaphor of a blank screen—analyst as subdued, almost erased figure—to a more colorful image, moving analytic "function" from abstinence to sustenance, a quality of aliveness in the analyst that is sustaining, rather than a re-presentation of a deadened mother.

Contemporary conceptualizations that describe the analyst's activity in contributing to the development of a symbolic narrative emphasize the analyst's use of her own mind to generate imagery as a key component in helping patients who are limited in this ability. Analysts do not solely "read the text" presented by a patient in any given session. Yet, as Harris (2014) astutely points out, in order to be curative, our verbal narrations in the clinical encounter must be grounded in embodied experience and alive with that which is "outside the sentence" (p. 1030) by calling on "our receptivity to the sensuous, embodied aspects of speech and communication" (p. 1030) in order to create "some of the most salient and mutative moments in treatments" (p. 1031).

Writing on the acquisition of language in children, Call (1980) stated: "Some of the most important messages sent between people are beyond words. The poet and creative writer utilize language to create images and to define the wordless territory of subjective experience" (p. 261). De Cortinas (2009) similarly noted: "The adults that have the faculty of using one or many of these lost sensitivities are the ones that are specially gifted, such as composers, musicians, and dancers" (p. 11). Analysts must also utilize language in this artful way, going beyond, beneath, and before the word. I suggest that analysts become dancers. (This should be no more challenging than the things we ask of our patients.)

We see that not only do analysts contribute to narrative representation in the symbolic realm, such activity must be registered within *the analyst's*, not solely the patient's, embodied affective responsiveness. This capacity in the analyst is an important ingredient in *all* treatments, wherever a given patient might be—frozen or flowing—in relation to this aesthetic dimension of the mind (see de Cortinas, 2009). We are not the audience to our patients; we need to feel the rhythm, the emotion, the motion, and to co-choreograph a series of movements into a ballet that can be meaningful for many years to come. Even patients with well-developed symbolic capacities—quite capable of dancing and choreographing—want and need an analytic partner who can both follow *and take the lead.* This reciprocal bodily and affective engagement presents a different image of what analysts are doing clinically from the typical conception of providing "a container."

I propose that it is the erotic that contains, unites the container and the contained, vitalizing the field of clinical engagement. We are connected by, and within, a libidinal matrix. If not, something vital, embodied, is missing. I highlight the activity of the analyst derived from her erotic self—an inner vibration, a vibrance, a poised alertness, just as a dancer in standing still on stage is poised, not passive, at the ready, full of potential movement, momentum. These are desirable qualities in a clinician. We cannot expect to foster the development of healthy passions in our patients without these aspects of self palpably alive and embodied in *our* presence in the clinical encounter. We are poised receptivity, not a receptacle: we act, respond, and not solely from an intellectualized theory but out of our own embodied, ardent energies—something of the alive moment, momentous.

We tune in to certain strands of feeling that catch our attention, move us to move in a particular manner: to jump in, or sit quietly, to speed up or slow down the rhythm of the session, to develop a theme or motif based on our intuitive leap—striding ahead, circling back, becoming more expansive or carefully balanced, tiptoeing. Sometimes we are still, but still "dancing." Might our analytic container be a womb of conception, a dance of gestation and delivery, where an analyst's embodied *eros* pairs with, and facilitates, a patient's ability to feel and express her own personal rhythm?

This ability to improvise from a spontaneous impulse and then to productively shape an emotionally evocative narrative, rich in symbolic meaning, is a choreographic capacity developed in the patient that can then be carried forward out of the consulting room and into life. Such clinical choreographies will need to be works in progress, repeatedly shaping communications that incrementally reach their affective mark with a patient who can feel within the analytic situation the rhythmic flow and movement of the analyst's eroticism as well as his or her own. This creative endeavor of the dyad, sustained and developed over time, promotes confidence, tenacity, and even courage, *in both patient and analyst*. Each member in the clinical dyad must dance to this primal mother–child rhythm in order that either, and hopefully both, can develop and grow.

Winnicott (1971) wrote that it is "creative apperception more than anything else that makes the individual feel that life is worth living" (p. 65). Freud (1915) had posited: "Sexual love is undoubtedly one of the chief things in life, … one of its culminating peaks" (p. 169). Might we think of the two intertwined—creativity and sexuality—as that which makes *psychoanalysis worth doing*, for both analyst and patient—a spirited union of bodily and psychic engagement. Creating is how we feel engaged. I doubt that analysts could bear to do analytic work if it did not elicit our creative engagement. The analyst has the reward and the fulfillment of developing her own personal expression rather than following a theoretical and technical script. This creative use of self is our gift to each patient and the gift of psychoanalysis to each analyst. It is the path by which our work life becomes richer, more vital, over the years, rather than routinized into a dulling repetition.

Although historically, analysts have tended to think of patients as shaping the hour, leaving the analyst to interpret what is presented, I believe that analysts are now becoming increasingly aware of how our own creative force shapes a session. Patients often say, "I had no idea we would be talking about this today"; they are correct. A patient typically begins with a direction consciously in mind, but the analyst may take the lead in a direction unanticipated by either. Their combined creative interplay has the potential to develop a meaningful theme that can gather momentum through that session and beyond. Yet clinicians often continue to try to master increasingly more sophisticated theoretical conceptualizations in the hopes of gaining an ability for more astute technical interventions. Though likely acknowledged tacitly, less attention is given to the idea that developing one's talent as an analyst might involve something ambiguous, intuitive, artistic—something that cannot be taught by or learned from an expert, but only found within one's unique being.

In the analytic space, the analyst needs to dance in the place of expressive movement in order to foster the same in a patient. Otherwise, one might be encouraging spontaneous gestures (Winnicott, 1971) in a patient, but not in contact with them in oneself—a "do as I say, not as I do" model of psychoanalysis. An analyst's capacity to relate within and through a personally creative modality provides a particular environment that supports the patient's access to her own creative self. Such creative aliveness allows one to dance on the tiptoes of a spontaneous melody, living life to the fullest, with passion and zest.

Conclusion

I have proposed that we think of analytic eroticism as stimulating, a stimulus—providing for both patient and analyst a flexible foundation, a springboard with movement, motility, momentum (see also Elise, 2015). As with a diving board, there is give and take. It is flexible and firm, something to bounce off, as well as into. Envision those exquisitely anticipatory steps the diver takes in intimate, kinesthetic relation with the board, that bounding leap into and away from, up into space, outward (swan dive as aerial dance), and then back down into the deep, only to surface again and have another go. There would be no diver without that board, no diving board without the diver—mutual reliance.

Invoking maternal eroticism, with its analytic counterpart, we can envision an expansive exuberance—the ongoing creation of a sensually based atmosphere in which we imaginatively experience our bodily and psychic selves, our minds. This lusty experience of being in the world extends beyond the maternal orbit and beyond the purely sexual to a more general *joie de vivre*, a passion for life in its ups *and downs*. This is of course an ideal picture of what we might hope to be the case, yet often is not. Then we see patients, like Sue, presenting with familiar problems of depression, meaninglessness—loss of joy, vitality, eagerness, and responsiveness. The "diving board" is now just a flat object with no spring; it cannot be made use of; it seems useless to try, indicative of a deadened versus creative relation to the self and one's objects.

Drawing upon the choreography of dance, I have linked this art form with a clinician's creative impulse in shaping the movement of a session. This clinical investment and responsiveness, expressing the unique libidinal connection and excitement of an analytic couple, I refer to as *analytic eroticism*. The aesthetic dimension of the mind must be rooted in the erotic dimension of the body. The *capacity* to choreograph or compose—in art, in psychoanalysis, in life—requires a confidence in personal expression to give shape to one's inner feeling through creative impulse, spontaneous gesture. I have described how such expressive confidence may greatly increase the effectiveness of the work and the personal reward for both patient and clinician. Each partner in this duet gains increasing access to her own choreographic capacities. When both participants are in the realm of personal creativity, together they co-create the unique choreography of that analysis, allowing the patient eventually to dance her own life.

Note

1 This chapter is based on my 2017 published paper, "Moving from within the Maternal: The Choreography of Analytic Eroticism," *Journal of the American Psychoanalytic Association,* 65: 33–60.

References

Alvarez, A. (2012). *The thinking heart: Three levels of psychoanalytic therapy with disturbed children.* London: Routledge.

Call, J.D. (1980). Some prelinguistic aspects of language development. *Journal of the American Psychoanalytic Association*, 28: 259–289.

Civitarese, G., Ferro, A. (2013). The meaning and use of metaphor in analytic field theory. *Psychoanalytic Inquiry,* 33: 190–209.

De Cortinas, L.P. (2009). *The aesthetic dimension of the mind.* London: Karnac.

Elise, D. (1998). Gender repertoire: Body, mind and bisexuality. *Psychoanalytic Dialogues,* 8: 379–397.

Elise, D. (2002). Blocked creativity and inhibited erotic transference. *Studies in Gender and Sexuality*, 3: 161–195.

Elise, D. (2015). Eroticism in the maternal matrix. Infusion through development and the clinical situation. *fort da*, 21(2): 17–32.

Elise, D. (2017). Moving from within the maternal: The choreography of analytic eroticism. *Journal of the American Psychoanalytic Association*, 65: 33–60.

Elise, D. (2018). A Winnicottian field theory: Creativity and the erotic dimension of the analytic field. *fort da*, 24(1): 22–38.

Elise, D. (2019). *Creativity and the erotic dimensions of the analytic field*. London: Routledge.

Fairbairn, W.D. (1944). Endopsychic structure considered in terms of object relationships. *International Journal of Psychoanalysis*, 25: 70–92.

Ferro, A., Civitarese, G. (2015). *The analytic field and its transformations*. London: Karnac.

Fonagy, P. (2008). A genuinely developmental theory of sexual enjoyment and its implications for psychoanalytic technique. *Journal of the American Psychoanalytic Association*, 56: 11–36.

Freud, S. (1905). Three essays on the theory of sexuality. *The Standard Edition*, 7: 130–243. London: Hogarth Press, 1953.

Freud, S. (1915). Observations on transference love (further recommendations on the technique of psycho-analysis III). *The Standard Edition*, 12: 157–171. London: Hogarth Press, 1953.

Harlow, H. (1959). Love in infant monkeys. *Scientific American* (June) 201: 68–74.

Harris, A. (2014). Curative speech: Symbol, body, dialogue. *Journal of the American Psychoanalytic Association*, 62: 1029–1045.

Kristeva, J. (2014). Reliance, or maternal eroticism. *Journal of the American Psychoanalytic Association*, 62: 69–85.

Laplanche, J. (1992). *Seduction, translation, drives*. London: Institute of Contemporary Arts.

Levine, H. (2012). The colourless canvas: Representation, therapeutic action and the creation of mind. *International Journal of Psychoanalysis*, 93: 607–629.

Levine, H., Reed, G., Scarfone, D. (eds.) (2013). *Unrepresented states and the construction of meaning*. London: Karnac Books.

Ogden, T.H. (1997). Reverie and metaphor: How I work as a psychoanalyst. *International Journal of Psychoanalysis*, 78: 719–732.

Ogden, T.H. (2018). How I talk with my patients. *The Psychoanalytic Quarterly*, 87: 399–413.

Thomson-Salo, F., Paul, C. (2017). Understanding the sexuality of infants within caregiving relationships in the first year. *Psychoanalytic Dialogues,* 27: 320–337.

Torsti, M. (2000). At the sources of the symbolization process: The psychoanalyst as an observer of early trauma. *Psychoanalytic Study of the Child,* 55: 275–297.

Winnicott, D.W. (1971). *Playing and reality*. London: Tavistock Publications.

Chapter 9

Vitalization as a case-specific emergent process

Steven Stern

The concept of vitalization (or enlivenment) put forth for consideration by Amy Schwartz Cooney and Rachel Sopher in this volume, and their work which inspired it (Schwartz Cooney, 2018; Sopher, 2018), falls within a broad and welcome trend in contemporary relational theory and practice—one that recognizes the analyst's active role in the co-creation of new, needed relational experience. I have long believed there is a forward-tending dimension of both the analyst's conscious and unconscious participation in the analytic exchange—a dimension that responds to the patient's unique needs and implicit aims for the treatment (Stern, 1994, 2007, 2009, 2017a, 2021). Ultimately, I believe every fully engaged treatment calls forth uniquely personal responses and affective provisions from the analyst that are progressively fitted (Sander, 2008) to what the analyst senses the patient needs in order to move both inward and forward in their therapeutic journey. More recently, an expanding group of relational and intersubjective authors have proposed a range of ways of thinking about this more personally engaged, forward-tending dimension of the analyst's participation and the (conscious and unconscious) analytic dialogue (e.g., Aron & Atlas, 2015, Atlas & Aron, 2018; Boston Change Process Study Group, 2013; Davies, 2018; Grossmark, 2012; Hoffman, 2009; Stolorow, 2014; Tolpin, 2002).

The concepts of vitalization and "vitalizing enactment" (Schwartz Cooney, 2018) emerge from and creatively expand this developing trend in relational theory. Contemplating these concepts set in motion (for me) a swirling sequence of questions and paradoxes, which tells me that they represent a generative area for thought in our current psychoanalytic moment:

- Are only certain patients lacking in vitality/aliveness, or, as Ogden (1997) has suggested in his book-length consideration of the issue, is this a feature of all or most patients who are in need of intensive analytic treatment?
- Are "vitalizing interventions" a specific class or form of analyst participation, or, again, following Ogden (1997), are we always seeking to somehow facilitate movement toward greater aliveness, both within the therapeutic interaction and in the patient?
- Is vitalization something we intentionally seek to bring about, or is it a transformation that emerges from unpredictable, unique movements in the intersubjective field that are made possible by our more general, highly complex orientation to the analytic process and our intuition of what the patient (or the process) needs from us in a given moment, session, or period of the work?
- If we find ourselves inhabiting states of boredom, disengagement, deadness, or the like in a session or over longer periods, do we work to re-find a sense of vitality or "stay with" the deadness that *is* happening, with the faith that our personal, or the relational, unconscious will ultimately yield some emergence of meaning or aliveness "within" or "from" the deadness?

Interestingly, the two papers that provided the inspiration for this book—Schwartz Cooney's (2018) paper on vitalizing enactment and Sopher's (2018) paper, "An allegience to absence: Fidelity to the internal void"—together contain both sides of the paradox. Schwartz Cooney is more focused on the analyst's initiation of case-specific forms of intentionally vitalizing intervention, whereas Sopher's focus, more in the spirit of Ogden (1997), is on emergence from repetitive enactments in which the analyst finds herself participating in the patient's active, unconscious perpetuation of internal absence and deadness. Through the analyst's reverie process, and reconnection with her own history with absent objects, a new space opens for connection and aliveness that is not immediately and automatically undone.

My own effort to delineate a general clinical methodology under the rubric of *the co-creation of needed analytic relationships* (Stern, 2017a) suggests a both/and, dialectical or paradoxical solution to these questions set in motion by the concepts of vitalization and enlivenment.

My approach emphasizes the uniqueness, and the unique complexity, of the evolving needed relationship with each patient—a uniqueness that simultaneously transcends theory while potentially making use of multiple theories or frames of reference as "selected" by a given case and the present analytic moment. Thus, for example, Schwartz Cooney (2018), influenced by Alvarez (2012), has introduced a new theoretical frame of reference with her construct of "vitalizing enactment"—a construct with a number of conceptual and clinical dimensions which, in her hands, proved to be transformative in the case she describes in her paper. Because of my tendency to privilege the uniqueness of every patient and analytic dyad, I would not assume that I could directly or fully apply this new frame of reference, as construed by Schwartz Cooney in the context of her specific work with her patient, in the context of my work with a different patient. However, I could easily imagine that, in my work with a different patient, my *take* on Schwartz Cooney's construct could *emerge as an inspirational element* in a given moment or period of work with a patient who seemed to share certain characteristics with the kinds of patient she was focusing on in her paper.

This may seem to amount to my simply making explicit the way many contemporary relationally oriented analytic clinicians think of themselves as working—that is, making selective use of, and creatively integrating, multiple theories and frames of reference as a given case seems to evoke or require. The reason I make a point of it in this context is that, for me, the process of vitalization begins with the presumption of uniqueness in every case and my belief that, in effect, we need to generate a *uniquely vitalizing theory of therapeutic action with each patient*, which is shaped by non-linear processes in the dyadic system over time, leading to progressive "specificity of recognition and connection" (Sander, 2008). At the same time, our assimilation and use of multiple pre-existing analytic theories and frames of reference, such as Schwartz Cooney's theory of vitalizing enactments, or Ogden's (1997) more general approach to the emergence of deadness/aliveness in the transference–countertransference relationship, *are* what enables us to locate our patients analytically and generate (co-create) the necessary specificity of recognition and connection that makes vitalizing interactions possible. What we already know provides the necessary substrate for engaging that which is new and not yet known, and for generating a needed response.

Cooney is aware of and holds the paradox I am describing in her understanding of vitalizing enactments. She emphasizes that they are not techniques, but rather “relational events” that arise uniquely and creatively in response to a certain kind of analytic impasse. Even so, there is always the problem with any theoretical model, including one that I might generate, of its taking on a categorical existence that would cause one to have thoughts such as: is my patient suffering from the same kind of inner deadness that Schwartz Cooney’s or Alvarez’ patients were? Is what I did today with my patient a vitalizing enactment in the sense that Cooney means it, or was it something else? If I can’t see its roots in my own traumatic history with “deadened objects,” will it be missing something essential? A question, therefore, that has seemed increasingly interesting to me is how we hold such constructs and models such that they help us without interfering with the vitality of our own creative and co-creative processes with each patient (Stern, 2017a). Or, to state it differently: what is the right “level of abstraction” for abstracting from one clinical context into another (Stern, 2021)?

The patient I have chosen to illustrate the emergence of unique (case-specific) forms of vitalization is characterologically very different, at least “on the surface,” from the patient (and type of patient) Schwartz Cooney wrote about in her paper. He is not the empty, disconnected, unformed, or “undrawn” (Alvarez, 2012) patient, which Schwartz Cooney focuses on as in need of vitalizing forms of participation from the analyst. In many respects he is one of the most alive, engaged, and *enlivening* people I have ever known. But, at a different level, he is not fully alive to his inner life—his traumatized, abandoned “child self”—and, as a result, lives a subtly isolated, half-deadened existence that no one, including himself, knew about until he stumbled into analysis.

Sam and me[1]

Now in our 10th year of working together, it took Sam and me a long time to understand the totality of his dissociative self-organization. It has always been a mystery to me how some children have the precocity to grasp the realities of their early relational worlds and devise often-ingenious strategies of psychic survival. Sam's mother died of cancer when he was 3, leaving him in the care of his financially successful but mildly sociopathic, pleasure-seeking, sometimes impulsive father who remarried three times during Sam's childhood and adolescence. This meant that Sam had *no parental*, let alone maternal, figure to help him cope with the overwhelming trauma of the loss of his mother. Thus he sensed at an early age that not only could his father not be relied on to recognize or attend to his emotional needs, *he* would have to be the one to watch after his father because, whatever his father's shortcomings, he was "the only person who stood between me and oblivion." Sam also understood very early that the closest he would come to having his own needs met was to be sure to protect, and take care of the needs of those on whom he depended; and later, the needs of those who depended on him. For example, a memory that stands out was the night, at age 8 or 9, Sam had to hold and calm his father, who was having a bad drug trip. He also became a confidant to several of his stepmothers, who would tell him about their problems with his father.

Sam, in short, developed a hyper-competent, hyper-vigilant self-organization he calls his "exoskeleton." His exoskeleton can walk into any business meeting and size up both the motivations behind, and financial ramifications of, anything he might be presented with, then quickly and instinctively figure out how to position himself in such a way as to secure enough positive gain for himself while remaining respectful of the needs of his "counterparties," wanting everyone to leave feeling they had gotten something. He is a business genius, but it's very important to him not to be unscrupulous like his father. He describes himself as a "capacitor": judiciously building enough resources to take care of himself, those he loves, and the many people from the community who come to him for advice or help of one kind or another.

Sam and I know that inside his capacitor-self lies an emotional core of unspeakable pain and loneliness, which he had never dared allow himself to dwell in for more than a few seconds. Like Superman's kryptonite, Sam—The Capacitor—only saw it as a threat to the hyper-competent adaptation he unwaveringly sustained. Moreover, Sam has an uncanny ability to lift himself out of these momentary states of loneliness, pain, and panic through a kind of self-administered endorphin high that requires no external drug or exercise routine. In the therapeutic context, however, this capacity constitutes a double-edged sword: because it functions as such an effective "anti-depressant" or "emotional anesthetic," it eliminates the subjective pain and urgency that motivate many patients to bring their pain forward into the shared space of analytic dialogue. Although Sam and I were able to talk, even joke, about who wanted him to go into his painful feelings, him or me, this had no effect on his ability to tolerate them.

For years the needed relationship (Stern, 2017a) took the form of what Les Havens (1989) called "loose holding": allowing Sam to create the space he needed to connect and feel safe. He would mostly tell me stories demonstrating his business acumen and unusual generosity, while I listened attentively and admiringly—joining him in a kind of dialogical high: a light-hearted, humor-infused repartee that we evolved over time. It was clear that Sam was coming to trust and feel very warmly toward me. Some months into the analysis he asked if he could hug me at the conclusion of some sessions if he felt like it. I would ordinarily be quite uncomfortable with doing that and have, in the past, actually refused certain patients' similar requests. But I found myself willing to try it with Sam. Very soon he was hugging me on his way out of every session, and I came to experience it as a comfortable, meaningful ritual in our relationship.

Influenced by Galatzer-Levy's (2002, 2009) application of non-linear dynamic systems concepts to the analytic process, I came to think of Sam's and my pattern of relating as a "coupled oscillator"—a kind of "in-sync-ness" that has its own therapeutic properties, not unlike Benjamin's (2002) (following Sander, 2002) concept of a "rhythmic third." According to Galatzer-Levy:

> Oscillators are said to be coupled if they are connected in some way ... The resonant vibrations of piano strings, the coupling of two weighted springs by a rubber band, the coupling of two neurons through connections in a neural network, and the back and forth movement of dancers, all are usefully conceptualized as coupled oscillators.
>
> (Galatzer-Levy, 2009, p. 988)

The main point of Galatzer-Levy's paper was that an analyst and patient, functioning as a non-linear dynamic system, can evolve powerfully therapeutic forms and patterns of connection through processes that take place outside the area of linear, cognitively grounded, cause-and-effect relationships posited in psychoanalytic theories of therapeutic action. I found Galatzer-Levy's thinking somewhat reassuring and freeing: there *was* a kind of vitality, connectedness, and pleasure in Sam's and my engagement. Yet I slowly came to feel troubled by a sense of circularity and directionlessness in our sessions. Although a strong self–object connection was forming, there seemed to be little therapeutic traction or movement.

Over a period of months I started to feel a sense of urgency around this—a feeling that I was somehow being remiss by simply going along with Sam's way of relating to me. Schwartz Cooney (2018), following Alvarez (2012), writes about this sense of "urgency in the countertransference" that can develop with profoundly withdrawn, disengaged patients—a desperate sense of needing to connect with them that can be the impetus for vitalizing enactments. Things were more complex and confusing with Sam because he was not exactly, or at least not manifestly, withdrawn and disengaged. It wasn't just that nothing was happening: it was that something was both happening and not happening at the same time.

First vitalizing enactment

My first vitalizing enactment with Sam began with the arrival of an unbidden, emergent thought, which set in motion a cascade of interactions over the next few sessions. One day in our second year, toward the end of a typically unsettling session, I had the thought: he speaks but I can't locate the *author* of his speech. It's as if speech happens, but without an inner speaker. Or, if there is an inner speaker, "he" is not speaking primarily through the content of his words but through their impact as a kind of enactment or emotional communication. I told Sam that *he tells me stories, but I can't tell who the author is, or what his purpose is in telling me*. His reaction seemed to be somewhere in between being taken aback and lighting up. But we didn't have time to discuss it.

He began the next session making a joke indicating that what he had taken from the last session was that I was against "story telling." I wondered if he felt wounded by my comment about authorship, as if I were criticizing him for not doing analysis right. I tried to clarify that this was not the case: I sensed behind *all* of his speech, not only his story telling, a kind of directionlessness. He said he operated with the understanding that I would learn something from his story telling that would be useful. I said that demonstrated my point: he didn't sense a direction within himself. He spoke of wanting, at some level he knew wasn't realistic, a guru who would point him toward truth and direct him about how to live. He denied that I was that person, and claimed he wouldn't want me to be: he would just reject it. I said the wish for a guru also suggested he feels he doesn't have a clue and needs outside direction. Yes, he agreed, he was starting to see that, while he was the master of outside reality in certain ways, he felt cut off from his own reality—he had no internal anchors. We revisited a comment of his wife, Carla, he had told me about previously: that he lives in an isolation tank, as in the 1980s film, *Altered States*. I said I felt that with him too. It's not just that he's cut off from inner reality, but also, in a subtle way, from others. It's the same basic barrier.

His acknowledgment that he was cut off from his internal reality and didn't know how to navigate felt like the truest, most real thing he had ever said to me, and I told him so. He then brought up that maybe both of us were swimming around in such complexity that we would just flounder together. I interpreted this as his worry that I wouldn't be able to help him, just as no one ever had. He agreed, but also reemphasized his trust and faith in me. He became almost tearful at this point, in obvious gratitude. He wondered what could help us. His dreams, he wondered? Yes, I answered. He got out a little notebook in which he had apparently jotted down some dreams—he'd been dreaming heavily, he said. As background to telling me about one of his dreams (which we never got to), he reported about his irritation with Carla in Washington D.C. on a recent vacation with their kids. On a number of occasions she had "rattled on" in complaint about being stuck in long lines waiting for things. This irritated him enormously. He felt like he was dealing with another child rather than a partner. He had gotten very critical and superior with her around this. I said his irritation tells us about him too. He has an allergy to her childlike states because they remind him of his traumatized inner child. He said, "You mean the 3-year-old [the age when his mother died]?" "Yes!" I exclaimed. He said, "But I think I started to become thoughtful and self-controlled in the way I am today very early." Yes, I agreed, but not before 3. He reflected and said he remembered reflecting on certain issues (in an extremely precocious way) when he was 4. Yes, I agreed, he's been taking care of himself since then: "*There's the 3-year-old and the 4-year-old.*" At this, he became tearful again, and indicated that he was having a lot of feeling. The session ended and on the way out he hugged me more tightly, and in a more prolonged way, than ever before. I felt moved, and very close to him.

In the following session Sam revealed that he had dreamt about me for the first time. All he remembered was that I was with him and his family, as if I were virtually a family member. When I asked for his associations, he said it was about feeling safe with me. In this and the subsequent session I was aware of feeling more connected with him. He was more spontaneously reflective about his feelings, not just telling me stories but trying to locate himself in or behind them.

By the conclusion of this series of progressive revelations, Sam and I had a new purchase on the profound dislocation in his experience of life. It had become clear that while, since the age of 4, he had organized his life so that he was always taking care of others, there was an inner 3-year-old who was still floundering, reeling from a totally unprocessed trauma, and unconsciously waiting for someone, somehow, to provide the help, direction, and care he was just beginning to recognize he needed.

It seems to me this first vitalizing enactment, though prompted by a sense of "countertranference urgency," falls more in the category of an emergent, non-linear development in which I was mainly attending to what *was* happening between Sam and me as opposed to intentionally trying to make something more "vital" happen. In this regard, the process in this first enactment seems similar to the process Sopher (2018) describes in her work with Jennie. Somehow, from my prolonged state of unsettling ambiguity and worry, the thought that I could sense "no author" behind Sam's stories emerged unbidden from my unconscious reveries in relation to Sam (Galatzer-Levy, 2002; Ogden 1997;

D.B. Stern, 1990). This emergent metaphor felt immediately relieving because I finally had language that fit my complex experience with Sam. Sharing my revelation with him seemed to crack open the months-long stalemate and set in motion a cascade of relational events.

The new revelations precipitated subtle changes in our relational field. One of the therapeutic yields was a shift in how I listened to and heard Sam's monologue. I now heard moments in his narrative that glancingly referred to emotional pain he experienced in disappointing, hurtful, or frightening interactions with Carla and his children, and in his work life. The deprivations he experienced with Carla seemed to be increasingly painful and disappointing in ways that suggested she was becoming the stand-in for the mother who "abandoned" him at age 3, and the subsequent stepmothers, all of whom also ultimately abandoned him. These chinks in Sam's exoskeleton were windows into his inner turbulence which was still so frightening to him that when we touched on it he immediately dissociated into a hypnoidal state bordering on sleep. He could acknowledge his fear that if he let himself "go there" he would break down and cease to be able to function at the high level he made sure to sustain; and the level he felt he needed to sustain 24/7 to protect his wife and children should something catastrophic threaten any of them. In short, this first vitalizing enactment had expanded our field such that he was more able and willing to bring in his experiences of pain, anxiety, and aloneness when certain relational happenings would cause him to slip from his "exoskeletal" self into an overwhelmed self-state. But he would not allow himself to stay there for long. He would say he needed me to guide him, which in a way I tried to do. But I knew he would have to be the one to allow himself to "feel his feelings." I could lead by marking the moments when he touched on feelings, but then had to allow him to go wherever he chose, which was mostly, still, very quickly into a dissociated place.

The ongoing conundrum

What *do* we do, as analytic therapists, with such thoroughgoing conscious and unconscious resistance to the kind of processes we imagine necessary for the working through of early relational trauma? In a talk I once heard Steve Mitchell give, he said that analytic therapists, like good-enough parents, tend to *worry* about their patients and about how good a job we are doing with helping them. I worry about the stuck-ness I experience with Sam. In fact, I worry about it more than he does! The conundrum I struggle with is that it is a complex stuck-ness: we seem stuck in certain ways but not others.

This conundrum has haunted me in my work with Sam throughout our decade of treatment. I, for one, am extremely uncomfortable with, and, in general philosophically opposed to, leading patients into emotional territory that they choose to avoid. I am a believer in the "wisdom" of the patient's unconscious. I understand that patients may be unconsciously conflicted, but I tend to respect their current choices growing out of their conflicts, and look for the forward-edge motivations embedded in those choices. It was coming out of this philosophical orientation that I had specifically refrained from pushing Sam to stay with his disturbing feelings any longer than he could tolerate. Yet, I was becoming increasingly convinced that his fractured inner self was causing serious problems: in his deteriorating marriage; in his chronic sense of unrealized potential despite his growing list of accomplishments; and in his overall sense of not being fully, emotionally present in his life. Sam knew of my discomfort and concern, but claimed *he* was not concerned: he said he trusted that in time I would figure it all out.

Second vitalizing enactment

Then, one weekend in the fall of 2016, soon after a conference where I presented my work with Sam, I had a revelation. In my paper (see also above) I had written:

> While [Sam] organizes his life so that he is always taking care of others, there is an inner 3-year-old who is still floundering, reeling from a totally unprocessed trauma, and unconsciously waiting for someone somehow to provide the help, direction and care he is just beginning to recognize he needs.

It suddenly hit me that if I really took this statement seriously, I was going to have to abandon my usual therapeutic philosophy and take a more active role helping Sam risk moving into the feelings and need-states I believed were causing so much trouble. If he really *was* functioning like a 3-year-old in the dissociated part of his personality, I was going to have to assume a more parental version of my therapist role to help him at least get over the hump. And in order to assume this more active, directive role in good conscience, I would need to believe that, as painful and frightening as it might be for Sam, going into these feelings would not kill him, or even cause him to break down in the way he feared—at least, not as long as he experienced me as in it with him.

I began our next session by sharing these thoughts with Sam. Sitting behind him as he lay on my couch, I said I realized I had been too tentative with him about going into and staying with his dissociated feelings. If he really was operating at the level of a traumatized child in need of direct help dealing with traumatized states, I needed to take more responsibility for making that happen: "I know you can do this," I said. "What you're scared of is not what will happen. You *will* be okay. You need to allow yourself to feel and process these painful feelings in order to grow. So we're going to do it together."

SAM: You're my parent.

[I can see tears beginning to stream down his face.]

THERAPIST: Yes, in this context.

SAM: You can think of it however you want, but you're my parent.

THERAPIST: Yes, I'm your parent.

SAM: My first and only thought is, to do this I need to be held.

[Awkward silence. I know this is what he needs but I also know I can't really hold him.]

SAM: Will you hold my hand? It's really OK.

THERAPIST: [I hesitated, but quickly decided, and said] Yes, I will.

[He reached his hand back behind him somewhat awkwardly, bending his elbow in an uncomfortable way. I met his hand with mine, gripping it firmly—the needed "hold." We kept our hands clasped like that for the next 15–20 minutes.]

SAM: I'm in a dark place. There's no imagery. I wish there was sunlight. [It's very significant that he's not generating imagery, which is what he always does when he's dissociating painful affects.] … So, what do I do with these feelings?

THERAPIST: There's nothing you need to do. It's not a matter of doing. You just feel them. See where they want to go.

[He became quiet, but fully engaged, not dissociated.]

SAM: I don't know where to go.

THERAPIST: This isn't a place, it's *you*; this is the real you.

SAM: I'm scared.

THERAPIST: You can trust yourself; it will be OK. Allow it to be whatever it is. These feelings are where you live, your soul.

SAM: I don't know how to take care of myself.

THERAPIST: That's right, you don't. In this place, you can't take care of yourself yet. You need someone else to take care of you.

[I could sense something in him let go here, relaxing into it]

SAM: I need to breathe. [He had talked the day before about being able to exhale but not inhale.]

THERAPIST: Yes, that's right—breathe!

SAM: The only other time in my life I've been in this place was once with Carla. But then, it just happened—she wasn't taking care of me.

THERAPIST: Carla can't take care of you this way. It's not her job. It's my job.

SAM: [He referred back to a picture he had shown me at the beginning of the hour of his mother and father around the time they got married. He said] "She was 19—my age, a child! [He immediately realizes the Freudian slip: He's no longer 19, but rather 50!] I want to go back and hug her, to help her with the awful journey she was facing.

THERAPIST: That's your exoskeleton talking. It's not your job to hold your mother as a 3-year-old child. It's her job to hold you. She has other people to hold her. You need to be held—held throughout all the ordeals you were about to go through at 3, 4, 5 and beyond. But no one was there to hold you.

SAM: Is that the way it's supposed to work—being held throughout your ordeals?

THERAPIST: Yes! That's right.

[With each of these statements of mine he seemed to go more deeply into himself, his feelings, and grow calmer.]

THERAPIST: You are loved, Sam. Your children love you; Carla loves you. But you don't know it because you don't let them. You can't when you're in your exoskeleton trying to take care of everyone. They hate it when you're in that place. But they all sense there's more going on in you. If you let them in more they will be able to love you. But you can't let them in until you let yourself in, like this.

SAM: [crying]

[Several minutes go by, and Sam starts emerging from this shared space; he lets go of my hand.]

SAM: I feel lighter! lightened [he corrected.] Also, I need to pee.

THERAPIST: I'm proud of you.

[Both of us feeling moved by what we had done together—more intimately connected than at any time in our many-year history.]

SAM: My nose is clogged—I can't breathe. [The tone is lighter now]

THERAPIST: No wonder: you probably have years of mucus stored up—there have been so many messes you've never been free to make.

[Here he goes back to his need to pee.] I wet my bed until I was 12.

THERAPIST: That makes perfect sense. The 3-year-old was frozen in time even as the exoskeleton was developing.

I stood up, and he reluctantly, slowly, got up off the couch and rubbed his eyes. We hugged deeply on his way out.

SAM: See you tomorrow…

THERAPIST: You know where to find me.

This was the only session in which I took such an active, hand-holding role with Sam. Having done so once with such promising results, my hope was that he now would be better able to assume responsibility for bringing his emotional self into the room. And indeed, our sessions have changed to some degree. He brings his real problems and emotional pain into our sessions more readily, and has greater, though still limited, capacity to sustain an engagement with these problems and affects. Sometimes, when I am sharing a new insight regarding his trauma history or his current struggles, he will drift into a near-sleep state, often with dream-imagery. We both feel that these state-shifts are not simply defensive: they also reflect a deep letting go because the combination of my words and tone of voice signals to him that I am here taking care of him and he can trust me enough to relax his exoskeleton. When he emerges from these reveries, he feels renewed, strengthened, and more connected.

I view this second vitalizing enactment, in contrast to the first, as very much in the spirit of Schwartz Cooney's concept as developed in her 2018 paper and illustrated in her work with Joel. Like Schwartz Cooney with Joel, and Alvarez (2012) with Robbie, I came to believe I needed to actively "reach out" (or "reach in") in order to directly engage and "awaken" Sam's traumatized, dissociated, half-deadened, abandoned, un-held, underdeveloped child-self, and to co-create a visceral, enacted experience of the kind of parental holding and coaching he had never received but desperately needed. Though my intention to initiate such an experience was premeditated, beginning almost immediately—really, with Sam's stating the conditions under which he could proceed—what ensued unfolded spontaneously and unpredictably.

It had taken me a long time to reach the conclusion that I needed to do something like this with Sam in order to make any kind of sustained contact with his profoundly traumatized child-self. That's because such an analyst-initiated intervention went against all of my psychoanalytic training and instincts. Had I been exposed to Alvarez' or Schwartz Cooney's pathbreaking work, I probably would have felt emboldened to try something like this sooner. As it was (and is), I felt relieved to discover that the risk I had taken with Sam seemed very much in line with their cutting-edge thinking.

One thought I have about doing this kind of work is that it may seem in retrospect to have been relatively simple and straightforward—as though the main difficulty was that I simply hadn't thought to do it, or been willing to take the risk, sooner. In fact, I think this is a deceptive, or at least paradoxical, simplicity. In one sense, what I did with Sam does have a certain "simple humanity." But that simply human (Sullivan, 1953) aspect rests on a complex matrix of analytic understanding and experience. Just to take one dimension of it, while the role I entered into with Sam in this vignette had a strongly parental, really maternal, aspect—one which Sam needed to name and reify—it was important that I remain clear (within myself) about the differences between what I was doing with Sam and what an actual parent does with a child. Sam and I were not entering each other's real lives outside the analytic situation; and the "analytic parenting" I was offering needed to hold, and be clear about, a paradoxical tension between the real and the symbolic in what we were saying and doing. For example, when I said: "Carla can't take care of you this way. It's not her job. It's my job," those statements rested on my understanding that analysis can at most offer an analog of parental caretaking—one that relies on an unconscious collaboration between patient and analyst in the co-creation of symbolic, analytic equivalents of good-enough parent–child interaction. (See also Stern, 2021.)

Vitalization as progressive fittedness

The foregoing descriptions of two very different vitalizing enactments in my work with Sam represent turning points in our relationship—extended moments of dramatic dialogue (Atlas & Aron, 2018), precipitating shifts in the organization of our therapeutic system, and following which our relationship was not quite the same as it had been before. Yet I have come to believe that such dramatic, transformative moments need to be kept in perspective with regard to the broader, "deeper," and ultimately more determinative movement toward vitalization. This movement has to do with the progressive fittedness of the analyst's total analyzing subjectivity to the patient's total subjectivity-as-patient in an increasingly nuanced and complex process of therapeutic system formation. In this regard, my thinking has commonalities with the Boston Change Process Study Group (BCPSG) (2013), who find a forward-tending movement toward increasing systemic complexity and competence to be a characteristic of implicit relational processes in analytic dyads, evidenced most dramatically during enactments. They believe that enactments represent the emergence ("eruption") of new, more complex and therapeutically potent modes of interaction that had already begun to occur implicitly as part of the dyad's natural movement toward greater complexity and fittedness. I tend to view enactments—especially their forward-edge, generative dimension (Aron & Atlas, 2015; Stern, 1994)—as introducing new, discontinuous, but *needed* forms and areas of engagement, as opposed to expressing forms already implicitly occurring. Either way, both the BCPSG and I envision a dyadic, systemic process evolving to take into account more of the patient's complex and evolving subjectivity and needs, as expressed in increasingly complex forms of interaction.

The upshot (for me) of this way of thinking has been to recognize and locate the crux of therapeutic action and analytic interaction in the analyst's increasingly complex analyzing subjectivity, manifest in the here-and-now intersubjective interaction with the patient. That is to say, the critical movement toward needed vitalization is occurring "quietly" in the analyst's evolving capacity to respond to the patient in needed ways. This movement is present in the analyst's progressive grasp of "what the patient needs from me" (Stern, 2017a, pp. 9–11), and his or her total participation based on that elusive grasp—what I have come to think of as the analyst's *transformative presence*. I have noticed, for example, in the later stages of "mature" treatments, following many enactments and periods of frustration and seeming stuck-ness, that certain complex truths about the patient and our unique therapeutic frame and process finally come into focus in a way that affects virtually everything occurring in the moment-to-moment interaction, including the problematic situations that had precipitated significant difficulties in the past. I have a new, more encompassing, sense of "what the patient needs from me," one which trumps earlier understandings and sets in motion many "small forms" of vitalizing connection (moments of meeting) in many sessions. In Bionian (1970) language, I think of this kind of evolution as "a successive approximation of O"—an actualization of therapeutic processes that represent the patient's and my conjoint "learning from experience"—fitfully acquiring increasingly "true" knowledge of the patient's complex psychic reality. This is a humbling perspective in that it assumes that one is always, even in the later stages of treatment, standing at a cusp between that which is known and that which remains unknown, and perhaps unknowable. There is always the sense that there could be something new to discover or uncover that might crucially reorganize all that has come before.

So, where am I with Sam in our journey toward progressive understanding and fittedness, given the transformations that have already occurred through our two dramatic vitalizing enactments and all that we have "learned from experience"? I feel we have progressed a lot, but have not yet reached the place of "mature," deep fittedness I have just described. At the same time that I feel there is much I have come to understand, I still feel there are critical, necessary elements I have not yet understood—critical questions that remain unanswered or even unformulated. For example, I don't know whether to initiate more sessions like the one in our second vitalizing enactment or wait for a clear signal from Sam that he is ready to do that. I don't know whether there is greater wisdom in letting go of my ambition for Sam to process his still-dissociated, unprocessed trauma or continue to allow myself to be "pulled" toward trying to facilitate that happening. And I don't know if there are countertransferential blind spots limiting what I am able to see and grasp. Actually, I assume there are; I just don't know what they are.

Where I have come to at this juncture, as I finish writing this chapter, is a new, more disciplined form of listening. Within this "listening position" I find myself closely following Sam's spontaneous narrative, tracking the "logic" of his experience of his sense of agency in different relational contexts. In most of the contexts in which he is an actor he is a competent, if not brilliant, problem solver and strategist. He rapidly grasps the nature of conflicts or roadblocks in his projects and relationships (professional and social), and senses quickly and intuitively how to manage them and move things forward based, in part, on his ability to integrate his own "true self" experience. With Carla, however—Carla who is the main source of his feelings of helplessness, frustration, anger, aloneness, pain, and being overwhelmed—he shifts into a much more passive, intimidated, restricted position, stuck in patterns of expressing his needs he has been trying for years, and giving up when they predictably fail to produce new, desired results. When his narrative reaches this point of helpless, angry, hurt frustration he tends to rapidly dissociate away from Carla into some other experiential domain in which he is more powerful and effective.

I have to be tracking him very closely and intentionally not to miss these instantaneous dissociative shifts and "lose" him. If I catch one, I think about how I want to respond. I don't want to be in the role of affect avoidance police, which in a sense I have been. I want to "stay with" his experience of agency (or lack thereof) *in relation to* his emotional experience. I might say something like: "Unlike how I experience you in most of your interactions with people, here, with Carla, it seems you reach a kind of dead end of frustration, hurt, and anger and have nowhere to go with it." He might say something like, "I bet I know where *you* want me to go with it! You want me to go into those feelings." I might say, "Unlike virtually any other situation where you are able to figure out a path forward toward realizing your goals or needs, with Carla you become passive and defeated, as if the only path forward would be for her to change her responsiveness to you. We have seen over a long period of time that that doesn't seem to be happening. Yet you seem to have no way to take that fact into account and figure out some other approach." (As I say this I am thinking that I do think that probably the only path forward *is* "through" his traumatic, dissociated state, which is activated with Carla, because only such processing would free him to respond to her (and his internalized maternal objects) with greater agency and flexibility. Like Bion (1962), I see this processing capacity as an essential life skill for navigating intimate, interdependent relationships (see also Civitarese, 2019). But I feel it is essential that I honor and trust his agency in relation to his emotions, knowing that I would stay with him wherever his agency takes him). At that point, in one such recent conversation, he said he experienced something like a lightning bolt, which he knew was coming from his traumatized inner self, and had no choice but to turn away and shut himself down. He then became quietly tearful, and I decided to let things take their own course for the duration of the session. Sam did turn away into other topics, but remained tearful and subdued until the end.

I feel there is something new in what I am attempting here—something informed by all that has come before. It doesn't fall within any theory of therapeutic action that I could identify—except perhaps a Bionian openness to that which is not yet known or understood coupled with an intention to "meet" Sam in a "place" where he feels "met" (Sander, 2008; Stern, 2017a). But I am clearly "stumbling along" (Bromberg, 2011) with very uncertain results. It is a complex, "quiet" place, where I feel I am on a kind of path and making a kind of progress in grasping who Sam is and how "to be" with him. One of the implicit measures I am using to assess the promise of this current path is that I feel intermittently vitalized by it and see moments of vitalization in Sam as well.

Note

1 The following clinical material, including the first "vitalizing enactment," draws on two previously published accounts of my work with Sam (Stern, 2017a, 2017b). The second "vitalizing enactment" is published here for the first time. Moreover, in this account all of the material is integrated and recontextualized within the theoretical frame of vitalization and vitalizing enactment. The overall clinical narrative is specific to the context of this book, and both the introduction and last sub-section, as well as certain "linking" sections, are new.

References

Alvarez, A. (2012). *The thinking heart: Three levels of psychoanalytic therapy with disturbed children.* New York, NY: Routledge.

Aron, L. & Atlas, G. (2015). Generative enactment: Memories from the future. *Psychoanalytic Dialogues, 25*:309–324.

Atlas, G. & Aron, L. (2018). *Dramatic dialogue: Contemporary clinical practice.* New York, NY: Routledge.

Benjamin, J. (2002). The rhythm of recognition: Comments on the work of Louis Sander. *Psychoanalytic Dialogues, 12*:43–54.

Bion, W.R. (1962). Learning from experience. New York, NY: Aronson.

Bion, W.R. (1970). *Attention and interpretation.* London: Karnac.

Boston Change Process Study Group (2013). Enactment and the emergence of new relational organization. *Journal of the American Psychoanalytic Association, 61*:727–749.

Bromberg, P.M. (2011). *The shadow of the tsunami and the growth of the relational mind.* New York, NY: Routledge.

Civitarese, G. (2019). Bion's O and his pseudo-mystical path. *Psychoanalytic Dialogues, 29*:388–403.

Cooney, A.S. (2018). Vitalizing enactment: A relational exploration. *Psychoanalytic Dialogues, 28*:340–354.

Davies, J.M. (2018). The "once and future" focus of a relational psychoanalysis: Discussion of "vitalizing enactment." *Psychoanalytic Dialogues, 28*:355–360.

Galatzer-Levy, R. (2002). Emergence. *Psychoanalytic Inquiry, 22*:708–727.

Galatzer-Levy, R. (2009). Good vibrations: Analytic process as coupled oscillations. *International Journal of Psychoanalysis, 90*:983–1007.

Grossmark, R. (2012). The flow of enactive engagement. *Contemporary Psychoanalysis, 48*:287–300.

Havens, L. (1989). *A safe place: Laying the groundwork of psychotherapy.* Cambridge, MA: Harvard University Press.

Hoffman, I.Z. (2009). Therapeutic passion in the countertransference. *Psychoanalytic Dialogues, 19*:617–637.

Ogden, T.H. (1997). *Reverie and interpretation: Sensing something human.* Northvale, NJ: Jason Aronson.

Sander, L. (2002). Thinking differently: Principles of process in living systems and the specificity of being known. *Psychoanalytic Dialogues, 12*:11–42.

Sander, L. (2008). *Living systems, evolving consciousness, and the emerging person: A selection of papers from the life work of Louis Sander* (G. Amadei & I. Bianchi, Eds.). New York: Routledge.

Sopher, R. (2018). An allegiance to absence: Fidelity to the internal void. *Psychoanalytic Quarterly*, 87(3).

Stern, D.B. (1990). Courting surprise: Unbidden perceptions in clinical practice. *Contemporary Psychoanalysis, 26*:452–478.

Stern, S. (1994). Needed relationships and repeated relationships: An integrated relational perspective. *Psychoanalytic Dialogues, 4*:317–345.

Stern, S. (2007). The conundrum of self-care. *Contemporary Psychoanalysis, 43*:605–620.

Stern, S. (2009). The dialectic of empathy and freedom. *International Journal of Psychoanalytic Self Psychology*, *4*:132–164.

Stern, S. (2017a). *Needed relationships and psychoanalytic healing: A holistic relational perspective on the therapeutic process.* New York, NY: Routledge.

Stern, S. (2017b). Holistic thinking and therapeutic action: Building on Louis Sander's contribution. *Psychoanalytic Dialogues, 27*:89–103.

Stern, S. (2021). Analytic adoption of the psychically homeless. *Psychoanalysis, Self, and Context* (in press).

Stolorow, R.D. (2014). Undergoing the situation: Emotional dwelling is more than empathic understanding. *International Journal of Psychoanalytic Self Psychology, 9*:80–83.

Sullivan, H.S. (1953). *The interpersonal theory of psychiatry.* New York, NY: Norton.

Tolpin, M. (2002). Doing psychoanalysis of normal development: Forward edge transferences. *Progress in Self Psychology, 18*:167–190.

Chapter 10

Vitality, attunement and the lack thereof

Daniel Hill

Affects are the dynamisms of aliveness we experience in the body and mind. They vary in intensity. Dan Stern (2004, 2010) referred to them as "vitality affects," noting that they *move* across time and take on varying "shapes" or "forms": surging, bursting, accelerating, lingering, fading, etc. He understood them as the elemental life force (*élan vital)* and the fundamental components of the experience of one's existence. In devitalized patients we don't perceive these ebbs and flows of life within. They don't move us and are difficult to engage in therapeutic processes.

In this chapter I define vitality as a regulated state in which one is processing affect and able to use it adaptively. I've depicted the devitalized personality as a product of chronic dismissals and traumatic shaming that occur in the early attachment relationship and result in a failure to develop the capacity for affect regulation and awareness of subjective experience. I discuss affect attunement as a synchronization of affect states resulting in an enhanced, shared state of consciousness. It sets up optimal conditions for therapeutic actions. I end with suggestions for the treatment of devitalized patients, especially with regard to their deficiencies in regulating hyper-arousal and the difficulties attuning to them. I begin by reviewing necessary aspects of affect regulation theory.

Devitalized personalities suffer the dreariness of an affectless existence and pay a high adaptive price for their failure to process affect. Affect marks the adaptive value of objects (Damasio, 1994, 1999), communicates meaning and is crucial to assessing and navigating the socio-emotional environment. Self states are organized by and around affect (Emde, 1994; Hill, 2015). Schore (1994) proposes the regulation of affect to be the core executive function of the organism and gives primacy to affect in development, psychopathology and therapeutic action. Stern (2010) and Damasio (1999, 2010) propose affect to be the fundament of mind, consciousness and the self. In the consulting room, vitality, the ongoing processing of affect, is the lifeblood of depth therapeutic processes.

Most of the time affect idles in the background of consciousness, generating a sense of what Winnicott called going-on-being. When it deviates from a baseline state sufficiently to get our attention, we are perceiving positively or negatively toned, hyper- or hypo-aroused, somatic responses to internal and external objects. We are noticing the automatic preparation of the organism to engage (hyper-arousal) or disengage (hypo-arousal) the object (Damasio, 1994; Schore, 1994). Affect interests us in, links us to and establishes our relationships to our objects (Kernberg, 1975). It cathects objects.

We detect affect in others through movements in their facial expressions, bodies and voice—implicit/non-verbal communications. These implicit/non-verbal communications of affect stream alongside their words, mostly unconsciously, conveying their internal states; the flows and shifts of their subjective experience; their spontaneous responses to objects; what matters and how it matters to them. Affect is at the core of our subjectivity (Alcaro, Carta, and Panksepp, 2017; Schore, 1994; Stern, 1985). The continuous, mostly non-conscious reading and responding to affect in ourselves and others is the core transaction of intersubjective relating. Trevarthen called it "primary intersubjectivity" (1979).

We tend to think of vitality as a state of positively toned, moderate hyper-arousal; a state of heightened well-being in which one is alert and disposed toward engagement, present and ready to go, available for exploration and growth. In what follows I'll settle for this notion. But first, I need to make some important distinctions about vitality. It's not as simple as a positively toned, up-regulated state.

To be vitalizing, affect must be regulated and integrated. Although hypo-manic states are hyper-aroused and positively toned, they don't qualify because they are dysregulated and dissociated. Nor does someone qualify who manifests a chipper false self, even though we would agree that they are in a state of positively toned moderate hyper-arousal. On the other hand, someone in a *regulated*, negatively toned hypo-aroused state such as shame *is* vital in the most fundamental sense of the term. Their affect is flowing, being integrated into their sense of self and others and is available for adaptive use. In the case of shame, it's available for real-time self-correction and long-term growth. Albeit painfully down-regulated, and although the patient may wish to hide it, there is an inner dynamism. The down-regulated states pertinent to this chapter, those that impede therapeutic engagement, are static.

It's the inertness, expressed in the stillness of the face and body and the monotony of the voice, that makes devitalized/disembodied patients stressful to work with. Their lack of affective responses to objects is central to the difficulty we find in connecting/attuning to them. Attunement requires mutual affective responsiveness (Stern, 1985). Working with such patients can easily turn frustrating and the counter-transference ranges from a narcissistic-based anger at the repeated rejection of our entreaties to connect, to succumbing to a similar state of numbed, down-regulated, detachment, despair and uncaringness.

So, I would use the term vital for any regulated state in which one is processing affect and able to use it adaptively. The colloquial use refers to an up-regulated, positively toned state of vitality reflecting the flourishing of the organism and the disposition toward engagement and growth. The second part of this chapter is about the co-creating of an enhanced version of this type of vitality and the therapeutic possibilities it supports, but let me first continue discussing devitalization.

Dismissive-avoidant trauma

From the point of view of regulation theory, devitalization is a psychobiological disorder that originates in trauma that has altered the limbic-autonomic system[1] located in the brain's right hemisphere (Schore, 1994). The trauma may be single incident trauma, or developmental trauma involving recurring incidents of overt trauma (sexual, physical and/or verbal abuse) by caregivers (Herman, 1997; van der Kolk 2005, 2014). Or, the focus of this chapter, it may be early hidden attachment trauma (misattunements occurring at the micro level) in this case the trauma of avoidant/dismissive attachment.

Let me note that the most damaging developmental trauma is neglect. Recall Bowlby's studies (1973) of hospitalized children who, in accordance with sanitary measures of the time, were never touched and rarely visited by their parents.. Over the course of several months, they went from an initial stage of protest (hyper-arousal) to a state of despair (hypo-arousal) to a final, disastrous state of devitalized detachment; of down-regulated affect and lack of responsiveness to objects.

The limbic-autonomic system is responsible for the continuous assessment of internal and external objects and for sending instructions, via the nervous system and bloodstream, to increase or decrease the activation of the organs and musculoskeletal system—hyper- or hypo-arousal. The ongoing flows and punctuated moments of affect that we experience and communicate to others represent these activations and deactivations of the body.

In the case of avoidant/devitalized personalities the limbic-autonomic system has been biased toward hypo-arousal. The dismissive mother's insensitivity to her infant's internal states has resulted in an infant deficient in the capacity to process his/her own body based affects or to read and respond to the implicit communications of affect in others. This down-regulated, desensitized outcome of the neurological aspect of the trauma is accompanied by an avoidance of stressful stimuli that helps to maintain the down regulation. The autonomic imbalance also results in a deficiency in modulating hyper-arousal and a core anxiety of being overwhelmed by affect. Easily dysregulated, avoidant personalities suffer chronic hypo-aroused states of consciousness in which mentation is slowed or deactivated entirely and is accompanied by intense detachment. Such states can be subtle and difficult to detect, manifesting as absence rather than a positive symptom. At its extreme it shows itself as a blank stare.

In thinking about devitalized patients it's also helpful to distinguish between dissociated and repressed affect (Cardena, 1994, Holmes et al., 2005, Spitzer et al., 2006; Meares, 2012; Schore, 2019a). Dissociated affect is not processed above the amygdala (the most primitive and earliest evolving component of the limbic system), has never become conscious and is especially difficult to access. Compare this with repressed affect, which has been conscious and is subsequently defended against. The shadow of repressed affect can be sensed, the defenses against it are in plain sight and it is relatively accessible. Devitalized patients suffer from dissociated affect. Their affect isn't being processed and in some cases, due to avoidant defenses, isn't even being generated. The salient object isn't being detected or responded to.

While dissociated affect may be limited to the affect associated with a specific trauma memory, the problem for avoidant personalities, as a result of their neurological impairment, is pervasive. Most commonly, avoidant personalities are frightened of and defend against hyper-aroused categorical affects – anger fear, joy and pride. They are likely to be limited to the hypo-aroused affects – disgust, sadness and shame.

It's worth mentioning that single incident trauma tends to result in either hyper- or hypo-aroused sequelae. Due largely to the work of Ruth Lanius and her colleagues (Lanius et al., 2010; Lanius et al., 2012) the DSM-V now differentiates two types of PTSD. One is typified by a psychobiological disorder of chronic hyper-arousal driven by fear and/or anger, hyper-vigilance and flashbacks in which one is abruptly driven into states of hyper-arousal and total immersion into a memory of the traumatic event. A second type of single incident PTSD suffers from chronic hypo-arousal accompanied by numbing endogenous opioids, social withdrawal/avoidance and episodes of depersonalization/derealization—profound detachment. Note the association of hyper-arousal with immersion in experience, and hypo-arousal with detachment and affect numbing. The cumulative trauma of early attachment follows this same pattern but the sequelae are more diffuse and usually more moderate. Avoidant attachment may be thought of as a down-regulated type of PTSD.

Unless one is working in a setting focused on single incident trauma or recurring obvious trauma during childhood, the devitalization of most psychotherapy patients is likely to originate in avoidant-dismissive trauma. Chronic micro-interactions of dismissal when seeking regulation represent failures by the caretaker to detect and respond contingently to stressful affect states of the infant. Each misattunement is accompanied by a jolt of shame in the infant and followed by a failure to repair the rupture by the caretaker. Chronic rejections when dysregulated result in a disposition toward auto-regulation and an aversion to dyadic regulation.[2] Such dismissals accumulate into an overall neglect and result in a disposition toward hypo-arousal, detachment, over-reliance on auto-regulation, avoidance and, ultimately, a shame-ridden core sense of self. Along with this inadvertent hidden shaming, the intentional shaming that is appropriate to this stage of development is carried out coldly and without soon enough repair to the rupture in the attachment relationship. Dismissive/avoidant trauma is a shame trauma and pervasive dissociated shame is a key factor in the devitalization that ensues. Indeed, the chronically down-regulated state of the devitalized personality is a personification of shame (Hill, 2015).

Later in development, when the left brain comes online and the capacity for mentalization develops, there will be little attention by the caretaker to feelings or the inner world organized around them—little that would encourage introspection. In addition to the environmental failure to facilitate the development of an inner world, the fundamental strategy of the avoidant adaptation to the rejecting environment that shaped them was to keep their attention away from the sources of stress. Such avoidance impedes introspection and works against the development of an inner world. Of course, the emptiness of the devitalized patient is a fundamental concern, but for now, let's stick with the devitalization problem.

There is a spectrum of avoidant devitalization. Some patients may be pervasively down-regulated and detached, unable to benefit from the nourishments of laughter or play and unable to get excited or become immersed in the present much at all. Others may shut down only when stressed. It's worth keeping this in mind since avoidant patients tend to find the focus on their inner world threatening. They may have more aliveness in other contexts and may take considerable time to relax in treatment. There are also degrees of deactivation of affective life. Interacting with patients suffering from the most profound devitalization is like the discomforting effect of a sound-deadened room where there is no reverberation.

Avoidant patients face a daunting array of obstacles to growth resulting from their malformed limbic-autonomic system. Among them is an incapacity for synchronized micro-interactions necessary for attunement (Schore, 2019a).[3] Attunement is a primary mechanism of development that sets up optimal conditions for growth (Schore, 1994; Stern, 1985; Tronick et al., 1998). The shared states it generates are the opposite of detachment.

In the remainder of this chapter I will discuss affect attunement as a means of generating heightened states of vitality that support shared/enhanced states of consciousness and optimize therapeutic possibilities. I will end with the problem of attunement with avoidant/devitalized patients.

Affect attunement, growth-promoting states of consciousness and therapeutic possibilities

To understand affect attunement one must appreciate the general characteristics, functions and processes of the right brain. Attunement is mediated by a synchronization of right brains (Schore, 2011, 2012, 2019a).

The right brain

The right brain has different characteristics and serves different functions from the left. It employs implicit mental operations to process the present. The left brain uses explicit operations to process the past and future (McGilchrist, 2009; Schore, 1994). Let's start with the functions and general characteristics of the right brain and then take up the processes themselves. I'll point to the therapeutic opportunities stemming from being in a right-brain-dominant state as we go.

The right brain evolved earlier than the left and develops first ontogenetically. The critical period of development is from the third trimester of pregnancy to about 18 months. The left brain begins development at about two years of age. This becomes important clinically because later-developing neural structures inhibit the earlier-developing structures to which they're connected. Left-brain processes inhibit those of the right. Also, regression, understood as returning to processes developed earlier, may be seen as a return to right-brain dominance. Attunement, requiring right-brain-to-right-brain communications, may be understood as mutual voluntary regression (Schore, 2019a).[4]

The right-lateralized limbic system, sometimes called the "emotional brain," does the continuous monitoring and regulation of our body-based affect and integrates it with the stream of implicit communications expressing the affect states of others. We attune to one another by matching the ups and downs and hedonic tones of our affect states. We are synchronizing our limbic systems, reading and adjusting affective responses to one another.[5] This synchronizing of affect states creates a felt sense of merger.

The resonance amplifies and prolongs affect, increasing awareness of one's own and the other's subjective experience. This maximizes the therapist's ability to appreciate patients' capacities at any given moment. The matching/sharing of affect states provides the therapist with implicit knowledge that guides empathic responding. It informs the intuitive interactive regulation of the patient—our spontaneous implicit responses that increase or decrease their level of arousal and keep them in regulated states as they encounter stressful material, and that reregulate them when they become dysregulated (Schore, 1994). For the patient, it generates a sense of feeling felt and being recognized (Benjamin, 1990), that is not only reassuring but also pleasurable and uplifting, making for heightened vitality. Thus, attunement both stabilizes and energizes, thereby providing a sense of safety and well-being that encourages exploration of novel material.

Note that the processing of our own body-based affect and the processing of implicit communications conveying the affect state of the patient occur in real time at speeds below the threshold of awareness. In contrast, the explicit, conscious operations of the left brain that process the past and the future operate relatively slowly. The implicit/unconscious processes provide the first/primary, automatic, "gut" response to the object. The left brain does the conscious, deliberate, secondary processing.

So, the right brain manages the present with implicit/unconscious processes specializing in affective/subjective experience and intersubjective relating. I'll discuss these implicit processes in a moment, but first let's focus on some general attributes of right-brain versus left-brain processing. The contrasts illuminate the importance of activating right-brain processes in depth therapy.

The differences between the hemispheres are stark enough so that personalities can be differentiated as left- or right-brain-dominant. Ideally there's a balance and the left is available to inhibit the right when necessary and can be relaxed for voluntary regression.[6]

The left brain evolved to control events. Its processes are linear, logical and verbal (propositional sentences like this one are a good example.). It grasps experience and assimilates it into known categories delimited by words. It forecloses ambiguity. Its logic is intolerant of inconsistencies and contradictions. It uses focal attention, breaks experience into parts and analyzes it. It assesses objects as objects with an eye toward their use, and disposes us toward instrumental relationships.

Whereas the processes of the left brain are verbal, linear and logical, those of the right are non-verbal, non-linear and not constrained by logic. Actually, it's not constrained by words or linearity either. Right-brain processes comprise associative and analogical processes integral to play, humor and creativity, all of which facilitate therapeutic progress. The left-brain processes fit experience into known categories and are intolerant of inconsistency and ambiguity. The right brain is inclusive and accepts things as they are, including ambiguities and contradictions. The difference in openness versus closed mindedness is a good example of how the left brain may clamp down on the affective, primary processing of the right. The left brain suppresses affect to avoid dysregulation and preserve as much adaptive functioning as possible.

The right brain serves different, more basic functions than the left, creates an entirely different state of consciousness, serves up an entirely different reality (McGilchrist, 2009). It is responsible for survival and well-being. The fight, flight or freeze system is in the right brain. More generally, the right brain serves to keep us in regulated/homeostatic states in which we are maximally adaptive and able to respond to internal and external objects with maximum flexibility. It assesses objects as subjects and disposes us toward relationships with others based on how they are rather than their use to us.[7]

The right brain's continuous assessment and regulation of affect serve as the basic mechanism underlying what Dan Stern called the "subjective self" (1985). Whereas the left brain objectifies, the right brain processes inner states and subjectifies self and others. Bach (1985) has captured the difference of the realities served up by each hemisphere in what he calls subjective versus objective awareness.

Attunement generates a heightened subjective awareness. The matching of affect states generates feelings of empathy and nurturance and what Pizer (2018) calls the analyst's generous involvement. These emerge spontaneously, evoking trust in the patient. Ultimately, I am proposing that attunement is a golden road to vitality and therapeutic possibilities.

Implicit processes

What Stern called the subjective self, Schore (1994) calls the "implicit self." He is referring to the implicit mental operations of the right brain that mediate the generation, communication and regulation of affective/subjective experience in the present. Schore (1994, 2019a) has delineated three types of implicit processes: implicit communication, implicit cognition and implicit memory. They perform the functions of the right brain and assemble its state of consciousness. They play key roles in attunement, vitalization and in facilitating therapeutic growth.

Implicit communications of affect are micro-interactions of facial expressions, gestures and prosody of speech that communicate when we're not speaking and stream alongside the words when we are. They are the medium by which we convey implicit knowings and by which we regulate one another's affect states. They are the means by which we "hold" patients and by which we convey our positive expectations and encourage them. They construct the implicit therapeutic relationship.

Implicit cognition or implicit knowing is another right-brain process. Rather than breaking experience down into parts amenable to analysis, the right brain synthesizes information into imagistic gestalts. They are a non-verbal mentation in which all the information is presented simultaneously. Visual images are the most obvious example, but also images of any sensation or of whole clusters of thoughts. Episodic memories are a good example. If I were to ask you about a memorable incident in your life, the entire episode would come to you all at once as a non-verbal knowing. You would then translate that "image" into a verbal story with your left brain, a logical syntactical sequence meant for communicating with others.

Insights, intuitions and metaphors, key currencies of therapy, all arrive unbidden, unconsciously assembled and fully formed as implicit cognitions. They are dense with information and known all at once.

Implicit relational knowing (Boston Change Process Study Group, 2002, 2010) consists of implicit cognitions crucial for intersubjective relating.

To get a sense of the complexity of right-brain-synthesized gestalts, the speed of their construction and what's involved in taking in the goings-on of intersubjective life in real time, consider the notion of "reflexive self-awareness" (Aron, 2000). It is an integration of the self-as-subject and self-as-object with the other-as-subject and the other-as-object. The "Third" (Aron and Benjamin, 1999; Benjamin, 1999) includes all this *plus* the view of the other's reflexive awareness of oneself. As a result of the right brain's use of global rather than focal attention, such implicit relational knowings come equipped with a panoramic view capable of taking it all in. Consider also the complexity of now moments and the real-time socio-emotional intelligence required to turn them into moments of meeting (Boston Change Process Study Group, 2010). Attunement requires no less as we read and adjust to our own and the patient's shifting affect states. All of these are the domain of the implicit processes of the right brain and extend far beyond the capacity of the explicit processes of the left.

Finally, *implicit/procedural memories* are encoded and stored in the right brain. The internal working model of attachment is an implicit memory system responsible for the object relations and affect-regulating procedures that make up the attachment relationship. The memories of the cumulative traumas of insecure attachment and the defenses against their repetition, prime targets for therapeutic actions, are also inscribed as implicit memories in the right brain. The corrective emotional experiences of the secure therapeutic relationship are mediated by the right brain and stored as implicit/procedural memories. In this way new objects are internalized and new procedures for intersubjective relating and regulating affect are established.

To summarize, attunement involves a matching of the ebbs and flows of affect. It requires a mutual regression into and synchronization of right-brain-dominant states. It simultaneously stabilizes and vitalizes, maximizes subjective awareness and potentiates essential therapeutic actions for depth psychotherapy. I can find no better description of the growth-supporting qualities of attunement than this quote from Kierkegaard, cited by Sroufe (1979):

> The loving mother teaches her child to walk alone. She is far enough from him so that she cannot actually support him, but she holds out her arms to him. She imitates his movements, and if he totters, she swiftly bends as if to seize him, so that the child might believe that he is not walking alone ... and yet, she does more. Her face beckons like a reward, an encouragement. Thus, the child walks alone with his eyes fixed on his mother's face, not on the difficulties in his way. He supports himself by the arms that do not hold him and constantly strives towards the refuge in his mother's embrace, little supposing that in the very same moment that he is emphasizing his need for her, he is proving that he can do without her, because he is walking alone.

It all seems normal enough, but look at the micro-level to appreciate the marvel of what's happening as Keirkegaard's mother plays Ginger Rogers to her infant's Fred Astaire. You can see the power of implicit communication as she shores him up when he totters and in their shared joy as she amplifies his confidence and pride. She's fully immersed in the subjective experience of her toddler and this informs her every move, each intuitively calibrated and contingent to his. Never intruding, she's going about the job of growth-supporting interactive regulation, implicitly, without a word spoken. Only the right brain can perform such magic.

Except for intense moments, our immersion and sense of merger with patients are less complete. There is a spectrum of attunement depth. Run-of-the-mill attunement tends to involve an in-and-out sampling, but it does the job of informing us about our patients' subjective experience so that when they're tottering or avoiding stressful affects we know intuitively what relational moves to make. Such moderate attunement may often be prolonged and set up shared flow states.

On the patient side, run-of-the-mill attunement provides a sufficient illusion of merger to embolden them with the assurance that we're with them, shoring them up and communicating our positive expectations. Yet, as they allow themselves to experience dangerous emotions and as they modulate the intensity of affect to a tolerable level, like Kierkegaard's toddler, they have the experience of doing it by themselves. Such accomplishments often generate a bonding warmth and even a measure of pride that mitigates whatever pain is involved.

Working with avoidant devitalized patients

I've depicted a devitalized, inhibited personality with a fundamental regulatory disorder resulting from shame trauma in the early attachment relationship. Chronic insensitivity to and dismissal of the infant's affect states result in a narcissistically damaged, insecure self and object relations developed to defend against anticipated shame. At the neurological level the trauma results in an impaired limbic-autonomic system in the right brain and over-reliance on the left. These result in a down-regulated set point and down-regulated responses to stress, deficient capacity to regulate hyper-arousal and a fear of being overwhelmed by it, avoidant defenses against stressful stimuli that impede introspection and growth, an underdeveloped inner world, a disposition toward auto-regulation, deficient capacity to process one's own affect and affect states of others and little capacity for intersubjective relating. Together, they represent a formidable barrier to therapeutic engagement and to living fully.

I've argued that attunement is crucial to relationally mediated development. However, in patients with avoidant trauma, the limbic-autonomic system, which is responsible for attunement, is maldeveloped. Attunement, the thing they failed to get and most need, may be beyond their capacity. It's not just that avoidant personalities shy away from the affective intensity of connection; they lack the neurological procedures to accomplish it.

Now what? How do we connect to do our job? There is, I believe, an inroad through the left brain that facilitates an initial therapeutic alliance and lays the ground work for deeper treatment.

Therapeutic actions may be classified as bottom-up, referring to implicit/right-brain-dominant interactions, versus top-down, referring to interactions that are explicit/left-brain-dominant. The former engages emotions directly and relies on here-and-now experiencing for effecting change. Regulation theory proposes that right-brain-mediated, direct implicit exchange of affect is most efficient for repairing the affect-regulating and relational deficiencies resulting from avoidant/dismissive trauma.[8]

Top-down, left-brain-dominant therapeutic actions work through explicit cognition addressing affective experience indirectly through verbal reflective processes—by talking about experience. These processes include observation, psychoeducation and the mentalizing of affect and states of consciousness organized around it (Hill, 2015). This is where the treatment of avoidant trauma can begin. Rather than the deeper intimacy of direct exchanges of affect involved in subject-to-subject-attuned relating, the patient is engaged through the less intense, indirect, side-by-side intimacy of shared attention. While it lacks the expanded complexity engendered by shared states of consciousness (Tronick et al., 1998), it's a start.

Beginning at the verbal reflective level, where affects are seen from a distance and known before experienced, accommodates avoidant patients' fears of being overwhelmed and allows them to approach disturbing affects at their own pace, often outside of treatment and in private. (Recall that they rely on auto-regulation and shy way from dyadic regulation.) The intersubjective deficiencies resulting from the trauma are also respected. Beginning their treatment with explicit processes accommodates what avoidant patients can and cannot do.

Given the emotional fears and the regulatory and relational limitations of avoidant patients, an unobtrusive treatment is called for (Grossmark, 2018). Yet vitalization will have to come from the outside and we are inevitably looking for ways to connect with and up-regulate such patients; to breathe life into the intersubjective field. Director (2016), for example, proposes acting as a catalyst to amplify existing, but dimly lit, self-affirming/up-regulating internal objects, a creative solution to the problem of having to bring about vitality without being intrusive. From the point of view of regulation theory she is making a positive internal regulating object more effective. Schwartz Cooney (2018), acting as a new object and seizing a now-moment as an opportunity to connect and generate affect, makes the implicit therapeutic relationship explicit. In this way she solves the problem of devitalized patients' deficiencies in registering implicit communications of affect and is able to create what she calls a "vitalizing enactment." In what follows I discuss using the early phase of treatment to establish connection and moments of shared affect at levels of intensity avoidant patients can tolerate before moving gradually toward full intersubjective relating.

The initial phase of the treatment of avoidant trauma typically includes the exploration of the internal working model; i.e. object relations and affect-regulating patterns that developed to cope with a rejecting mother. This is fertile ground for top-down therapeutic actions that may serve as opportunities for an initial connection and up-regulating interactions.

Opportunities may emerge as the patient is giving us a first take on themselves and their lives, especially from their presentation of their past and present attachment relationships or any events in which the sequelae of the attachment trauma manifest. As we make observations, explore their experience and offer occasional possible explanations, we earn their trust in our nurturing intentions and competency. Importantly, we are also disconfirming their trauma-based expectation of being shamed when vulnerabilities are exposed. We are beginning the disruption of their insecure internal working model and opening the possibility of a new kind of attachment relationship that is available and safe for dyadic regulation.

Much of this is psychoeducational. Avoidant patients are often alexithymic and in need of an emotional vocabulary. Clarification of their attachment relationships is often eye opening (hyper-arousal) and may generate a subtle shared pleasure of discovery and hopefulness. The same is true of the observation of their down-regulated arousal pattern and how it plays out in their personality. Education about trauma in general and specifically relating to theirs is a critical aspect of the early stage of treatment. Avoidant patients don't think of themselves as traumatized so it's also eye opening. Understanding trauma gives them a cognitive grasp of what ails them and helps to lift the trauma-related shame that plagues them. Perhaps most importantly, such explicit formulations of inner states—the implicit goings on in their relationships, their fear of affect, etc.—while none of it pleasant, provides opportunities for shared positive affect and connection. There is shared hope and warmth that comes from understanding what's wrong and why, and it comes at a level of intensity they can tolerate.

Such episodes often begin with reports of events in a patient's life in which they are enacting their insecure attachment dynamics. Among them, there is none more vitalizing, nor with more pervasive effects, than the discovery of dissociated shame as it plays out in interpersonal functioning, and nothing is more appreciated than having its inhibiting weight lifted.

Shame has a special place in an avoidant patient's trauma. It is the affect that traumatized him/her. Dissociated shame is central to the sense of self and organizes relationships. Building the capacity to process shame is a central therapeutic aim. The initial pointing to enacted shame may be complemented by an introduction to pride. Because of their fears of being overwhelmed by hyper-arousal, pride also tends to be outside their affective range. Avoidant patients are disposed toward the low end of the shame–pride axis.

In my experience an introduction to shame and pride often comes, in mundane moments, by making explicit an implicit enactment of it outside of therapy. Shame and pride, experienced at a remove, set the stage for later moments when they may be dealt with in the moment, subject to subject. In what follows I first give an example of enacted shame observed in a gist memory of social anxiety and of the implicit being made explicit. I then give an example of an observation of repressed pride, the defense against it being interrupted in the moment and accompanied by interactive regulation that allows the pride to be experienced.

Tom is 40 years old and began once-a-week psychotherapy at the request of his wife who complained of being lonely. It was not a new complaint nor is it unusual for an avoidant personality to begin treatment at the behest of a spouse. He had his own concerns too. His work life had faltered. His early sessions were mostly about this. In his early 30s he'd started a business with a partner who dominated him and eventually forced him out. By the time I started to see him, Tom was working as a mid-level manager in a large corporation and "going nowhere." It sounded like he had been moderately depressed, although he didn't seem to know it. Although shame was laced throughout his presentation, I saw no opportunities to approach it.

An opportunity came in the fourth month of treatment when he received an evaluation at work in which he was described as aloof. It was arrived at through a system in which he was evaluated by colleagues. He thought the idea that he was aloof odd, and that they were misinterpreting his shyness. He'd always been socially inhibited, which he'd mentioned in the very beginning of treatment and not since. Our conversation went to his shyness and I asked him what he knew about it.

TOM: Makes it difficult at business conferences. I'm not good at working the room. Lack of confidence, I guess.

DH: Confidence? In what?

TOM: That they'll be interested.

DH: Interested?

TOM: In what I have to say.

DH: You think they won't value what you say—that they look down on you?

TOM: I guess.

DH: It sounds like you expect to feel ashamed.

TOM: I guess.

And that was that. He moved on to another topic.

All this transpired without any obvious emotion, but there were some pauses and no eye contact. This indicates mostly left-brain processing. However, the metaphor of being looked down on, which pictures shame and activates the right brain, may have been what blew on the embers of his dissociated/unformulated shame. I could sense as I said it that he'd seen shame from a distance and it had interested him. The next time I heard about shame was several weeks later when he mentioned an incident in which his wife criticized him and he felt ashamed in front of his daughter. He then said,

TOM: I know you've got this *thing* about shame. (Since the topic had only come up that one time, I thought he had probably been coming across it by himself.)

DH: I do think it's a thing for you. Let's make sure we know what we're talking about.

I then embarked on a brief description of shame; that it was experienced through the eyes of others, shuts us down and makes us want to hide, and that it's our most painful affect. I showed him the hypo-aroused posture of shame (head down or at least eyes averted, muscles flaccid, shoulders rounded, compressing the chest – a down-regulated expression of a diminished self). As with the metaphor, I am depicting shame and activating the right brain. I also took the opportunity to introduce pride as its opposite: head erect, chest expanded, a hyper-aroused display of the inflated self.

Both shame and pride were occasional topics over the rest of the first year, always using verbal reflection and talking about his history or events outside of therapy. I had observed that he didn't seem to take in compliments and suggested that he might fear being overwhelmed by pride's hyperarousal. After telling me that in his family pride was a sin, he told me that once, in high school, he received an unexpected honor. Asked to come to the front of the class to receive it, he was unable to speak.

Several months later in therapy the following incident occurred. Note the switch from verbal reflection to implicit communications and subject-to-subject relating.

Tom waved away a compliment that I had embedded, without much thought and as an aside, in a discussion of something or other. His wave popped out at me and struck me as funny. His dismissal of his feelings had been an ongoing topic but here he was doing it in broad daylight! I tilted my head, raised my eyebrows slightly, smiled warmly and imitated his wave. This was done spontaneously and, if I'm able to reconstruct what happened with accuracy, my imitation began before his wave ended. As we then laughed together his eyes filled with tears of pride.

The opportunity to disrupt a defensive procedure like this is as unusual as it is for the implicit communications to be so obvious. It's important to note that there were undoubtedly concurrent micro-interactions regulating Tom's affect and making it possible for him to risk experiencing pride. Surely the shared laughter offset whatever shame was attached to crying. This was all implicitly mediated, right brain to right brain, subject to subject, and I suspect that this moment had greater effect than all the words spoken about pride to that point.

Summary and conclusion

I have proposed beginning the treatment of avoidant/devitalized patients using left-brain-dominant, explicit reflection and engaging in the, for them, more tolerable, indirect intimacy of shared attention;

i.e. talking about affect states. This introduction to affect may serve as the basis for subsequent direct, implicit exchanges of affect and mutual regulation (primary intersubjectivity) and for intersubjective therapeutic actions that engender subjectivity. In severe cases this may be a lengthy process that can be as stressful for some therapists as obvious "difficult patients" who suffer from a hyper-aroused bias, are action-prone and are often enmeshed and in open conflict with their therapists. Avoidant personalities cope with the opposite and pose opposite difficulties: hypo-aroused bias, inertness, proneness to inaction and relational distance. In my experience, significant changes can occur, especially with regard to the regulation of the shame–pride axis, tolerance for stress, socio-emotional intelligence and the capacity for intimacy and self-experience.

It's not just intersubjectivity that is a developmental achievement (Benjamin, 1995). Subjectivity also develops. In devitalized/avoidant personalities, due to deficient affect-regulating capacities and diminished affective experience, the development of the implicit/subjective self may barely get off the ground and, to the extent it does, is often on shaky ground. Ultimately, we're treating a trauma-induced developmental arrest. Therapy must begin with the development of the capacity to regulate affect and, alongside it, the development of subjectivity. One avoidant patient told me that in good sessions he felt like he was giving birth to himself.

Notes

1 The limbic system is responsible for assessing body-based affect as well as the affect state of the object. It regulates the autonomic nervous system which has two parts. The sympathetic aspect is responsible for hyper-arousal, the parasympathetic aspect for hypo-arousal. Optimally the system is balanced, with each component serving as a counterforce to the other. The capacity to regulate affect depends on this balance. Trauma biases the system toward either hyper- or hypo-arousal.

2 We begin life highly dependent on dyadic regulation. The fundamental role of the caretaker is to keep the infant in regulated/homeostatic states. The patterns of such interactive regulation become internalized as the procedures for auto-regulation. Optimally we are able to use either auto- or dyadic regulation depending on the circumstances. Dyadic regulation is more efficient and the aversion to it is costly.

3 Chronic negative states of low arousal represent an additional handicap. Emde (1991, p. 24) has argued that "positive emotions are crucial for adaptation; provide significant incentives for learning, communication and development." The list could go on.
4 It's noteworthy that we *allow* this rather than make it happen. Recall that the left-brain secondary processes inhibit those of the right. We must give up this control and surrender (Ghent, 1990) to right-brain primary processes. Like Kris's regression in the service of the ego, dropping into right-brain-dominant states of consciousness is regression in the service of development, the difference being that attunement involves a mutual regression (Aron and Bushra, 1998).
5 Research on the therapeutic alliance has shown patient–therapist matches in bodily movements, levels of cortisol and oxytocin, breathing patterns and vocal pitches when patients and therapists are in synch (Koole & Tschacher, 2016; Zilcha-Mano & Ramseyer, 2020). Schore (2019a, 2019b) reports research using simultaneous functional magnetic resonance imaging (fMRI: hyper-scanning) and electroencephalogram (EEG) measures showing corresponding neurological activations and levels of arousal when unconscious communication is synchronized.
6 Importantly, the right brain is activated in states of hyper-arousal, the left in states of moderate and hypo-arousal (Schore, 2015). This may help to explain why avoidant personalities tend to be left-brain-dominant.
7 In *The Master and his Emissary* (2009), McGilchrist warns that civilization is becoming increasingly and dangerously left-brain-dominant.
8 Trauma-based body therapies are increasingly being incorporated into psychodynamic therapy (Eldredge and Cole, 2008; Levit, 2018; Rappoport, 2012) and, along with eye movement desensitization and reprocessing (EMDR) and neurofeedback are a consideration for severe cases of avoidant trauma, especially when it has been exacerbated by subsequent trauma.

Bibliography

Alcaro, A., Carta, S., & Panksepp, J. (2017). The Affective Core of the Self: A Neuro-Archetypical Perspective on the Foundations of Human (and Animal) Subjectivity. *Frontiers in Psychology*, 8:1424. doi: 10.3389/fpsyg.2017.01424

Aron, L. (2000). Self-Reflexivity and the Therapeutic Action of Psychoanalysis. *Psychoanalytic Psychology*, 17:667–689.

Aron, L., & Benjamin, J. (1999, April). Intersubjective Processes (Recognition and Identification) in the Therapeutic Action of Psychoanalysis.

Paper presented at the Spring Meeting of Division 39 of the American Psychological Association, New York.

Aron, L., & Bushra, A. (1998). Mutual Regression: Altered States in the Psychoanalytic Situation. *Journal of the American Psychoanalytic Association*, 46(2):389–412.

Bach, S. (1985). *Narcissistic States and the Therapeutic Process.* New York, NY: Jason Aronson.

Benjamin, J. (1990). Recognition and Destruction: An Outline of Intersubjectivity. In S.A. Mitchell & L. Aron (Eds.), *Relational Psychoanalysis: The Emergence of a Tradition* (pp. 193–200). Hillsdale, NJ: Analytic Press.

Benjamin, J. (1995). *Like Subjects, Love Object: Essays on Recognition and Sexual Difference.* New Haven, CT: Yale University Press.

Benjamin, J. (1999). Afterword. In S. Mitchell & L. Aron (Eds.), *Relational Psychoanalysis* (pp. 201–210). Hillsdale, NJ: Analytic Press.

Boston Change Process Study Group. (2002). Explicating the Implicit. *International Journal of Psychoanalysis, 83*:1051–1062.

Boston Change Process Study Group. (2010). *Change in Psychotherapy.* New York, NY: Norton.

Bowlby, J. (1973). *Attachment and Loss*, Vol. 2: *Separation.* New York, NY: Basic Books.

Cardena, E. (1994). The Domain of Dissociation. In: S.J. Lynn & R.W. Rhue (Eds.), *Dissociation: Theoretical, Clinical, and Research Perspectives* (pp. 15–31). New York: Guilford.

Damasio, A. (1994). *Descartes' Error: Emotion, Reason, and the Human Brain.* New York, NY: Putnam.

Damasio, A. (1999). *The Feeling of What Happens: Body and Emotion in the Making of Consciousness.* New York, NY: Harcourt.

Damasio, A. (2010). *Self Comes to Mind: Constructing the Conscious Brain.* New York, NY: Pantheon.

Director, L. (2016). The Analyst as Catalyst: Cultivating Mind in the Shadow of Neglect. *Psychoanalytic Dialogues*, 26:685–697.

Eldredge, C.B., & Cole, G.W. (2008). Learning from Work with Individuals with a History of Trauma: Some Thoughts on Integrating Body-oriented Techniques and Relational Psychoanalysis. In F.S. Anderson (Ed.), *Bodies in Treatment: The Unspoken Dimension* (pp. 79–102). New York, NY: Analytic Press.

Emde, R.N. (1991). Positive Emotions for Psychoanalytic Theory: Surprises from Infancy Research and New Directions. *Journal of the American Psychoanalyic Association,* 39S (Supplement):5–44.

Emde, R.N. (1994). Moving Ahead: Integrating Influences of Affective Processes for Development and for Psychoanalysis. *International Journal of Psychoanalysis,* 80(2):317–339.

Ghent, E. (1990). Masochism, Submission, Surrender: Masochism as a Perversion of Surrender. *Contemporary Psychoanalysis,* 26:108–136.

Grossmark, R. (2018). *The Unobtrusive Relational Analyst: Explorations in Psychoanalytic Companioning.* New York, NY: Routledge.

Herman, J. (1997). *Trauma and Recovery: The Aftermath of Violence- from Domestic Abuse to Political Terror*. New York, NY: Guilford.

Hill, D. (2015). *Affect Regulation Theory: A Clinical Model.* New York, NY: Norton.

Holmes, E.A., Brown, R.J., Mansell, W., Pasco Fearon, R., Hunter, E., Frasquilho, F., & Oakley, D.A. (2005). Are there two Qualitatively Distinct Forms of Dissociation? A Review and some Clinical Implications. *Clinical Psychological Review*, 25:1–23.

Kernberg, O. (1975). *Borderline Conditions and Pathological Narcissism.* New York, NY: Jason Aronson.

Koole, S.L., & Tschacher, W. (2016). Synchrony in Psychotherapy: A Review and an Integrative Framework for the Therapeutic Alliance. Frontiers in Psychology, 7:862. doi: 10.3389/fpsyg.2016.00862

Lanius, R.A., Vermetten, E., Loewenstein, R.J., Brand, B., Schmahl, C., Bremner, J.D., & Spiegel, D. (2010). Emotion Modulation in PTSD: Clinical and Neurobiological Evidence for a Dissociative Subtype. *American Journal of Psychiatry*, 167:640–647.

Lanius, R.A., Brand, B., Vermetten, E., Frewen, P.A., & Spiegel, D. (2012). The Dissociative Subtype of Posttraumatic Stress Disorder: Rationale, Clinical and Neurobiological Evidence, and Implications. *Depression and Anxiety,* 29:1–8. doi: 10.1002/da.21889

Levit, D. (2018). Somatic Experiencing: In the Realms of Trauma and Dissociation—What We Can Do, When What We Do, Is Really Not Good Enough. *Psychoanalytic Dialogues,* 28:586–601.

McGilchrist, I. (2009). *The Master and his Emissary: The Divided Brain and the Making of the Western World.* New Haven, CT: Yale University Press.

Meares, R. (2012). *A Dissociation Model of Borderline Personality Disorder*. New York, NY: Norton.

Pizer, S. (2018). Deep Listening/Affective Attunement. In R. Barsness (Ed.), *Core Competences of Relational Psychoanalysis.* New York, NY. Routledge.

Rappoport, E. (2012). Creating the Umbilical Cord: Relational Knowing and the Somatic Third. *Psychoanalytic Dialogues*, 22(3):375–388.

Schore, A.N. (1994). *Affect Regulation and the Origin of the Self: The Neurobiology of Emotional Development*. New York, NY: Norton.

Schore, A.N. (2011). The Right Brain Implicit Self lies at the Core of Psychoanalysis. *Psychoanalytic Dialogues, 21*:1–26.

Schore, A.N. (2012). *The Science of the Art of Psychotherapy*. New York, NY: Norton.

Schore, A.N. (2015). Book Review of *The Emotional Life of Your Brain*, by Richard J. Davidson and Sharon Begley. *Psychoanalytic Psychology*, 32(3):539–547.

Schore, A.N. (2019a). *Right Brain Psychotherapy.* New York, NY: Norton.

Schore, A.N. (2019b). *The Development of the Unconscious Mind.* New York, NY: Norton.

Schwartz Cooney, A. (2018). Vitalizing Enactment: A Relational Exploration. *Psychoanalytic Dialogues,* 28(3):340–354.

Spitzer, C., Barnow, S., Freyberger, H.J., & Grabe, H.J. (2006). Recent Developments in the Theory of Dissociation. World Psychiatry, 5:82–86.

Sroufe, A.L. (1979). Socioemotional Development. In J. Osofsky (Ed.), *Handbook of Infant Development*. New York, NY: Wiley.

Stern, D.N. (1985). *The Interpersonal World of the Child.* New York, NY: Basic Books.

Stern, D.N. (2004). *The Present Moment in Psychotherapy and Everyday Life*. New York, NY: Norton.

Stern, D.N. (2010). *Forms of Vitality.* New York, NY: Oxford University Press.

Trevarthen, C. (1979). Communication and Cooperation in Early Infancy: A Description of Primary Intersubjectivity. In M.M. Bullows (Ed.), *Before Speech: The Beginning of Interpersonal Communication* (pp. 321–348). New York, NY: Cambridge University Press.

Tronick, E. and the Boston Change Process Study Group. (1998). Dyadically Expanded States of Consciousness and the Process of Therapeutic Change. Infant Mental Health Journal, 19(3):290–299.

Van der Kolk, B.H. (2005). Developmental Trauma Disorder: Towards a Rational Diagnosis for Chronically Traumatized Children. *Psychiatric Annals, 35*(5):401–408.

Van der Kolk, B.H. (2014) *The Body Keeps the Score.* New York, NY: Viking Penguin.

Zilcha-Mano, S., & Ramseyer, F. (2020). New Approaches to Exploring Processes of Change in Counseling Psychology: Insights and Principles for Future Research. *Journal of Counseling Psychology*, 67(4).

Chapter 11

The analyst as catalyst

Cultivating mind in the shadow of neglect

Lisa Director

Introduction

I describe an effort to cultivate mind and deepen relatedness in patients who exhibit unelaborated thought and constricted relatedness, due to the effects of a certain kind of neglect.

In this effort, I draw on vitalization as viewed by Alvarez (2012) concerning unreachable patients. As she writes, some of these patients may be lost in despair, habituated to deprivation, and so, constricted by atrophied psychic function. Such patients need a "call" to psychic life, Alvarez says (1992), communicated by an analyst's urgent, formative attention to their feelings and needs.

I find that both subjectivity and intersubjectivity may be underdeveloped in some patients raised amidst absent or unresponsive care, which impedes affective aliveness and deepening of connection. To me, some of these patients require the analyst to serve as an enlivening object (Director, 2009a) – that is, a catalyst, who takes proactive steps to summon a psychic realm to the patient's experience, and forge components of dyadic bonds that sow continued growth.

Case illustration

At a glance, he appears unremarkable. I find him leafing through a newspaper, not looking troubled or fraught. I greet him; he does not reply. He never does. He takes his seat in silence, then slowly turns to me to begin. His face is impassive; it tells me he's in place, if not entirely a presence. My spirit sinks a bit, and I gird myself.

This early encounter with my patient – unalive, stamped by routine – provides an entrée to my theme: treating patients who seem very constricted in their relatedness, due to serious disturbance or, like my patient, encapsulated states of nondevelopment. All analysts would recognize the features: blunted affect, concrete thought, inner lives void of fantasy, more likely occupied by inanimate things. "It is what it is" – so dehumanizing an expression – captures the quality of their speech and asymbolic means of forming experience. Personalities that lack vividness and the play of imagination can make such patients seem dull. I am anxious writing about such patients – perhaps, in parallel, expecting the reader's lack of interest.

I am also addressing neglect, which has not compelled our attention as trauma has. While there are many degrees of neglect, some ordinary forms of neglect, arising from parental limitation, can cause whole swathes of subjectivity in children to lie undeveloped. Such parental limitation can result, as an example, if parents were raised amidst emotional unresponsiveness themselves, so, in turn, lack abilities to recognize affective signals or need, or know what to provide in response (Crittenden, 1993; Seligman, 1994). As stated, such neglect, while unmalicious, can foreclose growth of subjectivity in a child in ways that escape our notice. How? The marks may show up quietly, as areas of unrealization that do not cause gross nuisance (Music, 2009). *Unremarkable*, as I said, regarding my patient. Actually, research suggests that neglect may cause more damage to the developing brain than trauma (Perry, 2002; Music, 2009). Perry wrote that early lack of stimulation prevents the dendritic growth needed for systems that mediate bonding and communication. "Use it or lose it," Perry warned: the links never made neurally underlie the links that these individuals find it hard to make with other people.

How do we awaken their dormant potentials to build mind and relatedness? I first turn to object relations theorists, who have guided insight into primitive states or unrealized function through their interest in developmental failure. Broadly, the British Independent and Bionian schools mapped the early care needed to assemble cohesion and enable mental life (holding, containment), breaches of which could impair growth. While classical Kleinian theory was not based on provision, Klein's ([1959] 1975) stress on the introjected good object as the core of ego capacity made nourishment and love, phantasied and real, essential to mental development.

However, Mitchell (1988) criticized views of dysfunction grounded in earliest, unmet needs, for depicting the adult patient as an environmental victim and for confining such needs to infancy. Rather, in Mitchell's view, early conditions of care shape relational patterns with which, however maladaptively, the child-then-adult negotiates such needs throughout life. Dysfunctional engagement, to Mitchell, reflects an adult's complex approach, actively sustained, to conflictual interpersonal situations, including treatment.

While the relational school authorized a more complex, co-constructive role for patients, the emphasis, in some relational theory, on a capable if challenged patient seemed to leave out patients who lack such means. Some patients sit before us seemingly stranded in aloneness, unequipped for collaborative engagement. Even when such incapacity is not due to serious disorder as in autism, marked schizoid states or encapsulated nondevelopment can constrict thought and affect so that object contact appears limited, often mediated along practical lines. Patients who are dulled by concrete ideation and flattened emotion require the analyst to take initiative as an enlivening object, as I (Director 2009a, 2009b) described, to instill links to people and mentalized thought. Across schools, analysts working with unmentalized states are making use of active modes – for example, co-involvement in enactment, attention to affectivity, use of figurablity[1] – to sense and build on, or give first voice or organization themselves to a psychic dimension of the patient's experience (Levine, 2013). Here, I focus on neglect's effects in constricting patients, and propose that the analyst must serve as a catalyst to induce elements of a meaning-making mind and the dyadic bonds that promote such function.

Let me delineate my approach further by citing two object relations theorists whom I draw on. Anne Alvarez, post-Kleinian therapist, wrote (2012) that with patients limited to rudimentary thought and relatedness, "vitalizing" interventions, in her terms, take precedence before efforts at explanation. With long-deprived patients, lost to connection and mindedness, the first order of communication need be that their experience *has* psychic meaning – a "call" to psychic life, said Alvarez (1992) that she imparts with intensified tone, beckoning subjectivity. Feelings and wants need an urgent, formative attention, she explained of some cut-off patients. To Alvarez, interest itself spurs psychic growth in neglected patients, because it challenges the "dumbness" and indifference of their internal objects.

I also draw on Neville Symington (2007), British Independent analyst, who likewise believes that it is the analyst's job "to help the patient to grow [his/her] mind" (p. 1415), through the analyst's emotionally imbued thought. Symington noted that destructive tendencies are grossly visible in people, while goodness dwells in them quietly. Yet it is the patient's good attributes, more than his bad ones, that need our recognition. Why? To Symington, goodness forms the synthesizing basis of the process that he called "mind-building."

In my view, both Alvarez and Symington accord the analyst an agentic role in the growth of the patient's mind, through the analyst's affective, recognizing responses. They seem to emphasize and build on object relations notions of countertransference and Bionian principles of containment to derive their responsiveness (Alvarez, 1992, 2012; Symington, 2001, 2007). Even when enlarged, the frameworks of countertransference and containment tend to confine these analysts' signature interventions to being *responses* to their patients. But I see their distinctly generative forms of involvement – vitalization from Alvarez, "focused wonder" from Symington, as he called it (2007, p. 1421) – as expressions of their subjectivities informing their responses. The contribution of the analyst's own subjectivity to her responses to the patient and the analytic interchange is explicitly recognized and inherent in the relational model, in contrast to the object relations tradition.

It is because of my self-aware use of my subjectivity that I can expressly argue for the role of catalyst.[2] Moreover, I believe it is through the relational school's inclusion of the analyst's subjectivity that we can expand the application of object relations ideas. Let me add that, while the analyst's subjectivity is assumed to relationalists, it is seldom examined in its various aspects. Here, in setting out my intention to serve as a catalyst, I express my conscious purpose. As I proceed, I will identify other aspects of my subjectivity, including my "self-reflective responsiveness" (Mitchell, 1997; see also Cooper, 2014), which helps in my self-enlivenment, and ultimately, the unconscious interplay of my object world with my patient's (Bass, 2001, 2003, 2009; Cooper, 2012, 2014; Davies, 1999, 2004, 2005).

My subjectivity is always in play; indeed, my "otherness" is what I utilize to enliven. But as a catalyst, here at work with the sequelae of a kind of neglect, I place priority on using my subjectivity to awaken my patient's growth. Bion (1994) said that the analyst's goal is to introduce the patient to himself. It is my main goal here for my patient to take his own emerging mind and psychic self with interest.

States of unrelatedness/forms of protection

Joe, in his 50s, called me seeking family therapy for problems in his relationships with his six children (four in their 20s and 30-year-old twins), which had grown during his wife's illness and death a few years earlier. When I met with him for a history, Joe spoke about his children dispassionately, at times in blunt terms that were jarring to me. Reported without affect, businesslike in tone, Joe seemed opaque to his own impact. But his kids' alienation led Joe to this conclusion: "it's tough to be with me." I suggested we work individually on that. We've met twice a week for five years.

The silence that Joe entered sessions with, described at the start of my chapter, was not generative, but inert. He seemed depressive, often remote; his face never brightened from an inner source of robustness. Almost always, I initiated discussion. Joe lacked a procedural grasp of engagement, so, talking would lurch: he'd repeat himself with a wearing effect, interject subjects like nonsequiturs, or if the chronology of his account ended, come to a halt. I felt few affective or other cues, not because Joe fought such processes, but because, in his seeming self-enclosure, his capacity for projection struck me as limited. Without the chief link that projective identification provides in communication and comprehension (Bion, 1959, 1962a), I lacked crucial bases for responding to him, or "reading" him at all. However closely we were seated, there simply was no current running between us. There was no "thinking" within Joe, or in me on his behalf, at this juncture (Bion, 1962a).

Silence, however, did not bother Joe; to be an isolate in another's presence was his norm. I internally scanned material for ideas, sometimes feeling anxious, at times taxed by the effort of keeping us viable. When my thoughts felt stale, I'd flee my mind by asking questions – about his marriage, and so on – which Joe answered matter-of-factly to the end of his data. My questions fruitless and, to me, intrusive given his silences, I was sent back to my own mind. Eventually, my self-reflection would yield guidance. I'd hoped that Joe's exposure to my thinking about him would rouse his psychic activity, but that wasn't so. He showed no interest in me – outside my problem-solving role – which I could harness by training my focus on him. But I came to find that my thinking about his children captured his attention. So my thoughts about them produced the components that would register, amplify through words, link to other components with the onset of affect, and form roots for building mindedness in Joe (Levine, 2013).

But at first, his silence and stiffness made him look like an anomaly in a therapy suite. How would he – we – ever fit? His humble sense of his own lacks moved me: "I'm not a good communicator, I don't know how." For the modest goal of a "dialogue" with his kids, Joe was there to "fix" what he lacked. We may have joined through our superegos, at the start. Joe would work hard for his kids, I on his behalf: it made for a connection, of sorts. Unbeknownst to me, my diligence was an aspect of an internal object of my own which would emerge later in my awareness and figured into my response to Joe.

"We are not born with a mind but with the potential for creating" one through "reflective communication," Symington (2007, p. 1410) said. Joe is one of ten children of Italian Americans – his mother a home-maker, his father a manager, both observant Catholics (Joe is not). The number of children may partly explain his mother's habit of forgetting his name. Joe's father was short-tempered; he'd had hardship after his own mother died in his infancy. "He was all about survival," Joe said, "what to do to get by." Joe was shy, bad at sports and school, socially awkward. He felt he was disappointing as the oldest son. His father has been partly assimilated by Joe (as in his own anger), but remains a partly separable object – obtuse or disapproving. Joe's struggles didn't engage either parent. They only asked, "Did you do your chores, did you do your homework?" "There wasn't time for emotions," Joe said; to his parents, it was all about just "barreling through."

Joe, too, uses movement and physicality as a self-container (Bick, 1968). Movement, in place of joy, overrides his dulled affect, and gives him agency (Fonagy, Moran, & Target, 1993). An engineer, Joe succeeded at work, muscling through projects. He recalled driving his kids for hours to new homes or jobs without any complaint, but without any conversation.

How pained I was, picturing these silent car trips! – until I found an empathic view. Could there be any more graphic display of Joe's internal world than his driving his children to these meaningful destinations, and right beside them, exchanging no discussion of the journey? Alvarez (2012), drawing on Bion ([1962b] 1984), believes that an infant is equipped with a preconception of a responsive, engaged other, but if that expectation isn't met, a conception of people as "interested," or interesting, never forms. Minds like Joe's, she suggests, might be occupied by "useless" or "empty" objects, versions of caregivers who, however close by, never turned toward their children to delve into their minds. So, Joe lacked an inner fount of interest from which he could originate a current of curiosity about people to use to discover his own children. I began to muse aloud about his children's involvements, to share the way a thought, say about a young person's activity, could be joined to other thoughts to create an overture.

Complementing Joe's movement was an inertness which had hindered his growth. I sought any sign of affect to build on. For example, he attended an important job fair with a newly graduated child, and said, meagerly, it was "good" to go; I said it felt *important* to him, so he'd gone to the same job fair now for a third time. He sent a link about a bowling tournament to a distant son, "because it's his hobby"; I said he seemed *eager* to renew their contact. After months of such plodding efforts, I asked Joe what kept him coming? "I miss my kids," he replied, flatly. Could he say more? In his literal fashion, he said, "I'm their father, they should be with me. I don't know." I nodded, and added, I sensed that there was more to his motive.

Making contact with emotions and objects

My early efforts involved always stressing the psychic source of Joe's behavior, helping to build units of thought, and turning my "interest" from a standing attitude into a dynamic force whose vitality affects (Stern, D.N., 2010) might propel further thought. But these efforts would not have had the immediate effects that several crises did, which demanded more from Joe. Hardest was a daughter's abruptly moving abroad, amidst minor legal offenses.

Joe felt to blame for his daughter's problems, due to his marital unhappiness, which had hardened long before his wife's illness. I was now startled to learn that, while Joe felt guilt for his marital failure, he felt none for having started a new relationship, with a younger woman, during his wife's illness. To Joe, his marriage had "died" long ago, and his kids didn't "know." Since his wife's death, his companion had joined his life publicly, and Joe started getting emails from his children with questions about his relationship. Never having had his intentional acts framed within the views of others (Fonagy, Gergely, Jurist, & Target, 2002), Joe did not realize that his behavior could be seen as hurtful to his children, nor could he empathically grasp their sense of betrayal.

Our sessions became a primer on theory of mind, and to Joe, "the big takeaway of treatment." They were beneficial to me, too, because his incapacity for perspectivism, and nondefensiveness about it, defused my potential anger at him for his lack of consideration of his kids, in this context. I led Joe to grope for his feelings about his marital problems. But it was not only our formulations of his mental states that initiated mentalization, but also Joe's goodness that played a role, as Symington suggests. These discussions were laborious for Joe, but he was fueled by reparative urges. His effort in these sessions could not have been as noticeable to his children as his lack of consideration had been, but it was synthesizing in effect: Joe wrote back to his children to account for his behavior, and, having realized it himself, admitted failing them in mishandling his marital unhappiness.

Joe's goodness forged another crucial link – to me. Writing was hard, Joe said, which was obvious as he read aloud his draft letters and tripped over his bad grammar. He'd then crane his arm awkwardly around his paper, and in cramped script, correct himself. This simple sight and his halting explanations to his children touched me deeply. Joe's penmanship may have been crude, but he had decency written all over him.

Affect and mind grow in tandem, we might say. My warmth, now, for Joe opened a pathway for me to my own inner bond to my father – a man unlike Joe, but similar in humble, hardening origins, who could be tender toward his children. I wondered if I had drawn on a fondness, as well as diligence – both aspects of my paternal bond – to incline me toward Joe from the start? For Joe, assembling a more mindful coherence (Levine, 2013) from past, fragmentary events opened pathways to his affects – at times, painfully. The hardship he had caused his children now caused him regret and self-recrimination. But I consistently pointed out his restorative steps because, as Symington says, constructive processes need our recognition to grow. With my focus on his reparative longings, and his history a running narrative, further affect was stirred in Joe.

Joe found that, if he tried talking to his kids about his past behavior instead of writing, he'd "choke up." Joe said: "It's like I've got these feelings, and they're trapped." His observation itself conveyed augmented thought – *about* himself, *to* me. We were now talking.

A favorite neighbor then died. When Joe reported "choking up" while thanking a sibling for attending the funeral, I noticed aloud how he sometimes faltered over positive feelings. "Gratitude," as he called it, concerning his sibling, sounded like an experience close to love. I asked what it was like, in his family, expressing love? He replied, "I guess I knew I was loved, but nobody ever said it."

Joe paused, then said: "My father thought I was a crybaby. I just didn't have faith in myself, that I could *do* anything." His father had been motherless, and had gotten through it. "So he'd just say, 'What do you have to feel bad about? You've got two parents, and siblings.' It was like, 'Stop it!'"

A few moments passed between us. Then, I said quietly, "He made you feel weak for having feelings." "Maybe that's the reason I learned to keep feelings in," Joe replied.

Joe and I had spoken of his parents' failure to notice his aloneness, or to seek out his hobbies and skills. Now, compounding this awareness was the sense of shame Joe recounted with his father, for his inabilities. Joe became a big doer, in time, but his "glass half-empty" view of himself, in his words, persisted. His self-criticism still extended, at times, to his tone with his children, which I reflected. As he monitored that tendency, another dimension of Joe opened – as in this session, after Joe reported catching himself being negative.

He finished his account, and paused. Then, Joe began to tell me about "this guy named Don," who'd been a church member and family friend. Joe had begun to drink as a teenager because it helped with his insecurities, he thought. He had an incident of disorderly conduct, and Don had a talk with him. "Don said – you know, nothing judgmental. He didn't say, 'Stop doing those bad things!' He just put it across, 'OK, you did this, I understand where you're at. But – you know, this can't happen any more.'"

We were quiet. Then, I said: "He spoke to you with understanding. How come your parents didn't notice how you'd struggled as a kid? Don saw you were having a hard time, and spoke to you with awareness." Joe said, "He led by example." I nodded, then asked: "How do you make room for his influence? It feels like only your father's influence takes hold of you."

I was touched by Joe's memory of Don, who softened both of us with his entry. My easy empathy for Joe, and the kindness he had received, told me that projective processes were under way, reciprocally. If inchoate at the start, an unconscious link between us had gathered strength and continuity.

Joe's object world had now filled out. Alongside the internalized object of his father, there was another paternal object, courtesy of Don, offering acceptance. Joe's mother seemed a figure who furnished elementary needs. I began to talk with Joe about the inner presences that I sensed within him – his uninterested or disregarding father, and the facilitating, though less available, Don. Relational analysts who draw on a model of multiplicity might use the language of self-states, assembled in relation to objects, to identify the varying factors affecting a patient's self-experience. But in my attempt to talk with Joe about the effects of these inner influences, I alluded to his internalized objects for several reasons.

First, Joe's sense of self was too spare to support the framework of self-states. The otherness of internal objects offered a useful means of entry into his internal world. Of course, internalized objects occupy a person's own psyche; they are "split off parts of the personality," Ogden (2002, p. 768) suggested. With a patient like Joe, who has not yet claimed such "parts," and their place in his own selfhood, or even recognized that they are there, it seemed a fitting first step to name then, and explain their presence as possible effects (real or imagined) of a closely known "other." Ideally, my goals would be to raise Joe's awareness of these inner forces, to make possible his own exercise of greater influence over processes of identification and differentiation. Specifically, my aim would be to help Joe become aware of powerful inner forces that made him feel dismissed or unvalued, and continued to constrain him; much fainter experiences of acceptance and changeability; and the ways in which aspects of the stronger attitudes had made their way unconsciously into his own character as a subject – with the hope of enabling reorganization of inner influences, toward

Joe's greater attainment of his desired way of being a father himself. Admittedly, these were long-range goals.

Some relational analysts write of using metaphor (Cooper, 2014) or descriptive characterizations of variable "selves" (Davies, 1998, 2004) to address the grip of internalized objects on patients' self-organizations. These approaches assume a capacity for self-reflectivity (if inaccessible at times) beyond the effort to establish mentalized content that I was working on. With Joe, naming influences in such form `as "your inner Don" was a basic step – and the concreteness of internal objects, as originally conceived by Klein, gave me terms for talking about internal forces that were aligned with his manner of mentalization (Lecours & Bouchard, 1997). Another example of my use of such terms follows in an excerpt shortly.

Yet I saw the higher potential for building mindedness in Joe's object relation involving Don, because of its dynamic aspects of *listening*. As Alvarez (1992, 1996, 2012) said in post-Kleinian terms, the neglected patient poses a twofold challenge: not only does his self have deficits, but also his internal objects are remote or dumb. In other words, a patient with undeveloped thought might be further deadened by lack of expectation that what he thinks could be found important to anyone. In effect, Alvarez suggests, a meaning-making mind entails internalization of listening: thoughts have to have been given importance by a listening object for the self to find its own thoughts worth hearing (see also Laub, 1992; Fonagy et al., 2002; Stern, D.B., 2010). Invoking Don gave me a ready-made link to Joe's internal experience, possibly deepening the impact of my own listening voice. It may also be that Joe's memories of Don were revived by his work with me, a view I will return to later.

In sum, investing my presence with a vibrant interest, naming Joe's objects and their effects, and activating links to internalized experiences of listening responsiveness were part of my effort to augment mental content and associativity, and promote shifts in Joe's internal world.

Enacted experience/unconscious communication

Vitalizing Joe's feelings and expanding affective resonance (Demos, 1984) lay the ground of relatedness. Some gains occurred with his children; much strain remained. A few unanswered emails to them led Joe to ask if it would "be better for the kids if they don't see me at all?" – sounding a question about himself that, to me, harkened back to boyhood. I pointed out the importance of an outing with one child, his advice sought by another. Invigorating Joe with my conviction was expressive of my subjectivity and my premise: to enlarge his worth, as Symington might say, would strengthen his inclinations toward openness and seeking – in effect, his desire to *know* (Bion, [1962b] 1984) – again, building mindedness.

An upcoming performance by one of his twins, a musician, caused new tensions. The prospect of Joe bringing his new partner, when his deceased wife had been so supportive of the son's music, stirred intense distress among the older kids. When Joe turned to me, I asked if a family session with the older kids might help. Since Joe had sought family work from me, it seemed right for me to mediate such a meeting. Joe agreed to it; the twins and other involved sibling did, too.

I had Joe's children come early to address powerful concerns they'd raised, and help them think about ways of constructively conveying them; Joe was to come soon after for the session. The discussion with the children needed to be separate, but it wasn't separate enough, for as I was still attending to their exchange of opinions, my buzzer sounded Joe's arrival. I stepped into the waiting room to ask Joe for a minute, so I could wrap up with them. As he sat, I was struck. The incongruity of the situation – Joe, in the waiting room, and me, in talking with his kids – "woke me up" to the enactment that I'd been engaging in (Bromberg, 1998, p. 285; see also Stern, 2004). Joe had spoken of his inabilities as a boy, and the shame they had caused him with his father; he had spoken a few times of embarrassment when he struggled to express himself in session. But the portrait I now faced of his seeming diminishment, as I had managed to exclude him, however circumstantially, from his own children's exchange, made me realize how I must have made him feel inferior and inadequate as a communicator all along, even by the sheer nature of psychotherapy. After all, Joe had told me that he didn't know how to communicate; yet, our every session relied on it. Symington (2007) captured the experience Joe must have had of his therapy when he described the particular shame of "being seen ... in an undeveloped state" (p. 1413).

What accounts for my inattention to my own role in causing Joe shame? Different schools would offer varied views. I will focus on ideas stemming from the interface of object relations and relational domains. Remember where Joe and I began? In our joined superegos? Symington (1983) wrote that that position could lock an analytic pair in. I was working, in earnest, to help Joe reach a goal that he was pursuing conscientiously. He was making progress – which, however real, may have dimmed my awareness of my other effects. Cooper (2012) saw a split between the analyst's experience of himself as a supportive external object, and awareness of himself as an internalized object that endangers. The patient's very success can serve the analyst's resistance to finding himself as that endangering internalized object. Until my waiting-room realization, I hadn't actively looked for myself as an internalized object that posed a shaming threat to Joe – which may have suited Joe, who wouldn't have wanted to see me that way.

Maybe I should have just *let him be*, and accepted the obtuseness and distance that endured within him (Bergstein, 2009), including with his children. I step back from this unusual session to look at this question. I took a proactive approach with Joe because he seemed to have "given up" on relating, causing an "atrophy" of function in him, as Alvarez (2012, pp. 22, 133) has described. It is true that Joe found withdrawal to be of defensive benefit, but I don't think that was the source of his condition. Rather, I think his potential for engagement had not been fully developed, so a self-enclosed position, with its appearance of withdrawal, became characteristic.

Let me return to my unawareness of my part in causing Joe shame, which crystallized for me at the family session, to consider another source – my grandiosity. That is, I wished for Joe even greater success with his kids than he had managed, to date. To me, by now, Joe was not all *stop* and *go*: he had a genuine goodness in his love for his children – a willingness to do anything for them – that I'd fully felt, and hoped they might perceive as well.

But in serving as family mediator, which may have carried my wish into my role that day with its potential for advocacy of him, I had slighted him myself, not only by briefly excluding him. When I asked Joe to wait, he took a seat in my waiting room – quietly and unquestioningly. It was in the nature of Joe's goodness to be unassuming. Goodness, after all, is not perfection. Perfection commands attention in its show of excellence. Goodness, in its ordinariness, asks nothing for itself. Had I made an assumption of Joe's cooperation, in my inadequate attention to scheduling that day, and taken his goodness for granted? I believe so. More broadly, Joe's selfhood itself, of which goodness was a part, was not yet fully established, so he did not know to stand up for himself, including with me. Taking a seat quietly may have reflected Joe's tenuous sense of a right to anything better. That I attended to Joe's weakly held right to self-regard by assuming a role in his meeting with his children but lost sight of it myself in my arrangements speaks again to the split in my ability to hold awareness of both my supportive and abandoning effects – a limitation theorized by Cooper, as earlier noted. My careless handling of Joe's selfhood in this way, and his goodness, put me most in touch with shame in myself.

It may have been the internalized object of my father – a man whose unheralded acts of generosity defined him, along with his shortcomings – that helped me grasp the modest essence of Joe's goodness, underscored on this occasion. My more nuanced appreciation for Joe's character, which included his flaws, led me to a further consolidation: if adequately secured, Joe's goodness would be *good-enough*, to qualify his fatherhood as amply loving and, when needed, thought-ful. In the deepening of our unconscious connection, I could now identify with Joe: in my offerings as his therapist, I hoped that my own goodness, given my lapses that day and others to come, would prove good-enough as well.

Conception and conclusion

Over time, my discussion of shame opened up with Joe, as we now saw his habit of "choking up" as an effort to prevent shame, and ways of removing himself as also protective. I raised my own inattention to the way that *I* brought on his shame. Joe admitted that therapy made him face his limitations as a communicator, with me and his kids – but that was his agenda, not my doing, he said. My role, for Joe, was still fitted to category; he viewed me as his "therapist," someone seen for professional services. Efforts I made to raise aspects of our relationship failed, as yet, to strike a chord.

But we had some humor now. Another time, Joe said it still wasn't natural to communicate, and maybe the reason was, "a bad teacher." He had a mischievous look, and we bantered – playfully but with an edge. He closed it, saying he "wouldn't be here if it wasn't effective." But the exchange was a way that he brought in, and I acknowledged, my limitations.

In fact, my need to face my own limitations was Joe's offering to me in our work (Suchet, 2015). Embedded in his reference to me as a "bad" teacher, however jokingly, was his recognition of the errors and inadequacies that I might bring to bear on his growth. I had to temper my commitment to my efforts as a catalyst with a realization of my own inadequacies. People change within the bounds of our capacities, as well as theirs; that was Joe's humbling reminder to me.

Symington (2007) often advises a student to "sit back, stay further from [a] patient" (p.1409), for a *fuller* perception of him. Looking across at Joe through these years, I realize that my perception of him has shifted greatly: from my first impression of him as wooden anomaly, to my image of him as homespun writer, to my recognition of his non-narcissistic goodness at core. My perception has given way to a conception, in Bion's terms, of his meaning. Joe, who began for me in impersonal facts, has become a symbolic being. The idea of Joe, *who he is as a person*, has gathered form in my mind. Joe had eventually married his girlfriend, and recently, I asked if he'd want a child with her.

"I would, if she does," Joe said. He talked about their different backgrounds, hers Hispanic, his Italian American, before concluding, "I think a child we had would be an interesting person." I had warmed, as I listened to him, with associations to men in my life, not only my father, who had been nurturers. The phrase, "maternal men," came to mind – with some wonder, in Symington's terms, at its occurrence now with Joe.

I said, about his wanting a child, "It's a way of being creative. It's the 'Don' in you. In you, like him, there's a caring provider, who wants to raise a young person and give him the resources and opportunities to make his way in the world."

Joe squeezed his cheek to manage emotion. I kept him company, saying lightly, "It's emotional, I feel it, too." Once composed, he said, "You're right. How to bring a young person into the world and give him what they need, to be whatever they want – that is something I care about."

How do we, as analysts, make a difference in our patients' inner lives? In this exchange, I again risked serving as the bad object, potentially prompting Joe's shame due to his surging feelings and incipient tears. But, to use another of Cooper's (2010) ideas, maybe I brought "newness" to that bad experience, through my own message of tolerance for feeling and shortcomings, including my own. I also gave voice to Joe's potential for identifying with Don, toward an internal lessening of his father's influence.

Of course, along with my reference to the "Don" in Joe, was my awareness of my own role as a "caring provider" for him. As I raised earlier, the synergistic effects of my own caring attention and the humane wash of feeling that came over Joe in evoking Don cannot be precisely sourced. In partial answer to my question, in the preceding paragraph, I agree with Bromberg (1998) and Cooper (2014) that the analyst *creates* the object, as it emerges through her own engagement with the patient, which entails the activation of internalized experiences and her own authentic offerings, in the dynamic, affectively tinged here and now (Joseph, 1989).

But that is only part of my answer (here pertaining to the junction of my listening responsiveness and that of an internalized relation with Don). Where neglect or other damage results in a patient's unrelatedness, concreteness of thought, and associated atrophy of function, the analyst *creates* an object of a different order. The analyst-as-catalyst is wholly new, or a wholly new dimension of the object, featuring: a robust presence in a world formerly felt to be largely empty or isolating, exuding an enlivening interest and proactive intent to engender growth. In brief review of my work with Joe, I sought to rouse inceptive processes of relatedness, entailing such steps as: reaching for him and drawing him toward engagement (Alvarez, 1992); kindling affect and forging resonance; directing efforts at connection away from behavior into expression of feeling and other states. It was my aim to build mindedness by: infusing his statements with unclaimed motive and desire; encouraging him, at times, in his flatness to search within himself for another thought; undergirding thought with words, and once begun, reverie-born connection; above all, hearing, inferring, even giving prospective sound to a psychic register in his action and speech that I imported into my comments to him.

To date, I had seen the properties of Joe's thought progress, at times, from concreteness and discharge-through-action, to a higher degree of abstraction and elaboration within (Lecours & Bouchard, 1997). Ultimately, I hoped that Joe would gradually introject my containment, leading him to cull ideas from his experience, and further his own assemblage of a meaning-making apparatus.

Let me close with a recent production of Joe's mind. He planned a gift for a son, who had been awarded a plum job as a top recruit at his business school. The gift was a leather briefcase, embossed with the son's initials, and the school name inside. Joe mentioned that his own father had given him a briefcase for work when he graduated college, but he'd never used it. When I ventured a comment about his particular choice of gift, Joe snorted, "It's about briefcases!"

Some weeks later, I asked Joe if he'd given his gift. He unfolded a draft of the note he'd written his son. It said:

> When I graduated college, my father gave me a briefcase. But the school wasn't fancy, so the gift wasn't a big deal. Yours is a prestigious school. Your success is fantastic. You had a dream of that program, went after it, and made this happen. I hope this briefcase reminds you how you went after your dream. It could also begin a new tradition in our family.

I had tears in my eyes when I finished reading. Joe was pleased that his son had loved the gift, "but it wasn't the briefcase – it was the note." He went on, "It's a lesson, of how I have to reveal more, about where things come from."

I said, "A briefcase is not only a briefcase."

Acknowledgments

I am grateful to Joe for permission to publish aspects of our work, and I express my admiration for his honesty, spirit of determination, and willingness that he brought to all our work.

His given name is common; he is one of a kind.

Notes

1 It is beyond the scope of this chapter to cite the many analysts who write of enactment and affectivity, and their own participating roles, as phenomena that can render meaning from "unmentalized experience," so called by Mitrani (1995). Figurability refers to the process described by Cesar and Sara Botella (2005), whereby an analyst's regression from rational thought enables him to produce an image that captures an irrepresentable experience in the patient.

2 I (Director, 2009a, 2009b) used the term catalyst in elaborating my view of the analyst's role as an enlivening object. I then came across Levine's (2013) use of the term to describe an analyst's active role in helping to construct representations in patients who lack the means. He does not foreground the use of the analyst's own subjectivity as a principal factor, as I do.

References

Alvarez, A. (1992). *Live company: Psychoanalytic psychotherapy with autistic, borderline, deprived, and abused children*. London: Routledge.

Alvarez, A. (1996). Addressing the element of deficit in children with autism: Psychotherapy which is both psychoanalytically and developmentally informed. *Clinical Child Psychology and Psychiatry, 1*, 525–537.

Alvarez, A. (2012). *The thinking heart: Three levels of psychoanalytic therapy with disturbed children*. London: Routledge.

Bass, A. (2001). It takes one to know one: Or, whose unconscious is it anyway? *Psychoanalytic Dialogues, 11*, 683–675.

Bass, A. (2003). "E" enactments in psychoanalysis: Another medium, another message. *Psychoanalytic Dialogues, 13*, 657–675.

Bass, A. (2009). An independent theory of clinical technique viewed through a relational lens: Commentary on paper by Michael Parsons. *Psychoanalytic Dialogues, 19*, 237–245.

Bergstein, A. (2009). On boredom: A close encounter with encapsulated parts of the psyche. *International Journal of Psychoanalysis, 90*, 613–631.

Bick, E. (1968). The experience of the skin in early object relations. *International Journal of Psychoanalysis, 49*, 484–486.

Bion, W. (1959). Attacks on linking. *International Journal of Psychoanalysis, 40*, 308–315.

Bion, W. (1962a). The psychoanalytic study of thinking. *International Journal of Psychoanalysis, 43*, 306–310.

Bion, W. ([1962b] 1984). *Learning from experience*. London, UK: Maresfield.

Bion, W. (1994). *Clinical seminars and other works*. London, UK: Karnac.

Botella, C., & Botella, S. (2005). *The work of psychic figurability: Mental states without representation*. New York: Brunner-Routledge.

Bromberg, P. (1998). *Standing in the spaces: Essays on clinical process, trauma, and dissociation*. Hillsdale, NJ: The Analytic Press.

Cooper, S. (2010). *A disturbance in the field: Essays in transference–countertransference engagement*. New York: Routledge.

Cooper, S. (2012). Exploring a patient's shift from relative silence to verbal expressiveness: Observations on an element of the analyst's participation. *International Journal of Psychoanalysis*, *93*, 897–916.

Cooper, S. (2014). The things we carry: Finding/creating the object and the analyst's self-reflective participation. *Psychoanalytic Dialogues*, *24*, 621–636.

Crittenden, P. (1993). An information-processing perspective on the behavior of neglectful parents. *Criminal Justice and Behavior*, *20*, 27–48.

Davies, J. (1998). Multiple perspectives on multiplicity. *Psychoanalytic Dialogues*, *8*, 195–206.

Davies, J. (1999). Getting cold feet, defining "safe-enough" borders: Dissociation, multiplcitiy, and integration in the analyst's experience. *Psychoanalytic Quarterly*, *68*, 184–208.

Davies, J. (2004). Whose bad objects are we anyway? Repetition and our elusive love affair with evil. *Psychoanalytic Dialogues*, *14*, 711–732.

Davies, J. (2005). Transformations of desire and despair: Reflections on the termination process from a relational perspective. *Psychoanalytic Dialogues*, *15*, 779–805.

Demos, V. (1984). Empathy and affect: Reflections on infant experience. In: J. Lichtenberg, M. Bornstein, & D. Silver (Eds.), *Empathy II* (pp. 9–34). Hillsdale, NJ: The Analytic Press.

Director, L. (2009a). The enlivening object. *Contemporary Psychoanalysis*, *45*, 120–141.

Director, L. (2009b). The enlivening object. Evolving notions of the analytic role: Three generations of relational analysts. Panel at "Relational Psychoanalysis Comes of Age," conference sponsored by the relational orientation, NYU Postdoctoral Program, New York.

Fonagy, P., Moran, G., & Target, M. (1993). Aggression and the psychological self. *International Journal of Psychoanalysis*, *74*, 471–485.

Fonagy, P., Gergely, G., Jurist, E., & Target, M. (2002). *Affect regulation, mentalization, and the development of the self*. New York: Other Press.

Joseph, B. (1989). Transference: The total situation. In: M. Feldman & E. Spillius (Eds.), *Psychic equilibrium and psychic change: Selected papers of Betty Joseph* (pp. 156–167). London: Routledge.

Klein, M. ([1959] 1975). Our adult world and its roots in infancy. In: M. Klein, *Envy and gratitude and other works 1946–1963* (Vol. III, pp. 247–263). New York: Free Press.

Laub, D. (1992). An event without a witness: Truth, testimony, and survival. In: S. Felman & D. Laub (Eds.), *Testimony: Crises of witnessing in literature, psychoanalysis, and history* (pp. 75–92). New York: Routledge.

Lecours, S., & Bouchard, M. (1997). Dimensions of mentalisation: Outlining levels of psychic transformation. *International Journal of Psychoanalysis, 78*, 855–875.

Levine, H. (2013). The colourless canvas: Representation, therapeutic action, and the creation of mind. In H. Levine, G. Reed, & D. Scarfone (Eds.), *Unrepresented states and the construction of meaning: Clinical and theoretical contributions* (pp. 42–71). London, UK: Karnac.

Mitchell, S. (1988). *Relational concepts in psychoanalysis: An integration*. Cambridge: Harvard University Press.

Mitchell, S. (1997). *Influence and autonomy in psychoanalysis*. Hillsdale, NJ: The Analytic Press.

Mitrani, J. (1995). Toward an understanding of unmentalized experience. *Psychoanalytic Quarterly, 64*, 68–112.

Music, G. (2009). Neglecting neglect: Some thoughts about children who have lacked good input, and are "undrawn" and "unenjoyed." *Journal of Child Psychotherapy, 35*, 142–156.

Ogden, T. (2002). A new reading of the origins of object-relations theory. *International Journal of Psychoanalysis, 83*, 767–782.

Perry, B. (2002). Childhood experience and the expression of genetic potential: What childhood neglect tells us about nature and nurture. *Brain and Mind, 3*, 79–100.

Seligman, S. (1994). Applying psychoanalysis in an unconventional context. *Psychoanalytic Study of the Child, 49*, 481–500.

Stern, D.B. (2004). The eye sees itself: Dissociation, enactment, and the achievement of conflict. *Contemporary Psychoanalysis, 40*, 197–237.

Stern, D.B. (2010). *Partners in thought: Working with unformulated experience, dissociation, and enactment*. New York: Routledge.

Stern, D.N. (2010). *Forms of vitality: Exploring dynamic experience in psychology, the arts, psychotherapy, and development*. Oxford: Oxford University Press.

Suchet, M. (2015). Impasse-able. *Psychoanalytic Dialogues, 25*, 405–419.

Symington, N. (1983). The analyst's act of freedom as agent of therapeutic change. *International Review of Psychoanalysis*, *10*, 283–291.

Symington, N. (2001). *The spirit of sanity*. London, UK: Karnac.

Symington, N. (2007). A technique for facilitating the creation of mind. *International Journal of Psychoanalysis*, *88*, 1409–1422.

Chapter 12

What makes time fly?

Loewald's concept of time and the resuscitation of vitality

Christopher Bonovitz

David is ten minutes late for his session. He arrives in a confused, disoriented state, unaware of the time and preoccupied with a jumble of thoughts that are difficult for him to grasp. He feels like time is passing him by, and that he's unable to collect the pieces of his past and grasp how he has arrived where he is now, uncertain of any charted course towards the future. Several years before, David's wife Theresa died in a car accident at the scene of the crash—no warning, no goodbye. It was then that time was severed, the past amputated. Ever since, David has struggled to gather the pieces together and connect them with his current life. He has bouts of anxiety and dread, convinced that he too may die at any moment. He walks around in the world unable to fathom putting together the semblance of anything that might have meaning without her presence.

David loses track of time at various points during the day, unconsciously refusing to mark time and instead allowing it to pass him by unnoticed. He is generally preoccupied with somatic concerns, convinced that he is on the verge of contracting a terminal illness, one that would strip him of a life he is unsure that he deserves. It is not so much that time stopped when his wife died; rather he is ambivalent about continuing to live life without her, unable to understand how he can continue in a life that she may never know.

David experiences an absence of vitality that, for the purpose of this chapter, I understand as linked with the fragmentation of time which, according to Loewald (1972), morphs the world into bits and pieces where connections between past, present, and future disintegrate—with each instant losing its connection to the next. How can vitality exist within David if past, present, and future are splintered? In this case, analysis came to center on resuscitating the vitality that was obliterated when Theresa died. In order to restore vitality, the analytic process needed to reestablish the links between the past, present, and future, weaving them into a "nexus of interaction" (Loewald, 1972).

In this chapter I will explore the defensive function of fragmentation, such as in the case of David, and the threat of implicitly acknowledging the connectedness between the present, past, and future. As background, I will consider the concept of vitality in psychoanalysis according to Winnicott and Alvarez, and then use Loewald's concept of time, namely the two opposing poles of time—fragmentation and eternity—in discussing my concept of vitality and the interconnectedness among the temporal modes of psychic activity. Included in this discussion will be the idea that building the capacity for vitality means developing the capacity to "play" in the transference such that it connects the past and the present, as well as conscious and unconscious life. Transference becomes the vehicle through which the past is kept alive and made available to the analytic dyad for exploration, revision, and symbolization. If time is primarily fragmented, as in the case of David wherein the past has been amputated from the present, it moves glacially, disabling symbolic functioning and bringing forth a concrete mode of thinking (Bonovitz, 2016).

I will use the case of David as well as that of a child treatment to illustrate the process of threading the various dimensions of time with vitality, which rests on the tension between eternity (including what Loewald (1972) refers to as the "abiding instant") and fragmentation so as to establish a sense of continuity through time.

Concept of vitality in psychoanalysis

The concept of vitality is in some ways a perfect fit for psychoanalysis, beginning with what Freud (1920) referred to in his notion of Eros—the life instinct—and an emphasis on the sexual instinct embedded in the drive to live. Generally speaking, the associative meanings of vitality conjure up the idea of energy, life, meaningfulness, purpose, activity, dynamism, and passion—the various types of energetic feeling states that analysts on the whole value in their respective theories and therapeutic goals of psychoanalysis. Who could argue against the idea of a greater sense of vitality as a possible outcome of treatment? Yet one area where theorists differ is in the developmental roots of vitality, generating disparate narrative explanations in instances where vitality becomes muted, possibly replaced by deadness, and the various ways of understanding the processes by which vitality is resuscitated (or generated) in analysis.

For Winnicott, who was thinking about the mother–baby dyad from the beginning of life, vitality had a developmental energy that was fused with the erotic life of the baby, energy with an aggressive quality that existed independently of as well as in relation to the object (Winnicott, 1975; Phillips, 1988). Aggression remained a life force as long as it was modified by a relationship. For Winnicott, this type of aggression that in part made up vitality and the sense of being alive depended on an environment where the baby could come into being unintruded upon and with a "good enough" responsiveness to its needs. The feeling of being real and existing as a self in relation to objects was what Winnicott referred to as the "true self"; Phillips (1988) describes Winnicott's "true self" as collecting together the "details of the experience of aliveness" (p. 127). Vitality is embedded in Winnicott's true self and the potential that it holds, potential that becomes expressed through the "spontaneous gesture" and depends upon recognition and reflection back by the mother in order for vitality to grow. "The spontaneous gesture is the true self in action" (Phillips, 1988, p. 127). Aliveness for Winnicott is located in the baby's body and sensorimotor action and expressed through creativity.

Alvarez (1992), through her work with children on the autism spectrum, is particularly interested in how to restore vitality, or cultivate it for the first time, within a child who lives inside a deadened, rigid state which she describes as "glacializing," meaning attached to the old in a way that forecloses the new. These are children who sometimes dwell in psychic retreat (Steiner, 1996), existing inside a deserted landscape where nothing is lost as there was never any internalized object to begin with. In other words, they have not developed the capacity to internalize an object, leaving their inner world barren. In order to begin the slow, gradual process of "dissolving" deadness, Alvarez, similarly to a mother, pays careful attention to ways she may arouse the child through surprise, novelty, and delight—all of which the kids generally fortify themselves against in order to maintain the familiarity and safety manifested in their rigidity. The child here must develop the capacity to "think of" before he or she can "think about," meaning being able to know what one is thinking before being able to ascribe meaning to the thought itself. Alvarez (1992) stresses the importance of the mother trying to interest and attract the child in order to draw him out; he "needs input in order to be recalled to himself" (p. 95).

In her more recent book, *The Thinking Heart*, Alvarez (2012) describes how deeply disturbed children may experience objects as "useless," "mindless," and may have great trouble feeling their feelings and thinking their thoughts. In order to build the house of the mind (internally) so there is something to put into it, to use Alvarez's metaphor, action language (e.g., swishing, flowing) and intonation are critical in accessing preverbal emotions, as is working on what she refers to as the "descriptive level" before moving on to generating meaning and explanation. Where vitality is muted, working at the descriptive level means exploring the texture of subjective experience that Alvarez refers to as the "whatnesss of experience"—facilitating in the patient the articulation of preverbal, or pre-symbolic content, what something "feels like" rather than some sort of explanation. Only by working at the descriptive level first can we then move towards building the patient's capacity for introjection and internalization.

From a developmental perspective, these are patients who were deprived of being held in mind. Not having the experience of someone waiting for you undermines intention and the experience of sharing one's interest, which cumulatively over time may lead to the kind of deadness, or lack of vitality, that Alvarez is unpacking. Without the experience of being held in reserve in the other's mind, the patient is plagued with the feeling that things may disappear—thoughts, objects, or feelings. In this type of internal landscape, the patient may perpetuate the feeling that there is no space or time to think, needing to get everything out of his mind quickly before a thought can disappear.

Whereas the descriptive level correlates with "one-tracked" thinking—a type of thought without symbolic meaning—explanatory interpretations follow developmentally for Alvarez and involve the capacity to think two thoughts at the same time—being able to contain anxiety and turn "passive unresponsiveness" to something more active and agentic. In my own thinking about Alvarez's ideas with regards to cultivating vitality, I see it as embodying both the descriptive and explanatory levels of experience, meaning the "whatness" of experience and ascribing meaning through explanation. If a patient is only able to experience feelings at a preverbal level, then vitality is unmediated and ephemeral, with feelings existing as fleeting, coming and going from one moment to the next. Feelings at this level do not carry a history and symbolism that give them depth, context, and background. At the preverbal level, feelings are not connected to memories through time, and yet it is history and memory that function as the foundation of vitality.

Resistance to the play of the transference

Loewald (1972) understood transference as a vehicle that keeps the past alive in the present relationship with the analyst, activating past experience and coloring how it is remembered. For Loewald, transference reintegrates the past through the modifications of the analytic relationship which has bearing on both the patient's psychic future as well as how the past lives on inside of him. Memory is a "memorial activity of the mind"—a "living activity"—in which connections are formed between the past, present, and future (p. 144). It is this connectedness that imbues time with meaning and restores continuity across time, an essential achievement for the development of vitality.

In applying Loewald's concept of time, if we understand vitality as embodying memory and history that give the feelings, energy, and creativity associated with vitality meaning, then connectedness with time and its continuity is essential for the expansion of vitality. Vitality is a living activity, and to live with vitality is to embrace the immediacy of an experience while also allowing the past and future to influence that immediacy through temporal context.

I would argue that, without the various modes of time contextualizing vitality, it is experienced as short-lived and discontinuous. In other words, the creativity and energy associated with vitality only endure if the connectedness between the past and present allow for memories to imbue vitality with meanings carried forth from the past. Without the fusion of vitality and memory, there is no felt passage of time nor an accumulated collection of experience that accrues over time; psychic life remains static, akin to Fairbairn's (1963) closed endopsychic system, frozen across the temporal tundra of the mind.

David and the collapse of time

Loewald was very much interested in unity and connectedness in relation to the past and present, specifically how the past is kept alive in the present and potentially infuses the present with vitality and meaning. Similarly, he was also interested in understanding how unity breaks apart, and where connectedness is, in the case of time, replaced by fragmentation. Loewald refers to the experience of "fragmentation" as one where "time is abolished in the annihilation of connectedness." Past, present, and future are disconnected from one another, severing meaning as each dimension of time comes to exist in isolation of the other. Loewald (1972) explains that the present in the case of fragmentation is experienced as a "meaningless now," without connections and links that form a temporal context.

Since his wife's death, time for David existed in splintered fragments, with passing thoughts, feelings, and memories scrambled and floating around without context. Consistently late for his sessions, it seemed our sessions had no beginnings. Rather, we began with the absence before his arrival. The endings of sessions were jarring to him, invariably leaving him with the feeling of being cut off midstream. It was as if there were an unconscious refusal to mark time, as that would mean acknowledging a past that he would not be able to recover or revise, a past that felt either too far away to apprehend or subsumed in its entirety in the morass of the present. While of course there was the shock of the trauma (death of his wife) that punctured the connectedness of time and in some ways existed on a dissociated island dislodged from his cognitive processing system, the fragmentation of time that permeated his everyday life extended beyond shock and dissociation. He literally lost track of time most days, unable to remember appointment times and sometimes "forgetting" sessions. And though there was an active psychic process that added to his confusion and one that served defensive purposes, his missed sessions sometimes caught him by surprise—showing up some days not realizing he had missed the prior session until I mentioned it. In general, moments felt empty to David, devoid of any inkling of vitality and with the predominant experience of estrangement and depersonalization stalking him wherever he went (Loewald, 1972).

With Loewald's conception of transference as part of the background, it is no wonder that David had great difficulty working in the transference. For instance, when I invited him to explore his experience of a missed session or a possible representation of me in a dream, he understood the idea behind my question intellectually, yet emotionally could not consciously allow himself to recognize its relevance. Instead, he would look at me in a state of bewilderment, unable to grasp passing thoughts that might relate to his experience. Though he did occasionally reflect on the past, especially concerning Theresa during their time together before the car crash, he spoke of the past as though it existed in isolation from everything else. Through the lens of the transference as a "memorializing activity," according to Loewald, David's attempt to avoid the transference was also an attempt to preserve the past as it existed prior to the accident. The present and future eroded after Theresa passed away. Explicit attention to the transference was a threat to the defensive function of fragmentation and the implicit acknowledgment of connectedness between the present, past, and future.

Interestingly, though, I started to notice that in my absence David sometimes emerged out of the fog and became more curious. On one occasion, he showed up for a session while I was away on vacation. Even though I had given him much advance notice of my time away, he arrived at the usual day and time as if I had never mentioned being away—that piece of our shared history had been erased. When I returned, he described the experience of arriving for his usual session and seeing that the gate to my office was locked. Exploring his reactions at that moment, he realized that he had thought he might have mixed up our longstanding regular schedule even though it was the day and time of our usual appointment. While standing outside the gate waiting and unsure what to do (not knowing if I might eventually show up), he recalled wondering where I might be—perhaps I had overslept, had a meeting I forgot to tell him about, or a transportation delay. As he continued to wait while time moved into the beginning of the session (now with me absent—a reversal of the dynamic in which he shows up late), he described observing the people walking by, seemingly with some sort of destination in mind. And though he was at his presumed appointed destination (and I was away), he had nowhere to be at that moment, no other purpose except to be right there waiting. He felt extremely alone, and bumped into the thought that he had "given up a while ago on having a destination." Instead, he lived his life aimlessly wandering around, "drifting" in and out of consciousness.

David's time spent waiting for me was the beginning of an incipient and momentary experience of vitality. For the first time he was observing people passing him by, perceiving the passage of time and becoming more aware of his drifted-ness as a means of trying to escape the prison of time. He became more aware of how he wrapped himself in a fog, clinging to fragmentation as a defense against acknowledging the movement of time. In being forced to confront my absence, he momentarily emerged from the fog and noticed the world around him living and moving forward in time.

David stood there thinking about the whereabouts of his analyst, what this all might be about, and began to construct symbols with the objects around him. For instance, as he waited, he associated the afterlife with my office gate and wondered if, in fact, his wife was waiting for him in some sort of afterlife just as he was waiting for me. Paradoxically, David's momentary connection to time arrived in my absence. It was in the process of waiting for my arrival—we might say memorializing me in my absence—that he became more aware of how he had been existing in the world in relation to time and memory. He could see in this moment that he had been avoiding creating some kind of bridge between the past and present as to do so would threaten the preservation of Theresa frozen in time. My absence forced him to reflect upon our relationship through time in order to make sense of the locked gate, and in doing so brought together the past and present and created a symbol (the office gate as the conduit to the afterlife) associated with Theresa's death that breathed new life into this profound loss.

The abiding instant

While fragmentation exists on one end of the continuum of time, at the other end is what Loewald (1972) refers to as the experience of eternity, one in which "the flux of time is strayed or suspended" and in which there is no differentiation between the past, present, and future. An aspect of this pole of time is the "abiding instant," a state where the person is fully immersed in a feeling to the point that everything else in the temporal surround falls away—whether it be in extreme joy, sadness, despair, heightened sexual arousal, and so on. This is akin to what Freud (1930) referred to as an "oceanic feeling," the timeless now where the complete absorption inside the depth of a feeling negates time.

In thinking about the relevance of Loewald's concept of the abiding instant, an aspect of vitality is the capacity to experience the depth of feeling, to fully inhabit it in that only by doing so can the feeling then gradually acquire meaning and words in order to be further symbolized. The abiding instant is comprised of the full force of a feeling, and only by allowing one's self to sink into the bigness of such a feeling can vitality expand.

For David, the abiding instant began to set in as he gradually explored the various anniversaries related to Theresa (birthday, wedding anniversary, the day she died, and so on). Initially, he watched as they passed by, unable to come up with a ritual or event that even began to approach the enormity of her loss. But by the third year after Theresa's death, David arrived at an idea: he would write her a letter and then attach it to a balloon that he would release from the roof of his house. The idea itself was a marking of time, the beginning of more fully acknowledging her death in the time that had passed and writing to her in her absence (not unlike his dialogue with me in my absence when he showed up while I was on vacation).

In the note to Theresa, he recalled his memory of dancing with her at a relative's wedding, delighting in their enthrallment with each other in that moment. It was a joyous memory, one of course that was also bittersweet as it called up an agonizing longing for her, yet was another step towards restoring David's capacity to hold intense affect and experience the energy, aliveness, and depth of feeling that is the flesh of vitality.

Memory here served the purpose, not necessarily of remembering and reliving the past, but rather of looking back on it from the present, thus partially reshaping the content and meanings attached to the memory. With his restored relationship to the past and its connection to the present, memory was newly re-contextualized through the linkage of the past and present. It was as though he were living out the memory for the first time as he emerged from the dense fog in which he had been encased for the past several years. Memory was both a "memoralizing activity" for David, as Loewald put it, as well as a vitalizing activity that began the process of imbuing the present day with his past life with Theresa. With the present and past joined together around his relationship with Theresa, the restored continuity of time and its accompanying memories instilled a greater sense of vitality in David, enriching and deepening his experience. Without such an integration, the present in isolation of the past suffocates vitality.

The urgency of time as a defense against linking the past with the future

In this second vignette I draw on the case of Jennifer to illustrate how the sense of urgency with time may be used as a defense against connecting the past mode of time with the future.

Jennifer, an 11-year-old girl, typically entered the consulting room with a slouched gait and a conspicuous grimace on her face, as if to say, "I so want to be here, but need to act this way in order to not reveal this. So, play along with my defense and experience the complementary role of feeling unwanted as I wait for the session to be over." After plopping herself down on the couch and staring at the floor mumbling curt responses to my attempts to engage her, Jennifer would motion towards the play area, my cue that it was time to adjourn to the safety of the games we played together.

Once we entered the play space, Jennifer moved a mile a minute, rushing through games, speaking at a rapid pace, and answering questions as concisely as possible and without much thought. If I took too long to pick a card or make a move, she either moved for me or exhorted me with something like, "You take so long to go, just go." One of the games that was in her wheelhouse was called BS (short for bull shit) which, interestingly, she never referred to other than by its shorthand "BS"—a relevant word for a kid who at this moment presumably deplored therapy and had to wade through a lot of "BS" between her divorced parents.

To start the game, we divided a deck of cards in half, and then alternated laying cards face down in numerical sequence. The person who got rid of their cards first won the game. So for instance, if Jennifer lay down 2s (as many as she had), then it was my turn to put down 3s. And there was always the choice each player had of bluffing, with cards other than the stated number. If I did not have any 3s or only had one, I could elect to put more cards down and make the claim they were 3s (in order to get rid of my cards faster). It would then be Jennifer's decision if she wanted to call out "BS" or let it go. If she called "BS" and in fact I had "lied," I would be forced to take the entire pile of cards that had accumulated. If she was wrong (e.g., meaning I did in fact lay down the stated number of 3s) then she would have to pick up the pile and add it to her stack. Not only did Jennifer briskly and swiftly move through this game, she was adept at assessing my facial cues to determine if I was lying about my cards and was often accurate in whatever choice she made about whether or not I was "BSing."

Jennifer's fast pace functioned in two ways. It enabled her to keep things out of her mind, such as her parents' messy divorce (which filled her daily life with a lot of "BS") or her brother's misanthropic and emotionally turbulent adolescence. It also served to maintain a disconnection between the past and the future.

Jennifer seemingly protested the future through her defense against loss in that she did not allow herself to remain attached to any interest of hers. As soon as anyone expressed an inkling of enthusiasm for what she was into at the time, such as a musical instrument or ice skating, she immediately distanced herself from the stated interest and rarely picked it back up again. The other's desire frightened her, so much so that her muted response and detachment were about self-preservation in that moment. The same held true for friends or a teacher that she liked. What would start as an initial enthusiasm inevitably waned rapidly. She was threatened by the possibility that she could become attached to something that might be ripped away from her at any moment in a manner similar to what she repeatedly experienced when relocated on short notice, having to suddenly change schools and leave her friends. In defending against loss, or any kind of change for that matter, she resisted investing in her future such as trying something new for any sustained period of time, as to do so could subject her to some sort of future dislocation in having the newfound object seized by the other.

In the case of Jennifer, I consider vitality as embodying desire and an attachment to someone or something that has importance and personal meaning to her. She maintained her detachment through disconnecting the past from the future and, in doing so, she could shed objects before she became too attached and dependent. Yet, the cost of doing so could become emotionally burdensome as she closed herself off to others even during times when she craved comfort. Her desire was channeled towards self-preservation and maintaining past memories (such as her prior homes) that were frozen in time. Novel friendships and activities were threatening as they could alter the fixed memories she held of the past.

I gradually learned to play my complementary role to her apathy, namely to "play along" with it not so much in the interest of undoing or interpreting it but rather to engage in an implicit dialogue without rushing to assign meaning. For instance, when Jennifer began our sessions with an exaggerated stance of lack of interest, after many failed attempts to engage her, I sensed that I was finally catching on when I said something like, "I get the feeling that I am the last person on earth you want to see right now" or "You are already counting down the seconds as you walk into the room and can't wait for this to end" (meaning "waiting" is akin to not skipping ahead to the end, as she did from the start). To say more than this would move closer to the explanatory level (Alvarez, 2012), whereas to clearly state the communication as it relates to the "whatness" (or descriptive level) of experience slowed time down, allowing for a pause instead of a skipped beat.

Though I had the sense that her apathy was a defense against interest and desire, I believed that interpreting this would not go very far. Alternatively, I tried to describe what she showed me through playing what I deemed as my complementary role to her apathy, inhabiting the position of the uninteresting object. Referring back to Alvarez (2012), it was more a matter of making contact at a descriptive level before proceeding to the explanatory level.

After several variations on this type of response to Jennifer's gestural communication, she looked up at my eyes (as if she were glancing at me for the first time) and held my gaze for a moment or two. I said, "I just noticed that you are thinking something but maybe you are unsure if you want to tell me." (I chose to name her ambivalence so as to let her know I knew, while also communicating that she did not necessarily have to lean into it. This gave her more of a choice in that moment to tell me or not.) She decided to take me up on my offer and said, "You know I lived in seven places before here."

I said, "Seven, that's a lot—do you remember them all?" With some hint of interest in describing the pictorial scenes of where she lived, she recounted in great detail the homes she lived in, the respective neighborhoods, and a few details about what she liked about each one. Interestingly, the one she focused on the most was the first home she remembered when she was six years old. This was because it sat adjacent to her best friend's house at the time. They could visit with each other "any time we wanted."

While much stood out from this unfamiliar type of exchange with Jennifer, I will narrow my focus to the connection between time and vitality. First, though she had spoken of the past in prior sessions, it was more in the form of snippets, whereas this felt closer to the semblance of a narrative letting me know where she came from, the numerous relocations, and her visual attachment to each place, some of which felt like "home." Jennifer's vitality emerged around the past and memories of living embedded in the past. What accompanied her lively recounting of her past homes was an intense interest in describing the details in order to help me see these places. She became more willing to show me her excitement, her enthusiasm, and her need for me to understand these past lives of hers. There was less of a necessity to suppress her interest.

Second, the phrase "any time we wanted" hung out there after she said it, as it was such a contrast to how she currently lived day to day—moving between her parents' homes every few days, school and its activities, and extracurricular commitments. Of course, this included me and our pre-arranged appointment—she could not come see me "any time she wanted." But sticking to the "whatness" of experience and therefore resisting the urge to translate time into the transference for the "time being," I said, "That must have been a great feeling to go to your friend's house *any time* you wanted!" Jennifer smiled and said, "I miss that so much."

I paused for a long moment after she said this. This was the first time I had heard Jennifer say the word "miss." To "miss" meant an implied past that she was thinking about as well as an experience of yearning in the present—she was not stuck in the past nor filled with nostalgia. Rather, her experience of missing in that moment carried the wish to experience that same feeling again, the desire to have or even possess someone she likes or even loves "any time I wanted." The moment conveyed a hopefulness that in the future she may allow herself to want something or someone—and to hold on to that desire—without the anxiety of having it ripped away. It was a convergence of memory, desire, hope, and the linkage of time—the central ingredients of vitality for Jennifer.

Generally speaking, while vitality contains desire, hope, creative energy, and aliveness, I have also tried to show its relationship with time and the linkages of time and affect. In Jennifer's case, the severing of the past compromised her sense of vitality in that it functioned in maintaining a detachment from people, places, and activities that had become important to her at one time. In the restoring of the past through fond memories of her former homes, it also restored the linkage between the past and present, therefore enhancing her feeling of vitality. Without this linkage of time, vitality could not exist in its full force.

In the transference and countertransference, there was the implicit communication that she might be able to sink into the "abiding instant" if she could connect memories of her prior homes with the infinite, timeless experience of being able to see someone "any time she wanted"—something akin to Alvarez' idea of the pivotal developmental experience of a parental figure who holds you in the back of her mind even when occupied with something else. Maybe Jennifer could hold on to the ticking clock (objective time) while also dipping her toe in the illusory, "as if" analytic space, where time might suspend itself and she could remain connected to me (and me to her) even after our time was up. The analytic space and its timeless dimension could aid in the construction of a psychic home within her own mind.

Linking past and future: a return to the game of BS

As Jennifer became more engaged, so too did the elaboration to our already established rituals and patterns of relating, making room for connections between the past and future that served to further develop her capacity for vitality through the linkage of time.

One of the twists she added to our game of "BS" was something she referred to as "peanut butter." Meaning, if one of us successfully fooled the other person by putting the next card or cards in the sequence into the pile without being called out as "BSing," then we could elect to state "peanut butter," making it known we had successfully tricked the other person. This new addition was important for several reasons. First, Jennifer had injected something new into our game on her own without any prompting, thus showing some investment in our "time" together. Second, she had created an element which resulted in each of us more fully revealing our intention rather than letting it remain vague or implicit.

When I explored with Jennifer the name itself, she explained that she "used to love peanut butter." When I asked, "What happened to your love for it?" she said, "it went away," but that she has grown to like lots of "different kinds of foods." Curious about the word "love" and the fact that it was not a word she threw around lightly or much at all, for that matter, I pressed on in asking, "What do you love now?" She paused the game of BS in that moment, looked up and said, "I don't know, but I think I will love something more than peanut butter some day. I just don't know what it is yet." As she said this, I glanced over at the clock and realized we were out of time—time was indeed moving faster, maybe even beginning to fly.

While on the surface this exchange may seem like any other ordinary conversation with a child patient amidst the ups and downs of everyday analytic work, in my mind this was an important step forward for a few "vital" reasons. Jennifer was able to acknowledge her prior love (albeit for peanut butter) that may have also been a stand-in for other things (prior homes, the days when her parents were married, the wish to be a young child or baby again, etc.), as well as her openness to the possibility of falling in love again with a new food (or substitute any object for food here). She was bringing together the various modes of time, notably the past and future, and her feelings were growing more intense (from imperceptible liking to love)—an intensity that contained the abiding instant, reflection on the past, and imagining the future, all critical variables of vitality.

Discussion: vitality, the imagined future, and the growth of the analyst's mind

Vitality is a confluence of temporal and affective integrations, meaning the integration of the various modes of time—past, present, and future—that often occurs through (or made for the first time) affective moments, actions, and memories in the context of the relationship between analyst and patient. My primary focus in applying Loewald's concept of time to the treatments of David and Jennifer has highlighted their specific relationships to time and vitality. It is this reintegration of time along with more fully living out the force of feelings in a given moment that has implications for the analyst and the dyad. With the amputation of the past, as in the case of David, or the severing of the link between the past and future with Jennifer, my mind was restricted in what I could think and imagine in relation to the patient. As the patient reconnects the various dimensions of time and restores the feeling of vitality along with the experience of ongoing continuity, the analyst may experience more freedom of thought and a greater ability to imagine the patient in the past and future.

Not unlike Winnicott's spontaneous gesture or Alvarez' idea of a parent holding a child in mind while occupied with another activity, David's active role in memorializing the past that made time more of a "living activity" created psychic space in my mind to imagine the various ways he might grow in the life that awaited him in the future. I could gradually be more spontaneous with David, reimagine scenes of his life with him, or refashion a memory or dream as it unfolded now in the present. In cinematic terms, we could enter the editing room together after the film was shot, take a "second look" (Baranger, Baranger & Mom, 1983) at what we filmed, and reflect on how we might shape it going forward, a process influenced by context and the transference–countertransference with the linkage of time holding the various scenes together (Langan, 1993).

Jennifer's vivid description of her past homes, filled with specific details of the house or her room, was one of those instances where I could begin to see what she was saying, what Levenson (2003) refers to as right-brain-to-right-brain communication (see Bonovitz, 2016). Prior to this exchange, her words often felt devoid of anything important or meaningful to her; instead it was if she were filling out a perfunctory status report to satisfy the adult in charge. When she revisited with great interest being able to see her friend "any time we wanted," her motivation here infused our interaction with vitality as she was showing me a desire that she had not revealed before, that in the past was squelched, especially if an adult responded with enthusiasm. When we returned to our game of "BS" this time around, the dyadic context had shifted in that we both now felt greater spontaneity and the freedom to create. The necessity to unconsciously construct a dyadic field that was organized around managing anxiety was no longer as much of an imperative—the "interlock," as Wolstein (1959) calls it (protracted impasse), had loosened its grip (see Bonovitz, 2009).

So when Jennifer creatively added the "peanut butter" element to the game of "BS," voiced her past love for peanut butter, and allowed for the possibility of falling in love with a new kind of food at some later point, the linkage of the past and future brought with it passion (at least temporarily) and an invitation for me to join her in playing with this new element within the confines of the game. In addition, the integration of the past and future enabled us to become more capable of surprise and delight in imagining what might come to pass. The linkage and gradual restoration of temporal unity not only infused our relationship with vitality, but also engendered the idea that we were both now more receptive to the prospect of being surprised with what might come to pass.

Conclusion

While the idea of vitality may imply an immersive experience in aliveness and the energy and passion that accompanies it, I believe this is just one aspect of vitality. When a person is able to experience both the "abiding instant" of time as well as achieve a sense of continuity *across* time in which the past, present, and future are in dialogue, then memory and narrative bolster the floor of experience such that experience may evolve and accrue meanings with time. From this perspective, then, memory and narrative that spring from the linkage of time lend vitality a depth and lasting power that imbue the present and revitalize the past while informing the future with imaginative possibility.

References

Alvarez, A. (1992). *Live Company*. London: Routledge.

Alvarez, A. (2012). *The Thinking Heart*. London: Routledge.

Baranger, M., Baranger, W. and Mom, J. (1983). Process and Non-Process in Analytic Work. *Int. J. Psycho-Anal.*, 64:1–15.

Bonovitz, C. (2009). Looking Back, Looking Forward: A Reexamination of Benjamin Wolstein's *Interlock* and the Emergence of Intersubjectivity. *Int. J. Psycho-Anal.*, 90(3):463–485.

Bonovitz, C. (2016). On Seeing What is Not Said: The Concrete Mode of Psychic Functioning and the Development of Symbolization. *Psychoanal. Dial.*, 26(3):280–293.

Fairbairn, W.D. (1963). Synopsis of an Object-Relations Theory of the Personality. *Int. J. Psycho-Anal.*, 44:224–225.

Freud, S. (1920). Beyond the Pleasure Principle. *The Standard Edition of the Complete Psychological Works of Sigmund Freud, Volume XVIII (1920–1922): Beyond the Pleasure Principle, Group Psychology and Other Works.* London: Hogarth Press, pp. 1–64.

Freud, S. (1930). Civilization and its Discontents. *The Standard Edition of the Complete Psychological Works of Sigmund Freud, Volume XXI (1927–1931): The Future of an Illusion, Civilization and its Discontents, and Other Works*. London: Hogarth Press, pp. 57–146.

Langan, R. (1993). The Depth of the Field1. *Contemp. Psychoanal.*, 29:628–644.

Levenson, E.A. (2003). On Seeing What is Said. *Contemp. Psychoanal.*, 39(2):233–249.

Loewald, H.W. (1972). The Experience of Time. *Psychoanal. St. Child*, 27:401–410.

Phillips, A. (1988). *Winnicott*. Cambridge, MA: Harvard University Press.

Steiner, J. (1996). The Aim of Psychoanalysis in Theory and in Practice. *Int. J. Psycho-Anal.*, 77:1073–1083.

Winnicott, D.W. (1975). *Through Pediatrics to Psycho-Analysis. Int. Psycho-Anal. Lib.*, 100:1 –325. London: The Hogarth Press and the Institute of Psycho-Analysis.

Wolstein, B. (1959). *Countertransference*. New York, NY: Grune & Stratton.

Index

www.ingramcontent.com/pod-product-compliance
Lightning Source LLC
LaVergne TN
LVHW021120300926
849160LV00010B/799
* 9 7 8 0 3 6 7 6 8 7 8 9 2 *